Classroom Countdown

Education at $\times$ *the Crossroads*

Books by Max Rafferty

Max Rafferty on Education

Suffer, Little Children

What They Are Doing to Your Children

Classroom Countdown

Education at the Crossroads

by MAX RAFFERTY

Hawthorn Books, Inc.   PUBLISHERS   New York

CONTENTS

FOREWORD

A GENERATION AND more of Progressive Education in this country has produced some interesting results, not the least of which is the odium which has come to cling about the word "controversial." Have you noticed, incidentally, how many formerly harmless English words have become villains of late? "Propaganda" and "indoctrination," for instance, were originally neither good nor bad in connotation. "Law and order," too, once occupied a spot in the semantic pantheon right next to "home and mother." Not anymore.

Today, all these have new meanings. Bad ones. Similarly, the word "controversy" has come to be a naughty one, especially among educators.

Not long ago, I got up to speak to a gathering of my professional colleagues and found myself being introduced as "the most controversial figure in modern education." The reaction was fascinating. Those nearest me on the platform eyed me askance with an air of respectful revulsion, and the audience shifted in its seats uneasily, murmuring behind its hands in well-bred but horrified attention, like a bird about to be charmed by a snake.

The very fact that I was up there in front of those people at all, especially being introduced to them as the superintendent of public instruction of the biggest state in the Union, was indicative of the phenomenal 180-degree change in direction that American education is now undergoing. In the past, as soon as a school administrator became in any way controversial, he found himself well on the way to becoming an ex-school administrator altogether.

Controversy was frowned upon, you see. It occupied the same doghouse as competition, and for the same reason. The Brahmins of my profession, who had imbibed Progressive Education like their mothers' milk from the abundantly flowing bosoms of their education professors in Teachers College, could tolerate almost anything except disagreement.

The "life adjustment" cult preaches cooperation at any cost. Anyone who has sat, as I have, in solemn conclave with the Progressive Educationists knows that the unpardonable sin in their eyes is ultimate disagreement. Oh, a little initial dissent is tolerated if only to make the inevitable happy ending more blissful and savory. But to rise from the council table before togetherness and in-groupness have been finally achieved? Unheard of!

Yet education exists to disagree, to prod, to stimulate. Once let the current yearning for togetherness pass the point of no return, and real education might just as well shut up shop. It looked for quite a while in my line of work as though the next generation were being conditioned to believe almost as an article of faith that agreement is always and forever good, and that disagreement is always and forever to be avoided.

It's against this backdrop, then, that the startling events of the last five years must be considered. For education has of late convulsed violently against this cult of gray-flanneled facelessness. Fireworks are going off all over the educational map these days—things that would have been absolutely unthinkable just a short time ago.

Dr. James B. Conant, for example, came out for more homework for pupils and less credentialing for teachers. Heretics have burned for less.

Then the National Council of Teachers of English announced that English teachers are ill-trained, and that many of them have never had a course in grammar. This is the first time in more than a generation that anyone has even cared, just so long as the English teacher could deal successfully with such units as "How to Talk on the Telephone," "Principles of Toastmastership," and "The Dynamics of Committee Membership."

In a good many elementary schools today, kindergartners are actually being taught to read. Why, it seems only yesterday when the slightest hint of formal instruction of any kind in this privileged sanctuary of nose-blowing and toilet-training would have brought every primary-grade supervisor within five hundred miles swarming to the attack like so many maddened barracuda.

More recently, Admiral Rickover has referred rashly to the ladies of the PTA as "infernal nuisances," thus demonstrating a brand of sheer, chrome-steel nerve that I for one would never dare to share, but which I presume has been standard equipment for naval heroes ever since the days of John Paul Jones.

Indeed, the winds of change are freshening. Rarely has education had greater incentives to mend its ways.

The choices are increasingly apparent. The crossroads offer clear alternatives. The great danger now is the rift that seemingly separates my ancient profession from the great majority of the American people who support and populate American schools.

It was not always thus. Until our own distracted time, we teachers went hand in hand with the nation's lay citizens. Their goals were ours. Their wishes for the future both of their children and of their country were our wishes.

As the busy, roaring years went by, the American people tamed and cultivated the land, and even as they did, the traveling pedagogue tamed and cultivated the people. America ripened toward greatness, and we teachers were part of the ripening. Indeed, we helped to cause that greatness, and because we were all marchers in the mighty parade that was the Great Republic, we loved our fellow marchers and were loved in return.

Recently there's been a fork in the parade route. Somehow, we educators took a different route from the rest of the marchers. What happened?

The answer is a flawed diamond, with many facets. Here, for the record, are six of those facets:

(1) We teachers have defined education as "life adjustment"; America's parents want education to be organized and disciplined instruction in subject matter.

(2) We teachers hanker after teaching the "whole child"; parents want us to concentrate on his mastery of the fundamentals of human learning.

(3) We teachers are tending to use the school as an instrument to reform society; parents regard it as a place where children become learned.

(4) We teachers are obsessed today with academic freedom; parents wish we would become equally concerned with academic responsibility.

(5) We teachers seemingly are reaching for the right to set policy in our schools; parents feel that only representatives of all the people can set policy for institutions owned and populated by all the people.

(6) And increasingly, we teachers are claiming the status of trade unionists; parents ironically are uplifting the tattered banner which we are abandoning, and they

stubbornly persist in regarding us as members of a great
and ancient profession.

Colleagues, I condemn no one. The rift exists. Daily it
widens and deepens. Parents want for their children the
same things they have always wanted, the same things
which in other, happier days we wanted with them. The
parents of America have not left us. We have left them.

The parade is going up another street. The sound of
the music and the cheers is growing fainter. Shall we continue trudging to our own lonesome drum, or shall we get
back to our proper place at the head of the marchers?

The past is prelude, however. What of things to come?
The most important spume-plume on education's wave of
the future is, oddly enough, skipping along on the crest of
the incoming breaker these days, almost unnoticed. It's
the declining American birthrate, swooning and collaps-
ing all over the country like a Victorian maiden aunt attending a typical 1969 movie.

The demographic charts plotted by my State Department of Education experts in California predicted five years
ago that the school year 1969–1970 would show a marked
reduction in the number of kindergarten enrollees. In
1970–1971 the subsidence will hit the first grade, and
from then on each year the class sizes will grow smaller.
By 1976–1977 the nation's junior high schools will be affected, and the school year 1978–1979 will see the mini-
enrollments reach the senior high level.

The implications of this unprecedented pupil drought
will be profound:

(1) Class sizes should grow smaller for the first time
in modern history. Maybe we can even achieve the Holy
Grail of my profession—an overall ratio of one teacher
for every twenty-five pupils.

(2) The long-term shortage of teachers should be over for a good long time. Perhaps as a result local school boards will acquire enough backbone and intestinal fortitude to set up salary schedules on a merit pay principle, and pay inspirational instructors more than they pay dull-as-dishwater ones.

(3) More attention will be paid to individual pupils, if only because there will be fewer of them to pay attention to. This should mean, among other things, that America's youngsters will be learning to read a lot better than they've been learning for the past thirty years. Reading skill is of necessity a highly individualized phenomenon. Ideally, I suppose, every beginning reader should have a special tutor. That's not about to happen, of course, but the lower pupil-teacher ratio of the Seventies may be the next best thing.

(4) Dramatically lessened school-building needs should enable more tax money to be channeled into such attractive instructional devices as closed-circuit TV, teaching machines, and learning laboratories. Gadgets of this sort can never take the teacher's place, but they can certainly help the teacher do a better, more interesting job.

Apart from the side effects attendant upon the falling birthrate, I venture to predict these developments in American education during the next decade:

(1) Much more emphasis on the social sciences, which are currently badly out of balance with the more glamorous—and more deadly—physical sciences.

(2) The continued decline of the school superintendency, with a growing trend to put the administration of local school districts in the hands of staff committees.

(3) A mushrooming of vocational education, with increased stress on on-the-job training for high school pu-

pils in cooperation with private business and with organized labor.

(4) Planned obsolescence of school buildings, with utilization spans calculated at thirty years so that the education of tomorrow's Americans will not be shackled by the limitations of today's architecture.

Two of the things I believe the Seventies will *NOT* bring are (a) Black or Brown or Yellow Power schools supported by public tax money but run by various minority groups and (b) massed compulsory bussing of children to achieve an artificial racial distribution within a given geographical area. The vast majority of the voting public in this country simply will not stand for either.

Speaking both as an educator and as an individual, I've been impatiently waiting for the Seventies to get here. Alongside the Sick Sixties, almost any decade in history would look like Paradise Regained.

Education's crossroads, then, hold mingled promise and peril, as crossroads so often do. It will be the task of this book to examine the alternatives presented by the proliferate forking of the highway that is American education, and to take a look back over our national shoulder to see how the main road was built in the first place.

Classroom Countdown

Education at ✕ *the Crossroads*

CROSSROAD #1

The Misconceptions of Modern Education

I BRING YOU IN this book the warmth and the bitterness, the passion and the partisanship, of the disappointed lover. Not the disillusioned lover, mind you. The disappointed lover. There's a difference.

For thirty years, I have been in love with education. Like all lovers, I have lived with my loved one, fought with her, forgiven her, and may yet live to be forgiven by her. And typical of my kind, I've spent an inordinate amount of time criticizing the object of my affection. The criticism betrays no lack of ardor on my part. Far from it. It springs instead from a zeal to see American education someday achieve the heights to which she should aspire but too often doesn't.

Ten years ago, when I was writing for the Phi Delta Kappan the essays that later became the book *Suffer, Little Children,* the great question of the day was, "Does education have a future?"

Today, in what seems almost a different century and

at least partly as a result of our failure to answer the first question, the query has escalated, horrifyingly and beyond all recognition, to "Does America have a future?"

Recently I got a letter from the U.S. Commissioner of Food and Drugs that made what's left of my hair stand right on end. It started out:

> During the past year a marked increase in the illegal use of hallucinogenic drugs throughout the nation, particularly around educational institutions, has been reported. Both students and members of the faculty are being secretly approached to engage in hallucinogenic "experiences." There is direct evidence of widespread availability of a number of drugs which have profound effects on the mental processes. I wish to alert all educational administrators to the gravity of the situation and to enlist their assistance in combatting an insidious and dangerous activity.

At first I must confess I had mixed feelings about this. If it were only the draft-card burners and the "Aid the Viet Cong" slobs who were munching the bennies and washing them down with libations of diluted LSD, I wouldn't get too excited, I'm afraid. After all, these relatively few young persons possess precious few mental processes upon which anything could have profound effects—even LSD.

But I'm assuming that the Commissioner was trying simultaneously to alert me to the fact that the hop habit is spreading from the unwashed pad-dweller to the serious scholar, and to ask for a wave of education's magic wand to solve the problem. I share his alarm, certainly, but I'm not at all sure that education has the answer. An analysis of the ailment and its historical background leaves me doubtful.

When I was an undergraduate 'way back when, during the Hungry Thirties, I could have understood and even sympathized with any of my classmates who might have started hitting the hashish. Lord knows we had plenty of cause in those days to resign from reality and to seek refuge in almost anything. None of us knew where our next meal was coming from, to say nothing of the next tuition check. Hitler was starting to raise what he raised so well in Europe, and Tojo was sinking our gunboats over in Asia. Every time we opened a pulp magazine, we were told with ghoulish relish and in considerable detail just how the next war would inevitably send us marching through nightmare forests that had been sprayed with tasteless, odorless, invisible gas fiendishly designed to rot the flesh right off our bones. Yet as I look back through the misty years. I can recall remarkably few of my fellow alumni who found it necessary to become habitués of opium dens just because the world was too much with them, as the poet says.

Instead of fleeing from life, we met it head on. We ended the Great Depression, we won the biggest war in human history, and we constructed the unprecedented prosperity that has endured now for almost a generation and which has made it possible for delicate draft-dodgers to nurture their neuroses in an atmosphere of luxury associated in my day only with movie stars and with the late Tommy Manville.

Contrast the sadsacks of my youth with the fat cats of today. Few of the placard brandishers have ever had to worry about eating. Fewer yet have worked for a living, a fact mutely attested to by their draggle-tailed, slovenly appearance. No employer in his right mind, after all, would take a chance on hiring them. Yet their rent is paid, many of them drive costly little foreign cars, and they have enough money left over to patronize the campus dope-peddler.

They worry about the Bomb, it is said forgivingly.

Who doesn't?

Atomic Armageddon threatens everyone, not just a few college students. But the rest of us are not noticeably hiding in corners puffing on marijuana and weeping tears of self-pity.

As I say, I'm not sure that education can do much to help this particular condition. I diagnose the current malaise as a kind of deficiency disease. It stems from not enough discipline at home, not enough faith in God, man, or anything else, and above all, not enough good, hard work anywhere along the line. It can be cured only by large injections of the indicated ingredients, not by the schools alone.

Unfortunately, we rarely hear or read these days about the overwhelming majority of sensible, studious scholars whose image is being so badly corroded by the capers of the kooks. One remedy for the Commissioner's complaint is for adult society to give greatly increased and impressive recognition to the decent and constructive elements among our youth, and the back of its hand to the indecent and the destructive.

Another remedy is for us to keep a close eye on our own kids. My son has gone into the Air Force since I got the Commissioner's letter, but at the time he was a college student and 1-A in the draft. I called him in and gave him the word:

"The day you start on 'pot' and LSD, my boy, you're going to be an ex-college student in one heck of a hurry, and 4-F in the draft to boot, at least until you get over the whipping I'm going to give you."

There would be fewer misconceptions and a much smaller generation gap if more parents would talk turkey to their own children. However, there is no denying that the misconceptions and the gaps persist. In my own profession, there are a few that amount to yawning chasms between educators on the one hand and the general public on the other.

(1) THE MORALITY GAP

If there's one thing that is guaranteed to raise my hackles instantaneously to a 45-degree angle, it's a teacher who deliberately panders to the worst in his students, instead of trying his hardest to bring out the best in them. Fortunately few in number, these prostitutes of my profession deserve to be drummed conspicuously out of education to a Rogue's March of public scorn and private revulsion.

Every so often, one of our more mixed-up instructors will fall by the wayside, betraying his calling in the process. The big black headlines that invariably chronicle the sorry event bear mute testimony to the rarity of the occurrence. Just the same, when it happens, it shouldn't. And it shocks.

A long-haired hippie in my home town of Sacramento recently got picked up by the hard-working constabulary for selling dope to his college classmates. This is par for the course these days, sadly enough, when so many of these grimy misfits are trying convulsively to destroy themselves and everyone around them.

What is emphatically *not* par for any course and what raised both my ire and my eyebrows simultaneously was the sentimental support given this dope-peddler by certain members of his college faculty.

One English teacher, apparently still under the narcotic spell of De Quincey and Coleridge, wrote this sort of unmitigated guff to the trial judge:

"Whatever Mike did, I am sure that he did out of love, out of a belief that here was a way to guide people to a truer way of engaging with each other. The law becomes then not a means of justice but a hindrance to justice."

Note the implication here. It's all right to break a law in our democratic society if you break it for the sake of love. Laws are thus presumably made for everybody but lovers. And the hoary old cry of the disappointed Frankie just after she has filled Johnny full of lead, "I did it because I loved him," takes on a brand-new and highly practical connotation these days.

When and if I decide to rob a bank, therefore, I have determined to do it with nothing but big, warm, wonderful love in my heart. I may even bestow a gentle kiss upon the flustered brow of the trussed-up bank guard as I step over him with the loot. This should guarantee me a whole flock of character references from my local college faculty. And who knows? Maybe even a demonstration or two down in front of the jail when the cops finally round me up.

Another mortarboarded mumblehead at the same institution lamented to the sorely tried court in regard to this convicted criminal: "His was a search for deeper emotional-spiritual values. He is as much a victim as a victimizer."

Next week, same time, same place, "East Lynne."

Sure, he's a victim. So is every scurvy dabbler in drugs who deliberately spreads his own filthy poison to others for the sake of a fast buck. Speaking for myself, I'd a lot rather associate with Typhoid Mary. At least she spread only the seeds of physical sickness. She never attempted to destroy the soul.

Come to think of it, I've never read any anguished letters from medical school faculties trying to get poor Mary out of quarantine because she distributed her germs affectionately and with the very best of intentions.

Can it be that our medical doctors are less sympathetic than our professors? Or just less stupid?

All of us make the laws that govern us. A teacher exists to show his youthful captive audience how to make desirable changes in those laws in an orderly way.

But a teacher who condones the breaking of democratically enacted laws by those entrusted to his care for any reason on God's earth is not a teacher. He's a Pied Piper of Destruction.

(2) THE PERSONAL-APPEARANCE GAP

The law, it is said, does not concern itself with trifles. Neither should education.

Just as if we schoolmen didn't have enough headaches these days, we find ourselves currently awash in the riptide of the Great Freak-out crisis.

Kids who couldn't care less about books and lessons can get frantically interested in a big hurry, it seems, if their school tries to make them dress decently. And parents who stay away from school elections and PTA meetings in droves are becoming all frothed up and wall-eyed because the principal won't let Junior come to class looking like an unmade bed.

My old friend and admirer, the American Civil Liberties Union, has predictably charged into courtrooms across the land, gallantly heckling various hard-pressed school boards whose sole crime has been a natural reluctance to permit the boy students from becoming indistinguishable from so many gorillas, and their female undergrads from looking like Main Street call girls.

Every so often, especially when earnest news is unaccountably scarce, the press regales us with a mock-serious account of some simpleton who insists upon coming to high school with a Mohawk haircut, or perhaps his female counterpart who has taken to wearing emerald-green makeup to class.

Naturally, the educational authorities feel obliged to take steps, and then there is a vast to-do about individual liberty and every person's right to make an ass of himself. A story of this nature, treated lovingly and attenuatedly, can sometimes keep an enterprising reporter or feature writer in business for more than the traditional nine days.

It's not always the kids who succumb to the fatal lure of easy headlines and photographs on page one. Occasionally an instructor will decide to cultivate an unkempt beard or perhaps grow long hair reminiscent of "When Knighthood Was in Flower." Quite often he will turn out to be a teacher who has been receiving poor competency ratings and is about to get the ax. What better way to confuse the issue and drum up sympathy than to pose as a persecuted individualist, martyred because of a little excess head foliage?

No matter how skin-tight the Capri pants on the sophomore girl or how revolting the insignia on the junior boy's black leather jacket, however, there always seems to be a superfluity of busybodies ready to spring to the defense of the poor harassed exhibitionist. I used to wonder where these crusaders lay during the prolonged intervals between silly seasons. Of late I have come to consider them a breed apart, hibernating regularly in order to store up excess indignation.

Why do school people play into the hands of these nuts by singling them out and proceeding against them? Because we have to.

Any teacher can tell you all about the fragile imper-
manence of classroom attention. It's hard to get in the
first place and exceedingly easy to lose. Yet without it the
most able instructor might just as well call it quits and
concentrate on research. It follows as the night the day
that anything that interferes with pupil attention is bad
for education.

Purple hair and shirts unbuttoned down to the navel
may simply be charming evidence of social immaturity or
adolescent bumptiousness, but whatever else they may be
they are undeniably attention-getters. Even if the teacher
turned out to be the lineal descendant and the virtual
reincarnation of Horace Mann, he would be hard put to
compete with this sort of three-dimensional psychedelic
prodigy. No. If the humdrum but necessary items of the
curriculum are to get from the instructor's daily lesson
plan into the skulls of the students, the school is going to
have to minimize distractions, not foster them.

It may be argued that an American citizen has the right
to grow a beard or wear a bikini or shave one side of
his head if he wants to, and this is true—as long as he
doesn't inflict himself upon others in an environment dedicated to scholarly learning. But our youngsters all have
to be in school and of necessity inflict themselves upon
each other. They are there to learn, not show off.

A school is not a freak show, nor is it a place to indulge distracting whims and crotchets. Its purpose is to
teach children enough so that in later life they will know
the difference between sincere individualism and phony
exhibitionism.

After all, even Abe Lincoln didn't grow a beard until
after he was elected President.

As a notorious advocate of individualism, rugged and
otherwise, I'm constantly being challenged nowadays

when I adopt an anti–fright wig and pro-bathing stance in controversies of this weighty nature.

"Why can't my daughter go to high school in a thigh-high dress?" one Mrs. Busty rasps via the U.S. mails. "She wears it to sing-ins."

I'll bet she does, too. And in some of our more confused churches today, she probably wears it to pray-ins. But not to a permanent teach-in, madam, if you don't mind. Unless she wants to turn it into a permanent leer-in. And the taxpayers might just cavil a bit at subsidizing four years of leering.

Enter Dad upon the scene, thundering off-key: "If my Junior wants to let his hair grow down to his waist and leave his shirt open to the navel, what business is it of the school?"

Well, Dad, I'm going to tell you. And through the exercise of what I consider phenomenal self-restraint, I'm going to overcome the temptation to ask in turn what kind of a character you have to be to let your son lurch around in broad daylight looking like Homo Neanderthalensis in search of a cave.

Under the very best conditions, a teacher has his work cut out for him. Positively his hardest job each day is to get and to hold the attention of his restless, revved-up, captive audience. His competition of late is pretty stiff. In addition to the World Series, the Super Bowl, and the Miss Universe contest, it now includes discotheques, go-go girls, the Monkees, and *Laugh-in,* not necessarily in that order.

Now, anything which makes it even a little tougher for the teacher to get his students to pay attention to him is bad for education. Period. So if your pride and joy ambles moronically into class wearing a beard or a Fu Manchu moustache done up in a snood—or a Mau-Mau bone in his nose, for that matter—he's not just making an idiot of himself; he's also making it hard for his teacher to do his job. And that's where we school people blow the whistle every time.

Whatever gives a conscientious, hard-working teacher a bad time is no good insofar as we're concerned. And anything that makes it tough for kids to concentrate on the job at hand has no place in the schools.

One final word of caution:

Don't get individualism mixed up with exhibitionism. It's one thing to want to stand out from the crowd intellectually and quite another thing to want to attract attention by adopting weird styles of dress and behavior. It's the difference between Henry David Thoreau and Timothy Leary.

(3) THE CULTURE GAP

We are going to have to decide whether we want educators to be skilled technicians or learned scholars. A former high school pupil of mine came back to see me shortly after the close of World War II. He had served four years in the paratroops and had seen duty in Italy, France, and Germany. His 1946 observations may be pertinent today.

"When I was in training at Fort Benning, Georgia, I used to travel around quite a bit on my leaves. I got into the habit of asking one single question in every new town I visited in the state: 'Who are your three most successful citizens?' The answer, nearly always, was: 'The bank president, the Cadillac dealer, and the Coca-Cola distributor.' The dollar sign was invariably the mark of success.

"Then when I got into Europe, and as soon as I could find someone in the many little towns we liberated who could speak English, I always asked the same question:

'Who are your three most successful citizens?' But there the response was quite different: 'The *maire*, or burgomaster; the *curé*, or priest; and [believe it or not] the schoolmaster.' The mayor because he embodied the civic conscience; the priest because he embodied religious truth; and the schoolman because he embodied the learning and culture of the community."

If my school district had had a superintendent sixty years ago, the odds are that he would have boasted a full beard, an impressive bay window (called in those days a "corporation"), and a big gold watch and chain with an elk's tooth hanging from it. He would have been superintendent for life, or its equivalent professionally. Today, a school administrator is lucky if he lasts out a four-year contract. My predecessor knew little about behavioristic psychology or acoustic tiles or standard deviations or drywall construction in school busses. In a dozen ways he was less competent than the fast-talking, fast-moving, fast-changing superintendent of today. Why was the old-time administrator an object of universal respect? Perhaps because although he was not much on public relations, he could read the *Aeneid* in Latin, the *Iliad* in the original Greek, and discuss Miltonic blank verse. The educator in those days was respected precisely because he *was* educated. He retained his position for decades because he symbolized supremely well the cultural ambitions for the community he served. When a stranger entered that community and asked to be taken to the most learned citizen in residence, he was lead proudly and unquestioningly to the leading schoolman. It is our misfortune that today this is no longer so.

Don't misunderstand me. It's not necessary in this day and age for a man to be a classicist in order to be cultured. But it *is* necessary for him to know how to write and to speak English in a manner at least relatively free from gross errors. It's advisable for him to know enough about American history to be able to distinguish between Andrew Jackson and Andrew Johnson, and enough about European history to explain the difference between Napoleon I and Napoleon III. And it's certainly expedient for him to react with some show of recognition when someone in the course of a conversation mentions Cyrano or The Wife of Bath or Uriah Heep. If the schoolman is unable to display this sort of minimum cultural competence, then who in heaven's name can we reasonably expect to do so?

That too many educators currently are at their weakest in this highly sensitive area cannot be attributed to any dropoff in the intellectual caliber of our school people during the past generation. Our teachers and administrators are just as talented and intelligent as they ever were—probably more so. But since the takeover of my profession thirty years ago by the burning-eyed, thin-lipped disciples of Dr. John Dewey, with their maddening and unshakable assurance that they alone were right and everybody else was not only wrong but slightly stupid, school people have been told by virtually everyone in authority over them that culture was of no consequence. The education major doesn't require any. No test is administered to the applicant for the teaching credential to see if he can even spell or knows the multiplication table. An administrator has to know psychology, curriculum, finance, and school law, but nobody cares at all whether he has ever heard of the Platonic Absolutes or the Nicomachean Ethics. And any schoolman can get a doctoral degree from any institution in the land without having anyone ask him if he can distinguish between Bizet and Puccini, Galileo and Copernicus, or the War of the Roses and the Flowering of New England. In such a philistine environment, under superiors who consistently sneer at and deride the importance of cultural content, exposed solely to a philosophy that holds that there are no lasting values, no eternal verities, no positive standards, it's a wonder that such a large number of our teachers and school administrators are as literate and cultured as they are.

(4) THE DEFINITION GAP

You didn't know, I'll wager, that a school system is good (a) if its lunch program is educational as well as nutritious, (b) if its teachers are all certificated by the state, and (c) if it spends at least twice as much per pupil as it did ten years ago.

Contrariwise, I doubt your awareness that a school system is automatically no good (a) if it uses merit pay to reward good teaching, (b) if it refuses to provide payroll checkoffs for National Education Association dues, and (c) if it doesn't take advantage of federal-aid programs.

I told you you'd be surprised. You question my criteria? I'm sorry. You simply cannot do that. They aren't my criteria at all, you see; they're the National Education Association's criteria, and arguing with the NEA is *lèse majesté* at best and high treason at worst.

I was, in fact, citing examples from an official NEA manual called "Profiles of Excellence: Recommended Criteria for Evaluating the Quality of a Local School System." There are 124 of these criteria, and presumably any school district lucky enough or sufficiently diligent to meet all 124 would qualify forthwith for education's Hall of Fame, with its superintendent a cinch for either canonization or apotheosis.

If by any chance you happen to be an educator, you're aware of the futility of questioning such an Establishment bible as this. Unthinkable.

However, to be purely hypothetical, here's what you might be saying if you did dare to disagree with the NEA's definition of what makes a school system good.

"A school district is superior not because it's big enough to provide all necessary educational services within its boundaries, as NEA avers, but because the educational services it does supply turn out graduates who are cultured, learned, and good citizens.

"And despite 'Profiles of Excellence,' a school system is not necessarily inferior just because it refuses to grab all the federal money in sight. It's inferior only if its pupils do not read and spell and calculate up to their own innate potentials."

I guess I'm a little bothered about a rating system for schools that refuses to concern itself with the only reason for a school's existence: the systematic imparting of organized and disciplined subject matter to its pupils in such a way as to insure their maximum mastery of the essentials of human knowledge.

This isn't so tough an outcome to measure, incidentally. In California, statewide annual tests in the "Three Rs" are required by law, and have been conscientiously administered by every public school since 1962. We know precisely which are our "best" school systems, and we are even now conducting research to find out exactly how they got that way.

Certainly America's schools need more money. Equally certainly, money alone will not make children learned. Beautifully kept school grounds are nice. Good teacher salary schedules should be the goal of every school system. Adequately staffed guidance and counseling services are highly desirable.

But confound it! A school can have all these advantages and at least 121 more, and it can still turn out graduates who can't tell the difference between Boyle's law and Gresham's law or between Moby Dick and Richard III.

The trouble with so many school districts is their penchant for first raising tax money and then funneling it into umpteen glittering, seductive channels, all glamorous, all attractive, but none of them having much to do with education in depth. What they should do, of course, is first adopt a sensible educational philosophy stressing mastery of subject matter and then raise the money to finance the program best calculated to flesh out the philosophy. First things first.

Remember this: If your school system's philosophy includes such concepts as abolishing report cards, using the "look-say" Egyptian-hieroglyphic approach to reading, abandoning history and geography in favor of the mishmash known as "social studies," then it won't make much difference how much money it uses to water its educational wastelands. The Sahara will remain obstinately dry. The only difference is that it will then be expensively dry.

(5) THE CONTROL GAP

Let's take a brief look at another misconception of our time, that someone besides the representatives of the general public should be running the schools.

We teachers walk along a branching highway as we shepherd our clamorous charges into tomorrow. Every so often, there's a fork in the road. Once in a while, we make the wrong choice. When we do, it's a devil of a job getting everybody back to the main turnpike again.

We were wrong thirty years ago when we bought Progressive Education and allowed ourselves to be converted to life-adjustment education by such anointed apostles of the Revealed Truth as William Kilpatrick, George Counts, and Harold Rugg.

We were wrong again in the late Fifties when we tended to pooh-pooh the message beeped by Sputnik and to insist that the only thing wrong with what we in our wisdom were doing to the children was that no one would give us enough money to do it in a more in-grouping, on-going, and forward-looking fashion.

We're wrong today when we listen to the winsome, warbling wood-notes of the teacher unionizers and permit the public to think of us as skilled labor when for at least the last two thousand years our goal has been to project the image of a learned profession.

But we're on the farthest out, loneliest dead-end street of all when we try to set educational policy for the schools in which we work, justifying our takeover on the grounds that parents aren't interested enough in their own children to set goals for their instruction or smart enough to know what's good for them.

Since the public school was first born on this continent, it has always been taken for granted that the electorate would lay down the objectives that the school would aim for, and that it would do this through the medium of its own locally elected school-board members. The general public would accordingly supply the *what* in education; we teachers would supply the *how*.

The relationship between teacher and parent was thus somewhat comparable to that between physician and patient. The patient, by telling the doctor what his symptoms are and what he wants the doctor to do for him and how much he can afford to pay for the treatment, sets *policy*. The doctor then uses his professional expertise to cure the patient, thus supplying the *how*.

The *what* and the *how*, then, have always been the two co-equal sides of the educational coin. But today we teachers too often are attempting to furnish both. And this just doesn't work. Not in a country like ours.

Florida recently proved my point. There the embattled teachers "resigned" their positions en masse to protest legislative policymaking in the form of a school-money package that they considered insufficient. To the accompaniment of much national publicity, they stayed off their jobs for three weeks. Then they went back to work, or in some cases tried to, under the exact legislative package that they had previously spurned.

To me, this whole proceeding seemed feverishly irrational at the time, but as the final returns filter in on this sun-kissed exercise in futility, it assumes even more of an Alice in Wonderland hue of unreality. Meditate if you will upon these developments since the end of the Florida strike:

(1) Each Lee County teacher had to pay a $100 fine to get his job back. Eight principals gave up $20,000 in total salary to get even this settlement.

(2) The Duval County school board screened 393 "resigned" teachers to determine which ones it wanted to rehire. Some of them didn't make it.

(3) In Broward County, seventy-four teachers stayed off the payroll for good.

(4) The Pensacola board rehired its "resigned" teachers on annual contracts only. More than a hundred lost their painfully acquired tenure as a result of their so-called resignations.

(5) Key West took back its teachers only after they had signed a no-strike pledge.

There were a lot more cases like these. Obviously, a strike that costs its participants as heavily as did this one just has to be a total disaster, especially since it ended with exactly the same money available as when it started. The implications for other statewide teacher unions that may be nursing an itch to summon the faithful to man the picket lines are portentous indeed.

What happened, of course, was that the Florida teachers came up against not General Motors nor CBS nor yet Alcoa, but eyeball to eyeball against the public itself— the public that elects the local school boards and runs the whole state. And the Florida citizenry was simply outraged at the idea of publicly employed professionals striking against the people. So the teachers took a beating.

This is what some of us were afraid of when this ill-omened walkout was first talked of. A teacher who isn't being treated properly by his employer has the immemorial right of every professional to pack his suitcase and seek out an employer who will treat him better. A Florida teacher can move to California, say, where the pay is higher.

But the one thing the teacher can't do and shouldn't do and darned well better not do is threaten or coerce or try to intimidate his fellow citizens who make the policy under which he holds his job. This pretty well rules out strikes, I'm afraid. May I suggest the more ancient and appropriate professional techniques of logic, reasoning, and persuasion? In short, educational techniques. After all, fellow educators, we're supposed to be able to educate people. If we can't, who can?

As a teacher, I'm sad that my Florida colleagues are suffering because they listened to irresponsible demogogues. But I'm even sadder that they were willing to adopt such unprofessional methods to attain an allegedly professional objective.

"Silent Cal" Coolidge said it once, and he said it for all time to come: "There is no right to strike against the public safety by anybody, anywhere, any time."

And there is nothing so unsafe as a nation with empty classrooms.

Fellow teachers, remember this:

We work for the people. They don't work for us. And in a democratic society, the people alone decide what's best for their own children. Anything else is fascism. No matter how you slice it.

(6) THE PHILOSOPHY GAP

In any discussion of the misconceptions of modern education, the most serious has to be the one that sells the children a spurious product. I've been seeing the evidence of just such a confidence game increasingly of late.

I often show up on a high school or college campus and try to field catch-as-catch-can questions tossed at me from all angles by the sharpest generation in American history.

Why do I bother to brave the beards and the barbs?

For one thing, it helps keep me in shape. After an afternoon spent with the kids, such reputedly hot historical gridirons as old King James' Star Chamber and even the Spanish Inquisition would seem cool and even clammy by comparison. A better reason is that I get an insight into the world of tomorrow by talking with those who are going to inhabit it.

It will be a smarter world, I think, but unless we teachers encourage students to use their brains to tune in on the accumulated wisdom of the past, it may well be a jaded, even a sick, world.

I happened to mention "absolutes" to a high school forum the other day. One bright-eyed senior girl challenged me immediately.

"Don't generalize," she commanded. "What exactly is

an absolute? Give me an example of one right here in
school."

"Glad to oblige," I replied. "An absolute in the school
sense is something universally true and of supreme importance to everyone within its framework of reference.
Here in high school, English is a curricular absolute. Without knowledge of the mother tongue, the astronomer can't
describe his novas nor the political scientist his ideal state.
The physicist is limited to formulas and the biologist to
color movies of fruit flies unless somewhere along the line
they are taught the stern beauty and the inner logic of
the English language. In France, of course, it would be
the French language."

The young lady reflected.

"Okay," she conceded. "But how about an international
absolute? A rule of conduct or morality that is equally
true in all countries and in all times? I don't think there
is one. No rule is equally true for all people."

"Oh, yes, there is!" I rejoined. "Try a negative absolute
this time. In no age and in no society has it ever been
morally correct deliberately to betray one's friend."

She was visibly disappointed. She had been all primed
by somebody for me to mention something like murder,
upon which she would have promptly brought up East Indian thuggee, or homosexuality, upon which she would
have triumphantly countered with a hair-raising description of Periclean Athens.

"Surely there must have been at least one place," she
murmured, frowning prettily.

"Name one," I challenged.

So I won an argument with a high school girl. Not as
easy as it sounds these days, incidentally. But that isn't
the point. What shook me was the fact that somewhere in
school the kid had been sold the tired relativist philosophy

that was old in Plato's day, and which he exploded for what should have been all time to come.

"There's no such thing as truth. All things are relative. All standards are variable. All values fluctuate from day to day."

This kind of cowardly, nihilistic excuse for not thinking has been kicking around the planet ever since man became man. You don't suppose today's youngsters who pride themselves so on rejecting the old ways are going to commit the supreme irony of falling for the oldest, moldiest thought system of all, do you?

Relativists are intellectually lazy. It's hard work to think in terms of absolutes, so the relativists drop out. They're the hippies of philosophy.

I guess what bugs me, as the kids say, is that somebody is spreading this worn-out bunk in the schools. We teachers can do better than this. In fact, we'd better, unless we intend to raise a generation indistinguishable from Pavlov's dogs.

Education exists to give youth the tools it needs to pursue the truth. And this implies rather strongly that there is a truth to be pursued. An absolute, if you will.

We educators had better believe it. Because once we kill off truth, we might as well take up some other calling. We will have scuttled our reason for existing.

(7) THE RACIAL GAP

There is an inordinate amount of twaddle being tossed around to the effect that the racial mess is going to prove insoluble and eventually bring public education to its knees.

Claptrap.

What we are facing is not the Frankenstein monster of racial bigotry but the Harlequin of stupidity. Plain ordinary horse sense seems regrettably to be the commodity in shortest supply these days.

For example:

I suppose this will have the usual effects attendant upon any deliberate poking into the wasps' nests that houses our buzzing racial minorities these days, but I have to say it. Some people are barking up the wrong stump in trying to improve their present image at the expense of past literature.

What triggered this observation was a mild spate of recent reports about requests to school boards and library commissions asking that Little Black Sambo's color be changed along with Shylock's religion before these two highly disparate characters are allowed to infect the kiddies with assorted unpleasant racial prejudices.

Regrettably this seems to be part and parcel of a misguided modern movement to scissor any reference to race at all out of our children's classics. And it's not just books, either.

"Swanee River" has to be sung: "Oh, people, how my heart grows weary," which is pretty silly.

"Old Black Joe" is conspicuous by his absence in most music books today, and it's too bad. When I was piping merrily and off-key in the third grade, Joe was always a particular friend of mine.

Then there are the movies. I can recall a few years back when the fine British cinema version of "Oliver Twist" was successfully kept out of the United States because Dickens had thoughtlessly made nasty old Fagin a Jew, and some of our Jewish organizations objected more than somewhat to the film for that reason.

This is a lot of applesauce. Not only are we looking

pretty silly around the world, which is really nothing new, but we're liable to end up bowdlerizing some of the best literature ever written.

Assume for the nonce that we decide to censor only the deep-dyed villains of our literary heritage so the small fry won't hook their villainies in automatically with their races and nationalities. We've got some immediate problems:

How do we keep Sax Rohmer's insidious Dr. Fu Manchu from being identified as Chinese?

Or Shakespeare's scheming Iago from being publicly known as an Italian?

Then, too, I always resented Sir Arthur Conan Doyle making his fiendish opponent of Sherlock Holmes an Irishman. We'll have to change Professor Moriarty's name to something like Smith, I fear, because every Moriarty since the Battle of Clontarf has been as Irish as Paddy's pig.

The Scotch certainly can zero in on bloody old Macbeth, and General De Gaulle would have a perfect case against Dickens's sinister French guillotine-watcher, Madame Defarge.

I can think of but one American Indian villain, and I seem to remember that he was only half-Indian, at that. Mark Twain dreamed Injun Joe up to chase Tom Sawyer through that nightmare cave with Becky Thatcher.

And aside from Ian Fleming's formidable "Mr. Big," I can't offhand recall any Negro villains at all. Simon Legree, that perfect paragon of villains, was to the best of my recollection a white Anglo-Saxon Protestant.

Really, fellow minority members, can't we agree among ourselves to settle tacitly each for his own literary villains, consoling ourselves the while with the comforting thought that ours are no worse than the other fellows' and maybe even a teeny bit better? More efficient, perhaps. Or with a certain flair and savoir-faire.

Because if we can't, we may end up with no villains in our literature at all. And this would be a shame. The thoroughgoing scoundrels are usually the most interesting guys in the books.

Of course, we could make them all Martians, I suppose. But what happens when we establish diplomatic contact with the Red Planet, and the Martian Anti-Defamation League begins to make itself heard?

I'm not much of a racist. Talk about black power or white power leaves me as cold as talk about green power or blue power. That's why I seldom agree with these superheated advocates of pigmented predominance who go around pounding their chests and associating all the cardinal virtues with the hue of their own hides.

When Floyd McKissick denounces the leaders of America's education establishment for saying, in effect, "Mix Negroes with Negroes and you get stupidity," I've got to go along with him. Too many of us are saying just that.

I'd like to file a rousing dissent.

There are plenty of good reasons for trying to achieve maximum racial integration in our public schools, of course, but to argue that an all-Negro school has to be a bad school just because the students are all black is as asinine as to say that an all-white school is automatically a good one, or even that a racially mixed school will perforce to be anything at all, good or bad, just because it's mixed.

The public school population in Washington, D.C., is practically all Negro today. There just aren't very many white kids around our capital anymore. Now, does this mean that all of Washington's schools are inherently doomed from now on to be snakepits of stupidity and incubators of inferiority?

Not according to a good many pretty knowledgeable

Negroes who have been speaking out increasingly of late. In New York recently, Herbert Ottley, of "Youth in Action," sounded off to this effect: "The Negro student doesn't have to sit right next to a white student to learn. Negroes can learn with Negroes."

And Dr. Allen Possaint, of Tufts, added, "There is no reason why we should have to join the white community to achieve our goals in education."

Amen.

Certainly there is every imperative cause for Negroes and whites to work together and for neither race to regard itself as intrinsically superior to the other. But a good school is a good school. If it has fine, inspirational teachers, small class sizes, good books, even-handed discipline, adequate buildings and supplies, and, above all, a philosophy of education that stresses learning to use the tools that the human race has found to be indispensable in the pursuit of truth, then the children who go to that school are going to learn.

Not too long ago, a high-cost federal study found that the amount of money you spend on a school has little if any relation to the amount of learning that gets into the heads of its pupils, and that even such a sacred cow as small class size didn't seem to help the youngsters very much. More significantly, it concluded that the out-of-school background of the children, particularly the socioeconomic level of their parents, was far and away more important in influencing scholastic achievement than higher teacher salaries, enlarged libraries, closed-circuit TV, and so on.

The recommendations of this "Coleman Report," named after its director, a Johns Hopkins professor, were resplendent and remarkable in their stark simplicity. There weren't any.

Instead, the worthy Dr. Coleman concluded somewhat

apocalyptically: "If recommendations had been requested, they could hardly have been given, for the facts themselves point to no obvious solution."

So why bother about good schools, decent working conditions for teachers, manageable class sizes, superior books, and all the other concomitants usually believed essential to above-average educational output? If the child comes from a well-to-do suburb, he'll do all right regardless; and if he happens to spring from a slum, it won't make much difference how much you spend on him, or indeed what you do to try to help him. He won't learn much anyway.

"Baloney," was my inelegant comment at the time.

If we have to wait until all the big-city kids are bussed into the suburbs before they can expect a decent education, the wait will approximate that which normally intervenes between two major planetary glaciation cycles. And if we delay until the middle-class suburban youngsters are bussed forcibly into the slum schools, we will wait until hell itself freezes over.

But my "Baloney" was occasioned by more than this obvious logistical fact. Professor Coleman, a teacher himself, came up in his report with this perfect whopper of a "research" finding: Teachers aren't really significant in slum schooling. Whether a child has a vital, inspirational instructor down in the grades is thus far less important than whether the child is sitting next to a middle-class schoolmate.

This "finding" is such obvious guff that anyone who knows anything at all about education discounted this portion of the Coleman Report as soon as he read it. The one ultimate reality in education is the impact of the personality of the teacher upon the personality of the pupil. This has been true, incidentally, since we emerged from Eden or came down out of trees, whichever you prefer.

And I don't care whether Junior is sitting next to Stokely Carmichael's son or Bill Buckley's daughter. If the teacher is the best in town, Junior is going to learn.

Comes now from the wings an equally prestigious professor, Dr. Samuel Bowles, of Harvard, to say that the Coleman Report findings are suspect, to say the least. Using the original Coleman data, Dr. Bowles finds that the quality of teaching is the most important factor in educating anybody.

"Were we merely to raise the quality of teaching resources devoted to the education of Negroes to the level of that currently devoted to whites, we would significantly improve Negro achievement," says Dr. Bowles.

Thank you, sir, for saying so well what some of the rest of us have been saying for a long time—namely, that we're simply going to have to get a substantial percentage of our top teachers into the slum schools, even if we have to resort to a kind of educational "flight pay" to do it. The importance of the teacher in any group-learning situation is so great that all other factors fade into relative insignificance by comparison. And I don't care whether the group doing the learning is Caucasian, Negro, Mongolian, Eskimo, or Berber.

Without belittling in any way the need for the races to mingle as Americans and to accept each other as human beings, I'm still compelled to recall that two thousand years before my own ancestors started speaking Gaelic and painting themselves blue on a barbarous island off the Northern European coast, the Chinese were providing excellent schooling for their offspring in schools that were (let's face it) highly segregated.

After all, what else can you call it when all the kids in school are Chinese?

Right here, let me introduce to you Dr. Seymour Gang, principal of Public School 192 in Harlem. His pupils are all "disadvantaged," to use the jargon of the day, although they come from different neighborhoods. They come out of the slum every morning and go back to it every evening. Yet under Dr. Gang's tutelage, his slum kids read almost one year ahead of the national average.

How is it done?

For one thing, each teacher is there on probation. His main goal is to have every child reading at or above level, with no ifs, ands, or buts. Seventy percent of them do just that.

For another, the school accepts complete responsibility for the child's reading ability. His poor home background, his bad heredity, his faulty English, his nonexistent home cultural opportunities, are ignored. If a new teacher uses these as alibis for failing to teach his pupils to read, out he goes.

Then there is the matter of class size. P.S. 192's pupil-teacher ratio is fifteen to one, but reading groups are even smaller. Two and a half hours per day are spent on reading, reading, and more reading.

Finally, an explicit study of phonics is included in every class. Each child learns the alphabet, the sound of each vowel and consonant, the importance of syllables as the indispensable building blocks of the language.

And just in passing, the school teaches standard English, not the bastard street-gang dialects that so many of our academic pinheads are hailing as vital and viable additives to the curriculum, presumably in compliance with the cowardly old adage "If you can't beat 'em, join 'em."

Where does this leave the Coleman Report? Partly shot down, partly intact. Shot down is its finding that the school cannot overcome the influence of the home. Intact is its assumption that money alone won't bridge the gap.

Any child not an imbecile can be taught to read. A

school that believes this and proves it with its pupils deserves all the money it can get. But if you're teaching reading via the tired old "look-say," Egyptian-hieroglyphic, word-recognition, configuration-contour method, fellow teacher, you might as well hold class in a swamp. Any money you spend will be down the tube.

It's not just Dr. Coleman and his achievement findings that are stirring up the racial pot, however.

Some fairly weird and way-out bats are currently fluttering and swooping about the formerly staid and orderly cave of intelligence testing, and I feel it my duty to make my readers aware of the critters, if only because an awful lot of education these days is based on the old IQ.

For one thing, my former home town of Los Angeles has found (a) that some teachers misuse IQ-test results by attributing to them the omnipotence formerly the exclusive property of Jehovah, and (b) that too many racial-minority kids end up in the "low track" in school because they test low in intelligence, thus perpetuating racial segregation in an otherwise integrated school. So Los Angeles has nobly done the obvious thing to avoid the unspeakable stigma of bigotry. It has done away with intelligence tests.

The mind boggles at the cosmic simplicity of this response. Aristotle would have constructed the syllogism thus:

Major Premise: All testing, no matter how valuable it may be for educative purposes, should be incapable of misuse and should be popular with everyone.

Minor Premise: Intelligence testing is capable of misuse and unpopular with certain groups and individuals.

Conclusion: Therefore intelligence testing should be eliminated.

Allow me, in the absence of Aristotle, to set up a parallel syllogism for the medical profession:

Major Premise: Thermometer readings should be incapable of misinterpretation.

Minor Premise: Some doctors misinterpret thermometer readings.

Conclusion: Therefore thermometers should be abolished.

This sort of wraithlike reasoning is so patently ludicrous, dimwitted and lame-brained that I refuse to pursue it further down the byways of futility. Instead, I propose to direct your attention to another aspect of the IQ question. It seems that a learned professor of educational psychology, one Arthur Jensen, has decided on the basis of a San Francisco study that white children are smarter than black children. To be more precise, he reports that white youngsters have a "significantly greater ability to grasp abstract concepts" than do their darker-skinned playmates.

Now, inasmuch as this particular kind of "abstract concept" intelligence is absolutely essential for higher education and indeed for most intellectual pursuits, Dr. Jensen's findings are presumably bad news for the Negro kids, gasoline on the black-power flame, tonic for the Ku Klux Klan, and big trouble with a capital *T* for the good doctor himself, I have no doubt, especially if he decides to open a branch office in Watts or Harlem.

Even more ticklishly, the professor has come right out and said publicly that the black inferiority in this field is probably "genetically based," and he winds up with the flat statement that the national IQ average is 100 for whites and only 85 for blacks. "The difference in scholastic performance," he states, "is comparable."

Sorry, professor. I doubt this.

I don't question your data. I think your thermometer is right, but your diagnosis is wrong.

Why do I think this? Because I have an uneasy hunch that about a century ago, if Messrs. Terman and Binet had been around then to invent intelligence testing, it would have been my own dirty-faced, freckled, barefooted, little Irish ancestors just off the boat who registered 85 on the tests. A couple of generations later, the low kids on the IQ totem pole would have been named Corelli or Orsini, and a generation after them the slow youngsters would have been Zbyshkos and Korizoffskys.

Frightened and belligerent, underfed and overtaxed, dirty and diseased, what would they have made of intelligence tests? I can't prove it, of course, but I'd bet my great-grandfather's shillelagh that he showed up pretty poorly alongside the well-scrubbed, well-poised Standishes and Cabots and Lowells of old New England in the 1870s.

For obvious reasons, I'd hate to think his inferiority was genetic. In fact, I *don't* think so. I don't think it about the Mexican-Americans in California who rate low on some of our standardized tests because they can't read English as well as the rest of us. And I don't think so about black Americans, either.

But we're not going to help cure the fever by throwing away all the thermometers. It's not that easy.

And as long as the race riddle is up for discussion, let me say right here that if I were a Negro, I'd be pretty riled at Dr. Charles Hurst, of Howard University. With the usual good intentions that always cause so much trouble, the worthy doctor is currently trying to persuade America's schools to accept Negro dialect instead of insisting upon everybody using correct English.

Teachers keep correcting children who use the dialect they grew up with, it seems, and this is traumatic for the small fry. I have my doubts. And they're king-sized.

Dr. Hurst points out quite accurately that the Negro is asked to learn a brand of English in school quite different from the kind he speaks at home.

So what? So was practically every immigrant kid who ever came over here. And so is every white child whose parents move north or west from Appalachia, incidentally.

In varying degrees, of course, this is true of all schoolchildren. That's what schools are for. There's not much point, after all, in going to school for twelve years just to be reassured that it's okay to be as uneducated as your parents.

One of Hurst's colleagues spells out the problem:

"Negroes living in Chicago's black belt have a language which for them is operable. They communicate among themselves with ease.

"Then they go off to school, and the school tells them their speech is incorrect, unintelligible, and just plain bad. They must cut it out.

"The kids, puzzled, say: 'The hell I will. Everybody at home talks this way.' "

Well, if everybody at home talks that way, everybody at home is speaking bad English. And the sooner the schools point it out, the better. Here Dr. Hurst provides the clincher:

"The schools simply have to stop dealing in rights and wrongs. They've got to accept the dialect the student brings with him."

And it's right here, too, that Dr. Hurst and I are going to go to the mat.

It is precisely education's job to deal in rights and wrongs. Because a child may count on his fingers and toes at home is no reason for his arithmetic teacher to let him keep doing it at school. And because a bigoted neighborhood may revel in racism doesn't make it okay for the civics instructor to neglect teaching the Bill of Rights to youngsters who call that neighborhood home.

Neither does the fact that Mom and Pop say "De cat ha jus split" when they mean "The man has just gone" make it right, any more than my Irish great-grandfather was permitted by his American teachers to go around voicing such Old Sod barbarisms as "Sure and begorra, 'tis a foine spalpeen ye are, bad cess to ye."

After his teachers had finished with him, Great-Granddad spoke English and he was thankful for it all his life. His parents went to their graves speaking brogue.

This is what schools are for. If they're just going to put society's seal of approval on the status quo brought with them by the kids from home, why bother to have schools at all?

Granted that Dr. Hurst is well aware of the need to teach culturally deprived Negro children "standard English," as he calls it. Granted, too, that English as a spoken tongue can be accented in innumerable ways, ranging from the drawl of the Deep South to the inimitable twang of New England.

But the Negro, over and beyond any other element of our polyglot population, has the right to demand that the schools tell his children that there is only one correct English grammar. One right way to spell. One right way to conjugate verbs. One right way to compare adjectives. One right way to decline pronouns.

Why? Because the Negro has the most to gain.

The mastery of the English language is the greatest gift that our schools can give to any of our children. Especially to our racial minorities.

The alternative?

Why, for the Negro to go through life talking like Uncle

Remus, the Mexican-American like José Jiminez, the Italian-American like an organ-grinder, and the Irish-American like Pat and Mike.

Oh, dialects make fine jokes. But who wants to be a perpetual joke?

Not so funny is the loss of jobs currently occurring because of our persistent inability to straighten out our misconception of what the race problem is. Without mentioning any names, here's an instance of bigotry in reverse, this time in athletics:

Once upon a time—but not too long ago you may be sure —there was a certain big-time college basketball coach. He ulcerated and agonized for a multiracial state university with stratospheric scholastic requirements, and he had to hustle to recruit enough fair-to-middling players to keep the huffing and puffing alumni from blowing his house in.

Under these mildly traumatic conditions, our coach was in no position to indulge in racial discrimination, or indeed in any other kind of discrimination on his slender if elongated squad, even if he had felt like it. A good 6-foot-6 forward to him was just about as unimportant as the 1960 Cook County vote was to Richard Nixon, and it didn't make any difference to the beleaguered mentor whether the forward in question was black, brown, or magenta. To him, a good player was plain 14-karat gold.

Just the same, Coach Smith had his disciplinary standards, and he stuck with them. One year he came up with the most promising bunch of sophomore whizzes that had ever graced his thin bench. He walked on air for about a month, and then was brought sharply back to earth by the discovery that several of his new nuggets were playing hanky-panky with his rules and regulations.

Sadly, Coach Smith suspended three of his offending

stars. Several key games were promptly lost, and our hero receipted for his full share of boos and dead cats from outraged booster clubs.

Note: All three players were white.

Additional Note: No one felt obliged to take up the cudgels for the canned culprits. The American Civil Liberties Union didn't mobilize its squadrons of lawyers. The several civil rights foundations didn't meet in special session to consider militant action. Even the National Association for the Advancement of White People failed to call for the ousting and excommunication of the offending coach. The remainder of the basketball team were good boys for the rest of the year, and eventually the erring brethren were restored to grace.

Now mark this: Two years later, another outstanding athlete on the same squad fell afoul of the rules. Coach Smith took the same rueful action he had taken before. The star was suspended.

But this time all hell broke loose. Half the team threatened to walk out. Political action committees all over the country hissed and spat. The board of trustees was memorialized. The coach was publicly threatened. Finally, the college administration intervened frantically and reinstated the offending player over the protests of the coach.

Note: This boy was black.

Additional Note: As a result of this application of racism in reverse, the white basketball players promptly threatened to strike the team, bitterness was engendered that may plague the college athletic program for years to come, and the poor coach is probably going to lose his job for daring to discipline a black player in exactly the same way he had disciplined white players.

As a matter of fact, demands are even now being circulated on this distracted campus that a certain quota of black coaches be hired to take the place of white coaches or all the Negroes on the squad will quit school.

I regard this sort of thing as positive poppycock.

A basketball team is not a New England town meeting, a session of the Athenian Council of the Areopagus, nor yet a "group dynamics" gabfest. It's a military-style benevolent dictatorship with the coach in the role of dictator. Everybody who goes out for basketball knows this, and if he doesn't like it he should go out for the horseshoe-pitching team.

The coach in this case treated all his players alike, regardless of color. For some of the black players to whine and threaten boycott, using their race as an excuse, seems to me as contemptible as did the antics of some of the "professional Irishmen" in the old days who used to whimper and whine for preferred treatment solely on the grounds that they were Irish.

As my shillelagh-swinging ancestor old Barney Rafferty used to say about these yellow maggots on the green shamrock: "The back of me hand to thim, the spalpeens!"

Now, don't get the idea that black educators themselves don't recognize the blind alleys that emotionalism is building so blithely for them to march down.

The comments of Ennis McDaniel are worth recording. McDaniel is something called an "intergroup-education specialist" in one of our larger California school districts, and unlike certain polysyllabically titled educators, he appears to know what he's talking about. To illustrate:

"Many so-called 'black history' teachers are wholly unqualified to teach. They are hired because school districts are under pressure from militant groups to offer the course."

And

"This is actually just another form of racism, just a switch of bias. It distorts the role and place of some of these minority people."

And finally

"I get leery of this type of thing. I want the truth told, but not just for the heck of it. I hope we have enough gumption to tell the whole story, Mexican, Negro, and Oriental."

To say nothing of Tartar, Basque, Polynesian, and Celtic.

McDaniel, it seems to me, has deftly pointed up the key difficulties encountered in the teaching of black history. Or of brown, yellow, and puce history, for that matter.

One of these difficulties is, of course, the question "Where does one stop?" If it's imperative to stress the culture and the contributions of one racial minority in order to salve the national conscience and to build up the minority group's morale, then we are presented with a king-size problem in logistics.

Surely the American Indian has a claim to attention that puts all others in the shade. Negroes were indeed enslaved and treated abominably years ago; but the original Americans were encroached upon, dispossessed, infected with alien diseases, corrupted with firewater and darned near exterminated.

Our citizens of Oriental extraction have a powerful claim on our history books, too. Chinese coolies were chain-ganged and brought to California a century ago by the shipload, only to leave their bones under almost every crosstie of the great transcontinental railroads as they fought their long way eastward across the continent. And a surprisingly large number of them were lynched by the rampaging California vigilantes of those vigorous days before they had been off the boat long enough to find out why they were being strung up.

How now, ye advocates of color history? Because the Indian was badly treated, are we then to require the next generation to take courses in Sioux buffalo-stalking, Mandan corn-cultivating, and the Song of Hiawatha?

And because our ancestors chivvied the unfortunate Chinese from San Francisco to the Sierras, must we consequently institute compulsory classes in Oriental history going back beyond the Chou dynasty?

As a practical educator, I'd like to inquire mildly just where in blazes we're going to find the time for such formidable additions to the curriculum of our already overburdened schools. We would have to keep the kids in high school at least until they were old enough to vote.

Then there is the whole question of where to get qualified teachers. It's hard enough to find teachers of good old American history. How to unearth enough authorities on Bantu culture and Amharic literature to man the nation's million classrooms is a mind-boggler and then some.

I think we teachers would be well advised to keep black history or any other kind of color history as important facets of the great diamond that is the story of America. All our minorities should be discussed and dealt with. All their contributions to the world's melting pot should be mentioned. But to confuse the facet with the diamond itself is to do a grave disservice not just to education but to plain common sense.

At least I gather that Ennis McDaniel feels this way. And it's going to be pretty difficult for Stokely or Rap to brand him a bigoted Southern redneck. He was born fairly far south, all right. But his neck isn't red, it's black.

Inasfar as college courses in black studies are concerned, the fuss seems to have been phony from the beginning. Here's what has happened in the biggest state of the Union, and in the biggest city of that state:

Los Angeles Valley College, under extreme pressure from militants whose hair fairly bristled with outraged indignation, launched an elaborate program of ethnically oriented courses a few months ago. The rioters and cop-cursers, who had done their best to turn California campuses into battlefields, won their fight. Their demands were met in full.

So what happened? Valley College gave an ethnic party, and nobody came. Half the bitterly fought-for classes didn't even open last fall. Reason: Hardly anyone wanted to take them, apparently. The Mexican-American courses attracted exactly four eager students. "Black studies" enrollments told the same deflating story, particularly in regard to "Afro-American Literature," a class in which only three students registered.

What happened to all the *sturm und drang*, fellows? Where's the proof of your half-baked pudding? In fact, where are you? Back in the old pad dreaming up some new non-negotiable demands?

The same phenomenon on a somewhat less spectacular scale is occurring at California State College at Los Angeles, which has a sizable enrollment of 21,000, of which 2,310 are Negroes and Mexican-Americans. All of Cal-State's ethnic courses together drew 500 students, about 2½ percent of the total student body.

There's nothing at all wrong with establishing college courses in the culture and history of our racial-minority groups. This is one of the many things colleges are all about. But there's one heck of a lot wrong when a mob of wild-eyed youths protesting their own perfect sincerity and denouncing their elders' detestable hypocrisy throw their weight around violently and obscenely all over a convulsed campus on behalf of a change in curriculum in which they themselves have absolutely no intention of enrolling and for which there is so little genuine demand that it can't attract any students.

Who are the hypocrites now?

And what kind of credence are we school administrators supposed to attach to the next batch of demands for "relevant reforms," when the last ones turned out to be so gloriously irrelevant to the real educational needs of the vast majority for whom the activists so confidently purport to speak?

I'm convinced that nearly all college authorities will gladly add new courses without any need for confrontations and Molotov cocktails when they are given any solid evidence of genuine student demand for said courses. I'm equally sure that ethnic-studies courses are really needed and will eventually attract their proper percentage of enrollees.

But as of right now, all last year's violence and venom, blasphemy, and brouhaha look pretty darned silly.

The activist mountain labored—and brought forth a gnat.

(8) THE MONEY GAP

Have you joined the rising chorus of gripes and groans about the high cost of public education? Voted against any school-bond issues lately? Felt your blood pressure go up right along with your tax bill, for all the world like a second Apollo project?

You need complain no more. I have the fellow responsible for all this expense, and I can show him to you in thirty seconds. Just go look in the mirror.

Who is it who squawks at the prospect of little Ronald having to walk more than four blocks to school? Who is it who demands high-priced dinosaurs of buses to transport him twice a day almost literally between your front door and that of the school? You know perfectly well who it is, and it isn't the school.

It's not just buses, however. Parents whose boys and girls don't get free diphtheria, smallpox, and tetanus shots in school these days feel positively discriminated against. The schools are expected to employ trained nurses to ride herd on this whole mass innoculation program, in addition to keeping health charts on all the children and giving advice to teachers and parents alike on problems of disease, hygiene, and general sanitation. This sort of thing isn't free, you know. But who kicks up a storm when it isn't available? It's not the faculty.

Then there is the whole adjunct of food preparation in the schools. If I may indulge for a moment in a weakness that I so often decry in others: "When I was a boy" I took my lunch to school in a brown paper bag. In that paper bag were a peanut-butter sandwich, a jelly sandwich, a cupcake, and an apple. I did not feel deprived or discriminated against or underfed. Everyone else, you see, had identical brown paper bags containing identical lunches.

Today, school nutrition experts would be appalled at the mere thought of any child so underprivileged as to be compelled to eat that sort of lunch every day. They would come up with a quick count of proteins, minerals, and vitamins, and they would prove incontrovertibly that no one could survive on that kind of diet much past the age of eleven.

These fine people are certainly correct, and I hope that no reader will imagine for a moment that I am advocating mass malnutrition. However, you were beefing about the high cost of schooling, and I'm just pointing out that the mere capital outlay involved in supplying a school with the complex and expensive paraphernalia of a modern cafeteria—to say nothing of the plant needed to house it—can be very great. And it's Mom and Pop who insist on it, every time.

One school district I worked for supplied the entire city with community recreation. It was a fine program, to be sure. It provided trained leaders and activity directors for Little League, touch football, junior basketball, stamp-collecting, sewing practice, yo-yo contests, and baton-twirling. It built Pony League baseball stadia and maintained badminton courts. To do it justice, it kept juvenile delinquency down and provided clean, healthy amusement for the small fry. But it was expensive as all get-out.

When one of the local schoolmen dared to diffidently suggest that Mom and Pop stay home in the evenings and play with Junior instead of using tax money to pay professionals to do this, he was shouted down and well-nigh burned in effigy by the same worthy taxpayers who just a month before had been emitting Macedonian cries of anguish at the size of their annual tax bills.

I'm not taking sides either way. But the next time your local back-fence griping club meets to compare invidiously the cost of schooling today with what it was in the good old days, you might remind the members of the extras that the schools have currently taken on. And remind them who asked for all this.

Another thing you asked for was more federal money. You've been getting it, too, for five years. Your own money back, of course.

Back in 1964, Congress in its wisdom reared back and passed the very first generalized "aid to education" bill in our history. The legislation slid through with little fuss and less opposition, and some of its sections were unexceptionable. Quite good, in fact, and in the best American tradition.

But there was one provision in it that should have rung all the alarm bells in the land, or at least those that have not yet had their clappers amputated by the professional spenders in Washington. That was the stipulation that school districts enrolling pupils whose parents are poor would in the future get federal money to help give these children compensatory education.

There are a couple of assumptions contained herein that we need to take a long look at. One is that a poor kid automatically is culturally deprived just because he *is* poor and that he therefore needs government money to keep him from growing up to be a bum. This bland, sweeping generalization would certainly have raised eyebrows on such ex-poor kids as Abe Lincoln, Tom Edison, Henry Ford, and quite a few others who managed over the years to figure rather prominently in the history of the republic and who did so without any noticeable federal aid.

The other assumption is far more expensive if not more serious in the long run. It is that because a given school district happens to have children attending its schools whose parents earn less than a certain amount of money per year, the district itself must therefore be poor as the proverbial church mouse and in dire need of government handouts to enable it to provide a satisfactory educational program.

From my own personal experience, to say nothing of the exercise of elementary logic, I can testify that this is a lot of bilge.

I used to work in a pretty wealthy school district that had huge utility installations within its boundaries and almost literally had money coming out of its ears. It provided a magnificent education for all its pupils and needed federal aid about the way the average American needs more mothers-in-law. Yet that's just exactly what it stands to get under the new law.

Why? Because it's located in an area where a large

number of chronic reliefers and poverty cases happen to live, and these folks have lots and lots of children attending school. So the rich school district will qualify for umpteen thousands of federal dollars it doesn't need at all because some of its pupils happen to have poor parents.

How many hundreds of school districts in my own state and throughout the other forty-nine are to be in the same delightful predicament with your money? Who knows? Only the bureaucrats. Yet this perfectly logical and legitimate objection to the new federal-aid-to-education bill has so far been completely ignored in the mad Washingtonian rush to put Superman Dollar to work in his current role of Mr. Fixit.

This is a classic example of what's wrong with generalized federal aid to education and illustrates perfectly why a lot of us educators take a dim view of the whole idea. A state can make a lot of mistakes and frequently does. Nevertheless, I know of remarkably few states that give away hundreds of millions of dollars to public agencies that don't need the money.

It's not that a state government is necessarily more frugal or more virtuous than the federal government. It's just that a state is apt to know more about its own local needs than does some far-off bureau in Washington. And the new aid-to-education bill proves this.

(9) THE AUTOMATION GAP

Americans have an Achilles' heel that extends roughly from toe to thigh. It's our inordinate love for mechanical gadgets and our national willingness to place a childlike if chuckle-headed reliance upon doohickeys and dinguses. If something whirs, clicks, buzzes, or hums, we're usually all for it, even before we know what it's supposed to do.

Thus the great wave of the future is right now supposed to be something called cybernetics, which my dictionary defines as "the science which treats of the principles underlying the common elements in the functioning of automatic machines and of the human nervous system." In industry, this means the fully automated plant; in military science, pushbutton warfare; in medicine, the electronic diagnostician.

What of education?

Theoretically, cybernetics is going to revolutionize the schooling of the young. Right now we have machines that ask questions, correct wrong answers, analyze the reasons for the mistakes, present the material again in a simplified form, and then retest for improved comprehension. They chime sweetly and turn on green lights when Junior salivates satisfactorily. They buzz harshly and turn all red-eyed when Junior goofs.

I supervise, in my own state, literally dozens of "automated learning" or "programmed instruction" experiments, most of them financed through Uncle Sam's unprecedented largesse in the form of the 1965 Elementary and Secondary Education Act. Thousands of youngsters, even as I write this, are pushing buttons, pulling levers, following taped instructions, and having a ball.

I'll make two predictions about all this right now, and you're welcome to check up on me a few years from now when the first fine flush of experimentation has faded from education's brow:

(1) The kids instructed by the motorized and softly purring chrome-steel versions of Our Miss Brooks will show spectacular rises in understanding and subject mastery as compared with those left to languish under the tutelage of the humdrum, flesh-and-blood originals.

(2) Teaching machines will not replace the real McCoy, because they don't really teach.

Paradox? Not really.

There's something called the "halo effect" in my profession, which means that the mere fact that a new program is being tried on a group of children causes them to be more interested and to work harder than they had been. Result: better achievement. Even if the new stuff isn't any better than the old. Sometimes even if it's worse. Catch: the "halo effect" doesn't last very long.

And I'm pretty confident that the human schoolmarm won't be scrapped in favor of the robot because of one thing. That's the underlying reality of education; the impact of the personality of the instructor upon the personality of the student. UNIVAC is estimable, durable, and even more patient than Job. Trouble is, he has no personality at all.

Oh, he can be a mighty big help to teacher. He can relieve her of age-old drudgery and time-consuming repetition. He can test and retest and correct and drill. Cybernetics in the classroom is going to be a godsend—but not a replacement.

As I've said, the teacher should approach his class as the conductor confronts his symphony orchestra. From the breathless whisperings of the strings, from the clarion peals of the brass, from the muted thunder of the percussion, the conductor will weave the very fabric of great music, threaded throughout with the polychromatic strands of his own genius. Even so will the teacher evoke from the myriad experiences of his pupils the chords that, laced and interwoven always with something of himself, will ring grandly in the harmony of life.

No machine, however versatile and ingenious, can do

this. Neither could it paint the *Mona Lisa*. And for the same reason.

Teaching is an art. The greatest and most ancient of all the creative arts. A machine may train. It may present facts. It may even evaluate and judge. It can never teach.

These have been a few of the minor gaps.

There remains the veritable Grand Canyon of misconceptions—the artificially nurtured belief that Progressive Education is now a purely historical artifact.

Progressive Education is like a cat. It's quiet and sneaky, gumshoeing around on padded paws and jumping on you when you least expect it. It has an uncanny ability to fall almost any distance and still land on its feet. And it possesses at least nine lives, as I can ruefully testify.

Historically, it's the offspring of John Dewey's "utilitarianism." Dewey preached relativism. To him, there was no eternal truths, no lasting values, no absolute standards. Education thus became adjustment to environment and was sold in that seductive package to a whole generation of educators. Subject matter became relatively unimportant, especially when compared with such glittering goals of the instructional process as togetherness, "life adjustment," and the happy, comfortable acceptance of the child by his "peer group."

This was the Gospel According to St. John as interpreted to the unwashed masses by Dewey's Three Apostles: William Kilpatrick, George Counts, and Harold Rugg. Catlike in this as in all things, it littered over the decades such educational oddities as "group dynamics," "fusion courses," and more recently "sensitivity training." It warred ceaselessly and stealthily on report cards, letter grades, phonics, classroom discipline, and examinations. If anyone believes that the ubiquity of Progressive Education for the past twenty-five years has no connection with the prevalence today of campus anarchy and obscenity, he has a far greater and more touching faith in the power of coincidence than I do.

The irony implicit in the whole much-ballyhooed movement was the sublime confidence of its protagonists that the widespread adoption of their philosophy by American education would produce the best-adjusted, most law-abiding young people in history. After all, the cheerful, easy adjustment of the child to his environment was the slogan and the shibboleth of the Progressivists. Surely the results of such an educational regimen would inevitably be a record crop of young Americans who would abhor violence, eschew crime, and cooperate with everybody.

Well, the results of the last quarter-century are now in, and I will leave it up to the reader to decide for himself whether the current generation is less violent, less criminal, and more cooperative than its predecessors.

What price Progressive Education if this is all it has to show for its years of power and the billions it has spent?

Here are some of those same slogans and shibboleths of "life adjustment" education. Each one is demonstrably and outrageously false.

(1) *"The aim of education is to work joyfully and find happiness."*
No. It isn't.
The aim of education is to give young people the in-

tellectual tools that the race over the centuries has found indispensable in the pursuit of truth. Working joyfully, finding happiness, making a million dollars, trapping a sexually attractive mate—all these consummations are, I suppose, devoutly to be wished and have in fact occupied a considerable fraction of human interest and ingenuity down the ages. But none of them has much to do with the main goal of education, which is the equipping of the individual with the arsenal he will need throughout life in his combat against the forces of error. Happiness is a by-product of education, not its be-all and its end-all. Education does not guarantee happiness. It merely enables one to be more discriminating in his quest for the elusive butterfly.

(2) *"Make the school fit the child."*

But will life in later years recast its iron imperatives to fit the individual? And isn't the school supposed to be, in the large, divine, and comfortable words of the Dewey Gospel, a microcosm of life, or at the very least a preparation for it?

If we deceive the child into thinking that life is going to adapt itself to him through all the vexing decades ahead, then surely we are lying to him in the most cynical and scoundrelly fashion. More, we are sowing the dragon's teeth of disillusion and defeat for every youngster who goes through his formative years swaddled in a cotton-batting environment of sweetness and light only to have the ugly face of reality thrust suddenly into his at the age of eighteen.

Sooner or later, a human being must come to an understanding with the world around him. Either he adjusts to it, or by dint of personality, intelligence, and force of will he shapes a small corner of it more closely to his heart's desire. In either case, he will be ill-fitted for the task if his teachers have convinced him since nursery school that the universe is going to accommodate itself to him.

The school must meet individual needs and differences, true enough. It should help the child in every possible way to prepare himself for life in a world diked and plowed by two hundred generations of men past. The school should be just. It should be kindly. It should by all means be as interesting as possible. But it should not and it cannot "fit" every child.

The Progressive Educationists conceive the school as Proteus. It isn't. It's Atlas holding up the centuries of human thought. Somehow the children of each generation must come to terms with the Titan.

(3) *"The absence of fear is the finest thing that can happen to a child."*

In Heaven, yes. On our imperfect earth, certainly not. It's one of the worst things that could possibly happen to a child.

One wiser than Dewey has said, "The fear of the Lord is the beginning of wisdom." This is one kind of fear, and a necessary one for sheer salvation's sake. On another level altogether, children should be taught to fear all sorts of earthly evils—from ant paste to sex perverts—if they are to grow up at all. Survival is the password here.

Assuredly the school cannot be an updated version of Dotheboys Hall, with assorted Squeers-instructors wielding terror weapons against panicked pupils. Fear as a motivation for learning is little better than no motivation at all. But fear as an ingredient of existence is as necessary for the survival of the species as is pain. Like pain, too, it has been a fellow traveler with man since the very beginning. When man ceases to be healthily afraid, he will be extinct.

The *unnecessary* fears are those that the schools should

war against unceasingly. Ghosts, werewolves, witches, broken mirrors, skin a different color from our own— these chimeras should indeed be exorcised instructionally. On the other hand, live wires, drunken drivers, venereal disease, atomic fallout—fears of these all-too-actual menaces had better be encouraged by the schools, not discouraged, or presently there will be no more pupils to instruct, or schools to instruct them, for that matter.

And so it goes. The common denominator in all those misconceptions is the inability of education to make people *want* to do what's obviously good for them. Education can give Americans the facts. It can teach them how to organize those facts. It can even build up certain desirable work habits and patterns of stimulus-response. But it cannot merely by holding up the good, the beautiful, and the true to its captive audience every day necessarily make that audience hanker after these fine old attributes.

What a lot of folks fail to realize is that the schools are up against some pretty stiff and even unprecedented competition these days.

Novels tell the world in four-letter words that every hero is in reality a villain, and vice-versa. This is a big help.

The stage today glorifies the "un-man"—the spiritual amputee—the adult crybaby who blubbers about the twentieth century without having the gumption to try to improve it.

The movies—many of them—are as sniggeringly and tastelessly vile as a stag party after the guests have become maudlin enough to hiccup barnyard quips at the overweight and somewhat jaundiced stripteaser.

And much of television should be commented on only by an authority on the mentally retarded.

We educators, in short, are doing our darnedest to

maintain an oasis of values in a vast desert of sometimes sparkling and occasionally seductive slop. But it would be unreasonable to expect us unilaterally to reclaim the entire Sahara.

There are some things education *can* do, however, and do it better than we have been doing, especially in regard to the teaching of attitudes. One of these is the highly important but generally overlooked little four-letter word "Love."

The self-appointed Pied Pipers of today's youth have been making a big thing out of hate. Hate is what is wrong with the world, they tell everyone who will listen: hate in Vietnam, hate in Alabama, hate among the right-wingers. If we could somehow just substitute big, wonderful love for all this hate, they say, everything would be real cool.

Maybe they've got something. Of course, I'd like to be around—though at a safe distance—the first time our bearded and sandaled friends tried selling the virtues of love as opposed to hate to that eminent peace-lover Mao Tse-tung. And I'm reasonably certain that the ghosts of the butchered Hungarian Freedom Fighters of a few years back would have a few things to say about the practical difficulty of loving Communist tank crews while they are busy crushing you to a jelly.

However, let's concede that our activist friends have a point. As the late Father Divine used to say: "Peace, it's wonderful." And so is love, of course. Which makes me wonder why, in all this talk about the positivism of love and the negativism of hate, no one ever seems to want to talk about love of country.

The official magazine of the Knights Templar recently discussed the results of two polls given to young Americans, one at the New York World's Fair, and one among the Big Ten universities. In both, 84 percent of the students questioned denied the importance of patriotism and described it as unnecessary.

I know this isn't necessarily the future speaking. The heroism and dedication of our young men fighting today in the slaughterhouse of Southeast Asia gives sufficient lie to any such contention as to make any feeble words on my part unneeded.

But there were other interesting findings in these polls. Sixty-one percent of the pollees rejected the profit incentive. More than half were for government ownership of the nation's industries. Seventy-one percent would deny an accused person the right to face his accuser.

Just as an aside to some of our creepier national newspaper columnists and editorial writers who have been doing their best in recent years to create a congenial climate for this point of view, 41 percent of the kids favored canceling freedom of the press altogether!

But it's the black eye hung on love that nonpluses me. That's all patriotism is, you know: just love. And with all the blackguarding and downgrading of hate that's going on these days, I should have thought that hate's opposite—love—would begin at last to come into its own. Apparently not, or at least in only its more trivial and superficial manifestations, to be found in any pad.

Perhaps a clue can be found in the recent statement of one young teacher who declined to lead his students in saluting the American flag.

"The pledge of allegiance mentions freedom and justice for all," he mused profoundly, "and I don't believe we have achieved freedom and justice in this country yet."

So we haven't attained perfect freedom yet. Your mother didn't give you perfect freedom either, did she? But did that prevent you from loving her? And telling her so? And being loyal to her?

Ideal justice admittedly is still somewhere in the dim future. Does your wife always treat you justly? And if, being human, she doesn't, are you going to stop telling her you love her? You'll have a fine, rewarding marriage, my friend. Just as you'll be a fine, rewarding citizen.

The schools should teach their pupils that it's good to seek after perfection. The very search cannot but ennoble those who take part in it. But the schools should also teach that to demand divine faultlessness as a prerequisite to love, or to the public expression of that love, is to banish love effectively from human affairs.

America is human, created by humans, populated by humans. As such, she will fall short of perfection. But with all her faults, she is still preeminently the fairest and the freest and the finest of all the countries of the world. She needs your love, and she needs to hear about it from you, even as your own loved ones do.

Why not tell her once in a while?

I have said that the old question "Does Education have a future?" has given way of late to a newer, more frightening query, "Does America have a future?" Given the knowledge that education has always been the indispensable mentor and handmaiden of the Great Republic, the escalation of the original question was inevitable.

I'd like to record my present answer to both questions as "Yes." When my profession clears its head and starts thinking hard once more instead of reacting impulsively to outside stimuli, it is capable of breaking through the iron paradoxes of the Misconceptions. Until it thinks more and emotionalizes less, it will continue to be held prisoner behind their rigid bars. The same thing is true of our country in this, the final third of the twentieth century.

The precious and unique function of the educator is to spur men on to think. And this we cannot do until we clear our minds of cant and see the causes of our present discontent clearly and without protective coloration. When we have done this as a profession, we will have earned our salt. Quite incidentally, we may also in the process have provided our country with a future that seems so darkened and so dim today but which education alone can so grace and illuminate.

CROSSROAD #2

The Life-Adjustment Cult

DOES JUNIOR TELL YOU that competition to get good grades is bad? A self-destructive pursuit of sterile status symbols? He learned this in school.

Does Susie believe that popularity with her peers and acceptance by her group are more important than learning how to spell properly? She learned this in school, I'm afraid.

Are both your children convinced that everything is relative—that what's good today may be bad tomorrow, and vice-versa—and that there are really no lasting values or eternal truths in this vale of tears? They learned this in school, too.

Oh, not in all schools, of course, nor from all teachers. But from entirely too many these days. For this is the tired old dogma of Progressive Education, with its bubble-headed jargon of "life-adjustment," "meeting felt needs," "relevance," "togetherness," and "on-going, forward-looking in-groupness." Since the mid-Thirties, it has clung to the body of American education like a barnacle to the bottom of a boat.

See the hairy Hell's Angel, unsavory, uncouth, a thrall to kicks. One reason he's this way is because his school taught him as a kid that rigid standards went out with high-button shoes, and that it's perfectly okay for each person to evolve his own moral code. So he did, God help him.

See the noisome hippie, diseased, debauched, degenerate. Down in the grades and with the same good intentions which pave Hell-road, his teachers let him get the idea that life is a ball where imposed toil is tyranny, where loafing on somebody else's money is everybody's right, and where happiness consists of doing your own thing. Sorry. It doesn't.

See the campus rioter, brandishing four-letter-word placards and Molotov cocktails with equal abandon. Some years back, his school told him a lot about individual freedom and nothing at all about individual responsibility. Now he exercises his own freedom at the expense of someone else's. Responsibility? That's Squaresville, man.

Good teachers the world over stress a moral code that places others' rights ahead of one's own, which emphasizes the duties of citizenship as well as its joys, and which condemns illegality and violence as ways to solve problems. Bad teachers say that morals are relative, that citizenship is all taking and no giving, and that violence is all right if you can't get your own way any other way.

Mind you, I've never known a teacher who came right out and said these things to children. But I've known too many of them who espoused and mouthed an educational philosophy that caused convictions like these to take root in the minds of their pupils as inevitably as the general amnesty that invariably follows the burning down of the university administration building nowadays.

How did all this get started?

It happened about three decades ago, when John Dewey's permissive pragmatism became the unofficial philosophy of the American educational establishment. Here's how it's affected the schools:

(1) *In regard to knowledge*

To Dewey, knowledge equals experience. There are no self-evident truths, no universals, no absolutes of any kind. Anything that satisfies a want is a "good." Otherwise the word has no meaning. Life is a stream of sensations to which the child must be taught to respond successfully, nothing more.

Understand now why so many of the kids live it up with raw sex and cooked pot?

(2) *In regard to the learning process*

Dewey taught that the child learns only what he lives. Education must therefore be an exercise in living. "Learning by doing" thus becomes one of the ritual responses in the litany of Progressive Education. The fundamentals of learning—the "Three R's"—are taught only as the child finds them necessary in helping him lead a "good" life.

Wonder any longer why the hippies stress the "back to nature" routine? And why so many of their protest placards are misspelled?

(3) *In regard to curriculum*

The Progressive Educationists term the curriculum the whole living experience of the child. So the school must interest itself in everything about the child and take the steps necessary to remedy any gaps in his experience that a foolish or shortsighted parent may refuse to fill up. The accumulation of knowledge for the mere sake of knowledge is not only unnecessary; it is probably actively harmful. Development of creativity is the important thing. The child must feel completely unrepressed and free from inhibitions so that his natural creativity will blossom and flourish.

Help you figure out why some of our teen-agers go around looking like unmade beds and exuding an almost visible aura of unwashed disinhibition?

(4) *In regard to education's aims*

The two main goals of Progressive Education are to aid the child to live the life of the group and to enable him to "adjust" to a constantly changing environment. The child is constantly reminded that he is merely one member of the group and that his success is being measured by how well he is accepted by his companions.

Remind you of the S.D.S. zombies prior to their recent split, all salivating together on cue like Pavlov's dogs, all breathing the same obscenities, all mouthing the same party line, knowing no life as individuals, experiencing only what the group experiences?

Indeed the Progressive Educationists have much to answer for. Most dangerous when they are most dedicated, they war against your children in the firm belief that they are helping them. They treat parents as though they were retarded first-graders, glaciating all over them in a fine mixture of contemptuous kindness and smug superiority.

But isn't Progressive Education as dead as Moses? That's what you've been told, isn't it?

Judge for yourself. Visit your local school. Look around. Listen closely. Above all, ask questions. Questions like these:

Do the people running your school believe "life adjustment" is the main goal of the instructional program? If they do, this is Progressive Education.

Does your school place primary emphasis upon the happy, easy, comfortable acceptance of your child by his "peer group"? If it does, your school is "progressively" oriented.

Is subject matter in your school paid lip service but relegated to a back seat? Are things like "social studies" and "language arts" and "orientation" being taught instead of history and geography and English? If these things are being done, it doesn't much matter what they call it. What you've got is Progressivism.

Do your teachers and administrators tell you that report cards are old-fashioned? Do they refuse to assign more than token homework down in the grades because it is "meaningless drudgery"? Do they teach phonics only as an adjunct to the "look-say" method of reading that has wreaked such ruin on a whole generation of functional nonreaders? These are all manifestations and outcroppings of Progressive Education.

A big-city reporter, fellow Gael Terence O'Flaherty, recently invaded one of our teeming junior colleges, intent upon an intriguing experiment. He wanted to find out what the younger generation thought of that blood-stained old nut Adolf Hitler.

He came away muttering to himself. Here are some of the representative comments from the finely honed college minds of all races and both sexes:

"I think Hitler was great. He carried out his plans. He did what he said he was going to do."

"There are atrocities in every war."

"I don't have any feelings, really. I don't know much about him."

"It's not for me to say. He may have been off his rocker, but then again he may have had a good idea."

"You can't really judge. I mean, I'm not a person who can judge another person because I don't think anybody has a right to do that."

Exit for a breath of fresh air the enterprising Mr. O'Flaherty, disgustedly concluding, "Apparently the philosophy of the permissive society has not fallen on deaf ears."

But just what spawned the permissive society? The thirty-year-old mismatch between behavioristic psychology and John Dewey's progressive education, that's what. This charmingly prolific couple had some other offspring, too. Tolerance of immorality. Willingness to compromise with evil. Acceptance of treason. Sympathy for crime.

It's quite a family.

For almost three decades now, I've watched the high priests of progressivism innoculate children with the germs of relativism. And as the injection begins to take, certain symptoms invariably develop that have to be treated immediately.

Toxin: "Society shouldn't try to judge anyone. Every person is responsible only to himself."

Antitoxin: Society has to judge its dynamiters, or it will quickly cease to be a society. Every person is responsible to every other person, to say nothing of being responsible to God.

Toxin: "Who's to say what's good and what's bad? Is there any validity to these terms anymore?"

Antitoxin: Oh, for Heaven's sake, come off it. You could reduce any value system to absurdity by this kind of lame-brained questioning. Is there any validity to such terms as "honor," "virtue" or "decency," for example? Or even "life" and "death"? Of course the terms are valid. Otherwise we might as well abandon language altogether, and go back to monosyllabic grunts punctuated by blows from a stone club.

Toxin: "What's wrong with marijuana? Alcohol is even worse."

Antitoxin: You can't justify a new evil by comparing it favorably to an even older greater evil. This kind of logic went out with old Pharaoh, who probably justified his wickedness to the Children of Israel by claiming that the Assyrians treated them even worse. As for marijuana, one question only: "Who the devil needs it?" And if no one needs it and if it can do no good but only harm, why legalize it?

The Progressive Educationists over the years have labored diligently to produce the permissive society. They have succeeded beyond their wildest expectations.

So now at last you have it: a culture where Hitler is acceptable, where Bonnie and Clyde are their own judges, and where everybody is as good as everybody else because there really isn't any reality to the word "good" anyhow.

How do you like it?

The deep thinkers of my profession, who regard me with the same lasting love and heartfelt esteem that they customarily reserve for Admiral Rickover, have been needling me in their learned journals because I keep throwing rocks at Progressive Education.

"Why doesn't Rafferty wake up and shut up?" one of them inquired testily the other day. "Progressive Education has been dead for years. He's just exhuming it for use as a political punching bag."

All right. Why not try a little experiment? Let's try it first on the sixth-graders, because in most states they represent the end product of elementary school education.

Get sixth-grader Johnny in off the Little League diamond for a few minutes. Stand him in front of you, with his soiled sneakers and torn T-shirt. Ask him to tell you something about Charlemagne. Get him to expound on Hannibal. Ask him what century Julius Caesar lived in, who knocked him off, and why.

Ask him who crossed the Delaware and what he did when he reached the other side. See if he ever heard of James Madison or Theodore Roosevelt or Henry Clay. You're going to be mighty, mighty interested in Johnny's answers.

Then get sixty-grader Mary in on the carpet. See what she can tell you about Evangeline or Silas Marner or the Lady of the Lake. Ask her to quote just the opening lines of "Paul Revere's Ride" or "The Charge of the Light Brigade" or "Old Ironsides." Get her to tell you something—anything—about "The Village Blacksmith" or "The Wreck of the Hesperus" or "Hiawatha." She'll probably think you've gone right off your rocker.

But don't stop here. Ask the same questions of the first eighth-grader you come across. See for yourself what "life adjustment" junior high schools are teaching.

Last of all, ask an average graduating senior in high school—not the college prep youngster but the average one. When you recover from the shock, don't blame the kids. Or their teachers. Blame yourself for permitting this sort of quasi-illiteracy to flourish unchecked in some of your own tax-supported schools.

And if you think Longfellow and Tennyson are old hat, try them on Browning or Dickens or even Homer— names that have stood the test of time and become part of the cultural heritage of mankind.

I've been looking through a moderately old textbook. It was written back in 1886 and adopted by my home state as a grade school reader. Here are some of its contributors, the men who wrote the material that the boys and girls were reading down in the grades in the days of Grover Cleveland: William Cullen Bryant, Lord Byron, William Shakespeare, Nathaniel Hawthorne, Sir Walter Scott, Edgar Allan Poe, Bret Harte, and a host of others.

These names have held up pretty well during the intervening decades, haven't they? The consensus among literary authorities would be that these writers have contributed significantly to literature. Great-Grandpa and Great-Grandma weren't so far wrong, were they, when they insisted through their state-adopted textbooks that their children be exposed to writing of such lasting value?

If you really want a shock, try these names on sixth-graders today. Or ninth-graders. Or even the great majority of twelfth-graders.

But apparently Grandma and Grandpa learned to read this sort of beautiful, valuable, interesting material, didn't they? And don't let anybody tell you that Grandma and Grandpa weren't in school eighty years ago. They may have missed high school—a lot of them—but they were certainly in the grade schools.

The reading consultants and the curriculum experts and the education professors will tell you that today's children aren't "mature" enough to grasp such "advanced" material.

Well, why aren't they? Our grandparents were.

Whose fault is it that they're not? Are our children more stupid than the children of eighty years ago?

Or are they just not being asked to tackle tough material because of a philosophy that has decided unilaterally that a child's mind exists not to be stretched but to be adjusted? A philosophy that preaches that the easy, comfortable, happy acceptance of the child by his "peer group" is the be-all and the end-all of education?

Johnny daydreams and refuses to socialize with the group. So did Shelley and Beethoven and Michelangelo, and even Winston Churchill. But the day of the lone thinker is past, it seems. Today, Johnny must learn to practice togetherness and in-groupness and democratic socializing with his peers even if it means that Miss Smith must construct a class sociogram and call in the district psychologist.

Ignorance, inaccuracy, unenlightenment—all the immemorial enemies and targets of education must take a back seat now to the new and supreme offense: unpopularity. But the purpose of a school is not to make pupils popular or well-adjusted or universally approved. It is to make them learned. It is to teach them to use the tools that the race, over the centuries, has found to be indispensable in the pursuit of truth.

It is said by some that subject matter is secondary to the main goal of education, which is acceptance and adjustment and appreciation. But I say that the schools exist to teach organized, systematic, disciplined subject matter to the children. For this they were created; for this they are maintained by the millions of Americans who support and populate them. I say further that the schools are the only societal agencies specifically designed to perform this function. And I say finally that if the schools do not so teach subject matter, the children are never going to learn it.

"Life adjustment" is taught by the home, the church, and by society itself in a hundred forms. Only the school can forge for the child the wonderful, shining, sharp-edged sword of subject matter.

The Progressive Educationists have long held the only

eternal verity to be that of constant change and flux. All values are relative. All truths are mutable. All standards are variable.

So the only thing worth teaching to youngsters is the ability to react to an ever-shifting environmental kaleidoscope. It is the philosophy of the man on the roller coaster.

It's a way of thinking and of teaching with which American democracy cannot coexist. Within it lie the seeds of the rumbles and the riots, the frantic search for "kicks," the newsstand filth and the cinematic garbage that mark the last descent into the cloying, clinging sickness of ultimate decay by every civilization that has ever permitted this infection to overcome its resistence.

Despite all this, my more turgid readers still take me to task for beating the dead horse of Progressive Education. The current party line on this, incidentally, is that (a) Progressive Education was always far more sinned against than sinning, poor thing, and (b) it's been completely extinct for years anyhow, so forget it.

For the devotees of party-line subsection (b) to mull over, I append the following recent statement by one of teacher Victor Harke's pupils in Hollywood, Florida, as reported by the faithful press:

> The first day of school was wild. Mr. Harke didn't say a thing. The lights went out and pictures started floating all over the room. On one wall was a movie about child molestation. On the same wall, superimposed on half of the first movie, was a travelog on Switzerland.
>
> On another wall, slides flashed pictures of famous paintings. Three tape recorders were going at once: one a Bible reading, another with music, and an-

other with weird electronic sounds. To top it off, when the bell rang, Mr. Harke got up and left without saying a word.

Queried by a presumably ear-plugged reporter with equally presumable dark glasses, Mr. Harke defended his own private version of Bedlam as follows:

"I try to make my classroom a part of the outside world, to get ideas of what the kids are interested in. This year it's psychedelics."

And next year perhaps it will be Molotov cocktails, or homosexuality, or maybe Murder, Incorporated. The possibilities, in fact, are fascinating and well-nigh limitless. Children do swing through quite a kaleidoscopic spectrum of interests, don't they? It would certainly be interesting to see Mr. Harke's classroom if he keeps it faithful to the good old outside world, which more and more these days resembles a cross between a hippie pad and a shooting gallery.

The news story concluded with a glowing report on how much Harke's students "like his unorthodox methods." Quoth one breathless graduate: "When we complained about the dull classroom, he told us to go ahead and do what we liked. In his class we even made our own lesson plans."

It's hard to pinpoint the first educational quack. I suppose the line of frauds goes back well beyond Jean-Jacques Rousseau, but that heartless mountebank will serve as a starting point.

Jean-Jacques, with an irresponsibility characteristic of his entire philosophy, fathered several bastards and thoughtfully shunted them into foundling asylums for his more humdrum fellow-citizens to support. At various times he practiced voyeurism, exhibitionism, and masturbation with equally feverish enthusiasm, preserving himself from any legal unpleasantness by pleading softening of the brain. He fought viciously if verbally with every normal intellect in Europe, and died insane.

Rousseau spawned a frenetic theory of education that after two centuries of spasmodic laboring brought forth a byblow in the form of John Dewey's Progressive Education. According to the confused Frenchman, education was running, jumping, shouting, doing as one pleased. The first impulses of nature are always right. Keep the child's mind idle as long as you can. And suchlike rot.

This sort of piffle is as old as the human race. The child is a Noble Savage, needing only to be let alone in order to insure his intellectual salvation. Don't inhibit him. Never cross him, lest he develop horrid neuroses later on in life. The cave children of the Stone Age grew up happier, better-adjusted, and less frustrated than do ours today, simply because they were in a blissful state of nature. So just leave the kids alone. They'll educate themselves.

Twaddle. Schooling is not a natural process at all. It's highly artificial. No boy in his right mind ever wanted to study multiplication tables and historical dates when he could be out hunting rabbits or climbing trees. In the days when hunting and climbing contributed to the survival of *homo sapiens,* there was some sense in letting the kids do what comes naturally, but when man's future began to hang upon the systematic mastery of orderly subject matter, the primordial, happy-go-lucky, laissez-faire kind of learning had to go. Today it's part and parcel of whatever lost innocence we may ever have possessed. Long gone. A quaint anachronism.

Except in Hollywood, Florida, apparently, and a few thousand other places.

The story of mankind is the rise of specialization with its highly artificial concomitants. Over the years, natural medicine gave way to anesthesia, antiseptics, and antibiotics. In the field of transportation, hiking sturdily along dim forest trails took a back seat to freeways, air routes, and eventually lunar orbits. Old Stentor himself, brass lungs and all, couldn't compete today with radio and the telephone.

So it is with education. When writing was invented, "natural" education went down the drain of history. From then on, children were destined to learn artificially, just as men around the world were increasingly to live artificially. This is civilization—the name of the game. When Rousseau and his cave-dwelling modern imitators cry out against artificiality, they are in fact down on all fours, mopping and mowing, hurling twigs and dirt at civilization. For all civilization is artificial.

I don't doubt for one moment that Mr. Harke's class is very, very popular with the kids. So is a discotheque. So is a penny arcade. So is a three-ring circus. So was Rousseau's "back to Nature" approach to education.

What I *do* doubt is that the youngsters are becoming educated in his class, or indeed in any other "class" where the pupils write their own lesson plans, horse around with colored lights, and spend their time on niggling trivia when all the while the whole vast ocean of human learning lies around them for the dipping into.

A school is not intended and was never created to reflect like a dime-store mirror all the jimcrackery and tawdry fustian of our present-day society. It's intended rather to be a beacon, generating its own laserlike beam and constantly urging its captive audience on to something finer and better than the mess we see around us every day. We don't need schools to show us what's going on. We need schools to show us what *ought* to be going on.

The purpose of education is not to sensationalize, not to entertain children, not to dazzle them with colored lights, not to deafen them with orgiastic sounds, nor yet to titillate them with discreet pornography. The purpose of education is to make pupils learned. Period.

Now, if anyone can tell me how teacher Harke's bravura boiler factory full of Roman candles, rock music, and child-molestation films is going to make anyone a learned scholar, I'll come back through for another look.

Failing that, however, I'll have to join Mr. Harke in his only action that I completely understand and with which I sympathize entirely. As the news story commented so cogently, ". . . when the bell rang, Mr. Harke got up and left without saying a word."

To take a tranquilizer, no doubt. After all, competing with three tape recorders and two motion-picture projectors going full blast would have been a tall order for Horace Mann himself. Or even for the tuned-in and turned-on Mr. Harke.

This sort of thing is symptomatic of something brand new and superlatively stupid in my profession—the compulsion to separate learning from discipline. Education is the first and only calling to go deliberately out of its way to make life miserable for its practitioners.

We teachers are masochists. We're like the nut who kept hitting himself over the head with a hammer because it felt so good when he stopped. We seek martyrdom compulsively, and if no lions are handy, we'll go out and dig some up.

At least I defy you to draw any other conclusion from a recent communique put out by the American Orthopsychiatric Association, which sponsored an institute for three hundred teachers and mental-health workers.

Topic: "Handling aggression in the classroom."

Conclusion: "The burden is on the teacher to establish a rapport with students so they can accept criticism without feeling rejected."

Now just a darned minute!

It isn't the teacher who's mouthing off in class, using four-letter words, running around in gangs, fighting in the halls, and generally behaving like a junior member of the Mafia. It's not most of the kids, either. But it's certainly some of them. Entirely too many of them. And they need to be yanked up sharply, before juvenile misconduct becomes adult thuggery.

Incidentally, some of the institute's other findings were perfectly fascinating, rather like a tape recording of an LSD trip. One Herman Schuckman, chairman of the entire proceedings, asked ominously, "How much pressure is there to have classrooms quiet?"

He followed this chiller with another accusatory question, for all the world like Zola inquiring into the Dreyfus Case: "How much pressure is there to have even the recess and hallways quiet?"

Frankly, I was aghast at such pregnant queries, dripping as they were with unspeakable innuendoes. Does Mr. Schuckman mean that some teachers are still so hopelessly reactionary after a generation of brainwashing by Mr. Schuckman and his ilk that they actually require quiet in their classrooms? Is he daring to infer that there are still schools in this enlightened land where the kids are compelled to keep the decibel level down to a dull roar while they're out in the halls?

Come, come, Mr. Schuckman. Surely everyone knows by now that the best way to solve the aggressive child's problem is to soothingly convince him that aggression isn't so bad after all. If Butch throws a tomato at the blackboard, smile and wipe it off. If he swears, write the naughty words on the board so everybody can learn them. That way, Butch won't feel isolated from his peers. If he beats up a less aggressive classmate, don't punish him. Establish rapport with him.

Above all, concluded the institute's far-out members, never send the aggressive child out of the classroom. This is the true sin against the holy ghost of St. John Dewey. It matters not that the other kids may be corrupted by the aggressive one's triumphant example. Less than nothing that the whole learning process for the vast majority may be smashed into smithereens because no one can hear anything except Butch's threats and obscenities. No matter. Cherish Butch. Establish rapport, whatever that is.

Tripe!

There have always been kids who acted aggressively in school, and who would have grown up absurd if their teachers hadn't lowered the boom on them. Churchill was an aggressive child. So was Tom Sawyer. Heck, so was I. If we had been allowed by our teachers to get away with it, Winston might in later life have become a seedy remittance man, Tom another Billy the Kid, and I the oldest living member of the S.D.S.

Society doesn't employ teachers to settle for the lowest common denominator of current behavior. It hires us to *change* that behavior. Our job is not to excuse nor to gloss over nor to establish rapport with youthful roughnecks. We're supposed to make ladies and gentlemen out of them, no matter how long or how tough the task. Above all, we're expected to make them learned.

Whatever it takes to make a school quiet and orderly and studious, we teachers had better do it and not fool around about it. Maybe if we spent less time in screwball "institutes" and more time brushing up on no-nonsense disciplinary techniques, we'd be better off.

In the long run, I know the kids would.

Then there is the recent press clipping from Seattle, describing a "new" program at Bellevue's Ardmore Elementary School. It seems the pupils there are being taught in ungraded classes. No more first-, second-, and third-graders, for example.

Purpose: To enable each child to progress at his own rate in the different subject areas of reading, mathematics, art, spelling, and the social sciences.

There's nothing wrong with this. I well remember, even across the geologic eons that separate me from my own childhood, how good I was at reading and how abysmally bad I was at arithmetic. A special program that would place me in a reading class with the advanced and in a math class with the severely retarded would have done me a world of good, and I only wish one had been in existence in those antediluvian days.

No, my ambivalence isn't caused by Bellevue's use of the ungraded-classroom concept. It's brought on by something else entirely. According to the press clipping: "Parents come visiting and expect to see neat rows of desks with quiet children. Instead, they find children sprawled on the floor playing checkers, laughing and shouting, and playing with guinea pigs . . . loudly teaching younger children how to . . . tie their shoes."

The reporter goes on to cite the shock felt by Ardmore School parents because the school had become so "noisy and unruly." They complained to their school board, which told them that the district's achievement tests showed the program to be just as good at teaching the fundamentals as the more conventional kind of instruction. The board invited the disgruntled parents to transfer their children to other schools, which several of them reluctantly did.

The news story is concluded with a couple of the usual "onward and upward" statements from parents and children, attesting to the worth of the program and how interesting it is for the enrollees. Finally, there is a big newspaper photo of one of the Ardmore classrooms, with kids sprawled all over the floor and nary a desk in sight.

And right here, gentle reader, is where my ambivalence wakes up, shakes itself, and starts thrashing about.

Meeting pupils' individual needs does *not* mean that order and decorum must automatically fly out the classroom window like so many peace doves fleeing from a summit conference.

Setting up an ungraded-class situation does *not* require the teacher to throw away the desks and let the pupils wallow around on the floor for all the world like hippies on a bad trip.

And teaching children arithmetic and reading on different ability levels does *not* necessitate shocking concerned parents with shouting, unruliness, and plain old horsing around until they have to send their kids to another, quieter school.

Years ago, I enunciated Rafferty's First Law of Educational Research, to wit: "Findings that fly in the teeth of common sense are for the birds." Today I unveil for your consideration my Second Law: "Innovative programs that permit pupils to loll on the floor and yell at their friends should be strangled at birth." And the results of achievement tests, to misquote Gilbert and Sullivan, have nothing to do with the case.

The thing that exasperates me so about this whole Bellevue affair is the obvious good will and dedicated teaching that have gone into it. I'm certain that the new program was thoughtfully conceived and planned. I'm equally sure that its "carnival atmosphere," as the reporter delicately describes the sound and fury, is completely out of line and absolutely unnecessary.

Fellow teachers, don't confuse confusion with innovation. Noise and running around are the oldest concomitants of education there are. On the pretty solid premise that you can't learn much in a boiler factory, they are also just about the worst enemies education ever had.

Somebody once defined ambivalence as the feeling that assails you as you watch your mother-in-law drive over a cliff in your new Cadillac. This is precisely the feeling I have about Bellevue's noble experiment.

I applaud the medicine, but I take a dim view of the side effects.

For those who believe that Progressive Education is as dead as Moses, what about this classic manifestation? Date: 1969.

The Harrison City, Pennsylvania, school system has been studying the problem of nonpromotion of pupils in the fifty states. It has announced that 5 percent of America's schoolchildren fail each year, and that it costs the taxpayers $1 billion annually to hold the kids back. This, according to the Keystone State researchers, is uneconomic, inhuman, and downright medieval.

Although I may seem somewhat cavalier with old John Q. Taxpayer's money, I don't really care if it costs $1 billion or $2 billion extra to give children a proper education. We're spending umpteen billions on things a lot less important than helping children learn. And Harrison City to the contrary notwithstanding, the only reason for making a youngster repeat a grade is to make sure he masters the subject matter and the skills he will need in order to succeed in the next grade.

Let's look at a fairly typical case. Johnny has been sick and out of school a lot while he was in second grade. He's missed out on most of his number combinations, and he's fallen behind in his reading. His teacher knows he'll be lost and unhappy in third grade next fall, so she decides to have him take second grade over again.

Sole object: To help Johnny.

Sole alternative: To make Johnny completely miserable next year and a probable high school dropout in about seven years.

Question: What else would you have the teacher do?

Oh, I'm familiar with the Progressive Education litany of old slogans and moth-eaten shibboleths:

"Nonpromotion places the child in a failure stereotype."

"Johnny isn't failing school; the school is failing Johnny."

and of course

"More money for education will eliminate the need for retention of pupils."

All these slogans are benevolent in intent, all are popular, and all are demonstrably preposterous.

A child does not become a pariah because he needs to stay with the same teacher for two years. If this happened to him frequently, of course, the "failure stereotype" would take on validity, but not on a one-time basis.

Retention doesn't imply "failing" anything or anybody, either. It simply means that Johnny, for any one of a dozen reasons, needs more time to learn than the other kids.

And all the school money in the world isn't going to make a sick child well enough to master subject matter as effectively as a healthy child. Even a full-time home instructor can't help too much if the youngster is feeling rotten most of the time.

What about the child who is physically healthy but who gets held back anyway?

What about him? Maybe he's immature. Maybe Mom and Pop are staging king-size rumbles at home every night and he's too nervous and downright scared to concentrate at school. Or maybe he's just plain slow.

No matter. Whatever the reason, Teacher thinks Johnny should repeat the grade. She's worked with him for a whole year. She knows what he's actually been doing, and she has a pretty good idea of what he's capable of doing at his best. She's aware of his IQ, his home background, and his work habits. Above all, she wants to do what's best for Johnny. And she happens to think retention is the best solution.

Now, friends, all this being true, who's going to argue with Teacher? Not I, believe me. Or at least only so long as it takes me to make sure that Teacher is qualified, trained, and experienced.

But the Dewey-eyed disciples of progressivism believe that everybody should be promoted regardless of whether or not reasonable achievement standards have been met, largely because they don't believe in achievement standards in the first place. Or tests. Or grades. Or subject matter, so far as that goes.

Money has little to do with the Harrison City findings. Ideology, on the other hand, has a great deal to do with them. And I don't like an ideology that kids people into believing that children should never do anything over again.

Least of all do I like the closely allied manifestation of Progressive Education that tells us that children should concentrate on things that possess "immediacy" and which are "relevant" to the newspaper headlines. This professional mythology regularly seduces some of my colleagues into the most harebrained antics found anywhere outside a monkey cage.

For instance:

Most local school superintendents are the salt of the earth. Oh, they're a little harassed these days. They tend increasingly to develop ulcers at a relatively early age, and they even have a tendency to be a bit snappish at the end of a hard day at the office spent largely in warding off the simultaneous onslaughts of integrationists and segregationists, taxpayers' associations, and teachers'-salary committees, sexologists, and anti-sex educationists. But by and large they're a pretty good bunch, excellent credit risks, loyal to their wives, and even fairly sane, which in itself is quite an achievement in this demented era.

There are, of course, a few conspicuous exceptions, at least insofar as sanity is concerned. One of them is superintendent of schools in Scarsdale, New York, and he's about as glaring an exception as you'd want to find, standing out like George Wallace at a Black Panther kaffeeklatsch. In fact, candor compels me to say he's just got to be so far out of touch with reality as to be totally disconnected.

It seems the superintendent is offering a regular high-school summer course in twentieth-century revolution intended for those of his eager pupils who hanker after the bloody laurels of the late Che Guevara. The course includes a field trip out into the verdant New York countryside so the kiddies can learn how to snipe safely from behind bushes, lay land mines designed to maim the malevolent military, and dynamite power stations, presumably in order to turn off the local citizenry in more ways than one.

The 1968 class, the superintendent announced proudly, wrote term papers on how to sabotage the entire community. His students, it seems, have become experts in guerrilla warfare.

The wire services carried absolutely fascinating photos of the youngsters scurrying about carrying water-filled balloons simulating grenades, and bristling with meticulous replicas of automatic weapons, for all the world like Nasser's commandos on a dark Nilotic night.

Their instructor, one Stephen Kling, summarized the course in a veritable lightning flash of understatement: "We found the village vulnerable to attack."

No doubt.

And I'm sure that if the schools were to start coaching first-graders on how to slip cyanide into the reservoir, the village would be vulnerable to mass poisoning, also. Really, Mr. Kling, old thing, no one is normally on the alert against the possibility of moppets murdering their moms, or even piglets poisoning their papa pigs, as the S.D.S. would so charmingly put it. Hitler and Stalin in their gloomiest spasms of paranoia never went quite that far.

I wonder how the good people of Scarsdale enjoy having their children brought up in the best traditions of Fidel Castro. I wonder, too, how the taxpayers feel about emptying their pockets once a year to pay the salaries of instructors who are out in the boondocks showing Junior how to pull the pin of a concussion grenade and Susie how to blow up the old covered bridge.

Isn't it strange—even downright eerie—how Americans can get so frothed up and apoplectic about high meat prices, escalating taxes, and the Washington bureaucracy's continuing imitation of a drunken sailor out on the town with everybody else's money, and then sit back smiling uncertainly while this Scarsdale-style slapstick goes on around them unchallenged?

I'm reasonably certain the Scarsdale folks are like everyone else. They complain about how much their schools cost them, but when the time comes around each year when they can inject a little horse sense into their school system via the ballot box, they stay home with their six-packs and let the nuts elect even bigger nuts to the local board of education.

I can't get too worked up over Mom and Pop in Scarsdale, I'm afraid. But I am a little concerned about the unsuspecting population round about. After all, guerrilla warfare is contagious. And if I were a resident of White Plains, for instance, and suddenly found myself booby-trapped by some brat, I would take precious little comfort from the belated discovery that my scars actually originated in Scarsdale.

And I would not burn my incense at the altar of old John Dewey, who thought up the whole concept of "permissivism" and "relevance" in the first place.

Closely allied with this sort of buffoonery, and one of the major and mischievous heresies of our time, is the contention that school ought to be fun and games, with all the participants constantly titillated and perpetually entertained. Another is the belief that children, if left to themselves, will of their own choice seek out the significant elements of our cultural heritage and diligently work to master them because, like Everest, they are there.

This just is not true at all. Nevertheless, the educational woods these days are full of strange gins and traps labeled "Let the Youngsters Educate Themselves."

One of the more glittering and seductive of these new devices was tried out Troy, Michigan, for four years. It's something called "flu e modular scheduling," and it works like this:

The faculty and administration of the selected high school start out by abolishing the traditional school day, which has always been composed of forty-five minute "periods." In its place, a series of fifteen-minute "modules" is installed, and the faculty decides how many of these periods per week each student should spend in the class-room in order to learn a particular subject. This work out to about 65 percent of a student's time each week actually spent in class.

The rest of his time theoretically is to be spent in free study, visiting the library, working in the laboratory, or presumably meditating on the Cosmic Oneness of It All. The youngster will be so interested in his school program that he will voluntarily eschew the temptation to spend his 35 percent shooting the bull with the boys, watching football practice, or following giggling blondes around the campus. Instead, he will spend it reading primary sources, writing research projects, and boning up for the term exams.

Sure he will. Just as you and I would have done when we were sixteen. Which is to say not at all.

Just a moment, now. Before you start reacting hysterically to my incredible cynicism, let me make two points:

(1) Some high school students will indeed study on their own, without supervision and without compulsion. Maybe 10 percent.

(2) In Troy, the high school principal reluctantly had to recommend the junking of the whole modular-scheduling experiment. *Reason:* His pupils were having an increasingly tough time getting into college and staying in after they got there. The proof of the pudding is in the eating, and Troy just couldn't eat this one.

There are several reasons why this kind of laissez-faire programming won't work. One I've already mentioned: human nature, sometimes known as "The Old Adam." Another is the fact that the typical school day is too short now.

Music and art, for example, are having a hard time these days holding their own in a typically six-hour high school day, which also includes such "must" subjects as math, science, foreign languages, history, English, and physical education. What our high school kids need is to spend 100 percent of their school time in class and then some, not just 65 percent.

This part of the problem is pointed up by a Michigan paper: "Many parents complained the students had too much free time." With school time and school money both in such short supply, the sight of students roaming about the grounds and lying on the grass while expensive classrooms are studded with empty seats is not a congenial one for harassed taxpayers to contemplate as they drive by on their way to the local Internal Revenue office.

The other side of the coin, of course, is that the kids like all this free time. Reporters came up with quotes like: "I've never felt so free"; and "I enjoy making my own decisions."

But this isn't really the point, I'm afraid. The primary purpose of a school is not to make people feel free; it's to make them learned. It's in just this crucial inning of the educational ballgame that modular scheduling has spectacularly struck out.

Please, now, no frothing fulminations from those of you who hanker yearningly after the fleshpots of educational gimmickry. Write to Troy High School's principal, who watched the kids' test scores go down for four years like a thermometer in Lower Slobbovia.

He will, in the vernacular, kid you not.

Then there's the matter of report cards, against which the "life adjustment" educators have warred so bitterly.

About thirty years ago the disciples of Progressive Education went into prolonged and agonizing labor. The Everest of the "life adjustment" establishment quaked and shook. Lightnings played around its snowy summit, limning in bold relief the nut trees that cloaked its flanks with such rich profusion and reached so exuberantly toward the lofty timberline.

Finally, after much thundering and fulminating, the sounding, quivering monolith gave birth to a little squeaking mouse that was promptly christened the Non-Report Card. Its growth and development over the years, to an obbligato of plaintive murmuring from puzzled parents, has produced at last a mature instrument as unwanted as a letter from the Department of Internal Revenue and as baffling as the Mayan Codex.

The old-fashioned report card used to be pretty laconic.

It was usually a rectangular card with one side devoted to a listing of the subjects to be rated plus A-B-C-D-F markings by the teacher in her best Palmer penmanship. The other side was reserved for the signatures of the parents, sometimes opulent and flowing with satisfaction, sometimes shaky with rage or disappointment.

Very occasionally there would be a terse explanation of the letter grades, with A equated with 90–100, B with 80–89, and so on down to the ignominious F, which generally meant below 60. Once in a while an E grade would come home, sowing consternation and necessitating an agitated parental trip to school to discover that it meant "Incomplete" and resulted from Junior's four-week bout with scarlet fever.

But aside from an occasional contretemps such as this, the report card was easy to understand. It didn't try to tell Mom and Pop how hard Junior tried or whether he came to school with his hair combed or even how adequately he was adjusting to his peer group. It simply told how well he was doing in reading and spelling and mathematics and history as compared to the rest of the class and in terms of the teacher's own standards of achievement.

The Non-Report Card has quite a different objective. Simply put, its goal is not to tell you anything you really want to know. Actually, the "life adjustment" folks would like to abolish report cards altogether in favor of parent-teacher conferences. Even the Non-Report Card, in their opinion, smacks distressingly of status-seeking with overtones of that unspeakable word "competition."

Since the long-suffering public, except in a few "avant-garde" school districts, has not been willing to hold still for the complete abolition of any written record of their offsprings' accomplishments, the high priests of Progressivism have settled for a multipage, footnoted, essay-type production that measures Junior's work only against some of Junior's previous work.

The old letter grades are out, and new ones like N for "Needs Improvement in Relation to Potential" and S for "Socializes Well" are in. Junior receives these grades in such esoteric "subjects" as "Participation in Sharing Activities," "Ability to Work Constructively With the Group," and "Response to Environmental Challenges."

This would be all right, if the world of tomorrow would judge us solely on how well we are doing in comparison with our own previous best efforts. Unhappily, it won't. It will continue to do as it has always done—reward those of us who do the most with what we know and punish those of us who falter in the race for success and even sheer survival.

It's what the other fellow does that we are measured against. In this kind of world, the Non-Report Card may be preparing Junior for togetherness with the dodo and the passenger pigeon.

During the same thirty years, schools across the land have been teaching something called "social studies," and in so doing they have succeeded in confusing millions of parents—who get it mixed up with social dancing—and thousands of irate businessmen, who confound it with socialism.

I taught social studies for twenty of those thirty years, and I have to confess to being confused myself. The social *sciences*, of course, have been around for years. They include the ancient and highly individualized subject disciplines of history, geography, political science, and several more. But what are we aiming for when we teach social *studies*?

Actually, it's the subtle mingling and hamburgerizing and homogenizing of various subjects into one ersatz end product. For example, I used to teach fifth grade "social living," which was a further refinement of social studies. The goal was the combining of every subject area under the sun into a single "unit."

Take "The Westward Movement," for instance. The history part dealt with Dan'l Boone and Davy Crockett, naturally.

We taught geography by tracing the course of the covered wagons as they lumbered through the Cumberland Gap.

Science was a little harder to work into the act—the pioneers not being especially known for their contributions in this field—but we at least managed to demonstrate the action of flint on steel as Dan'l lit his pipe while waiting for the Indians to attack.

Music was easy. We taught our pupils the whining, monotonous folk songs of the Kentucky hillbillies, thus giving rise in more recent years to that supreme American contribution to twentieth-century music: rock 'n' roll.

English I shudder even to think about, but we made shift to teach some spelling through the medium of such vital, meaningful "unit" words as "charivari," "Conestoga," "matchlock"—important words like these.

I remember one teacher who was the envy of our whole faculty. She and her class spent an entire week making soap out of ashes, just the way the pioneer women did. And so it went.

It wasn't the fault of the teachers. It was the fault of the nutty educational philosophy which held that the accumulated culture and learning of the past were best presented to children by hashing everything up and serving it in a sort of steaming, bubbling witches' brew instead of offering it in organized, systematic courses.

Now I'll get a rash of letters from teachers asking me if I don't think history should include a knowledge of geography.

Of course I do. But I don't think it's necessary to teach the two as a single subject, any more than it would be to combine algebra and physics into something called "quantitative studies" or even "quantitative living" just because an understanding of one is desirable before proceeding to the mastery of the second.

Social studies is on its way out in the upper grades. But the primary grade units on "The Home and the Community," "The Dairy," "The Trip to the Bakery," and so on are still very much with us.

In California I'm trying to persuade the folks who write our curriculum to turn these units out to pasture and to substitute for them units on such subjects as "Lives of Great World Leaders," "Events that Changed History," and "Landmarks of Democracy."

I hope we can swing it for the sake of the kids. Otherwise we'll be perpetuating a system that turned thousands of youngsters out of grade school who were adept at making igloos out of refrigerator ice cubes but unable to locate Greenland on the map; expert at constructing mud huts but unaware of where the Sudan is; authorities on soap-making but ignorant of the Monroe Doctrine.

Naturally, that old devil Homework was included with report cards, history, geography, and a lot of other things in the Progressive Educationists' onslaught on subject matter.

It must have been almost ten years ago that one of our great national publications announced with triumphant fanfare that educational research had finally proved that children who were assigned no homework in school did just as well in their studies, mastered subject matter as completely, and got just as good grades as did their unfortunate peers who sat up boning till all hours and burning the midnight oil over their assignments.

The implications were obvious. Why bother with homework? The Progressive Educationists had long regarded it with about the same enthusiasm that the Kremlin holds for a Red Chinese proposal to revise the Siberian boundaries. To no one's surprise, their researchers—all progressives to a man—had at last come up with findings to support prejudiced preconceptions.

Why didn't the life-adjustment cultists like homework? Because they didn't like subject matter, and homework just about has to be subject matter. It is, after all, rather difficult to turn in written lessons on environmental adjustment or peer-group acceptance, whereas multiplication tables and spelling can be learned very well at home.

With the declining emphasis on memorization and the rising stress on things like associational sharing and the dynamics of committee membership, however, homework became not only superfluous but downright embarrassing. After all, if Mom and Pop were conditioned to expect some sort of home assignment every evening and were used to looking it over before Susie went to bed, they might have some pointed questions to ask about the type of "studying" she was being asked to do. So homework had to go.

Now, like everything else in education, homework had always been subject to abuse from time to time. A few lazy instructors would give kids home assignments for which they had not laid the proper groundwork in class, and a few stupid ones would pile on reams of work on the general premise that if a little is good, a whole lot will be better. Once in a while Dad would get conned into working some math problems and Mom into writing an English essay. But these were abuses of a good thing, not reasons for abolishing it.

It's against this historical backdrop that the recent recommendations of Dr. James Conant must be considered. Dr. Conant came right out a short time ago for homework and lots of it, even in the lower grades. He didn't mean "busy work" or mere repetition or homework for the mystic sake of homework. He meant the invaluable experience of unsupervised, self-organized study in areas of subject matter that must be mastered but which the school day is too brief to encompass.

Largely as a result of this recommendation, the college preparatory youngster is doing up to three hours of homework a night, and a good thing, too. You don't have to tell me that a lot of them always have. I know this. It's just that now the vast majority are doing it. Ironically, we have to be careful now that we don't overdo it.

But what about all that so-called "research," I wonder? Those "proofs" that homework didn't do any good after all? Those triumphant magazine pieces sneering at the after-hour drudge?

"Rafferty's First Law" holds up pretty well, doesn't it?

The only real test of any educational philosophy is the ability to give an affirmative answer to the eternal question: "Does it work?"

Let's look at the record.

If life-adjustment education had worked, we would have raised a law-abiding generation devoted to peaceful and harmonious pursuits. Instead, we have raised the most lawless generation in history.

If life-adjustment education had worked, we would have by this time largely eliminated racism in the land. Instead, white racism still flourishes, and black racism —almost unknown until our own time—thrives and spreads across the nation.

If life-adjustment education had worked, there would today be peace in our cities, reason in our politics, and cooperation among our several groups and factions. Instead, our cities writhe and burn every time the weather turns hot, our politics is increasingly punctuated with rifle shots fired from ambush, and in this year 1970 there is more virulent hatred being preached in every corner of America than at any time since that other year of grim foreboding, 1860, when the nation stared helplessly ahead into the bloody face of approaching civil war.

Thus, by its own pragmatic standards, educational pragmatism has been the failure of the century. The only answer that can conceivably be given to the question "Does life-adjustment education work?" is "No, it certainly doesn't."

As a supplement to the failure of the aforementioned Gospel According to St. John Dewey, another thing that hasn't worked is the Apocrypha According to St. John Gardner. This attempted to change the definition of the American school from an institution dedicated to learning to an institution dedicated to political, economic, and social reform. No longer did the school exist primarily to make the pupil learned—a task sufficiently difficult in itself, incidentally, to have challenged to the very limit the finest minds of our profession for at least three thousand years. Now the school must exist to make the pupil an integrationist, an internationalist, and a liberal, though not necessarily in that order. The public has so far refused to hold still for this one.

Is the picture completely dark, then? Hasn't anything "worked"?

Quite a few rather impressive things have been working, are working, and will continue to work. To pinpoint a few:

(1) Music today is taught almost unbelievably well. Listening to a junior high school orchestra used to give

me both a tin ear and the cold grue. Not anymore. I've heard some within the past year that made me look carefully at the podium to see if Leonard Bernstein was conducting.

(2) Physical education is better that it's ever been. Oh, too many gym teachers are still being saddled with monstrous forty- or fifty-pupil classes. Granted. But even when well-nigh submerged by such hordes, the physical-education instructor these days is performing wonders with his tennis-shoed charges via weightlifting, isometric exercises, and individual physical-fitness testing. In my day it was pretty much, "Check out a ball, fellows, and start a game. I'll be around later to take roll."

(3) The delicate art of counseling a generation ago was very big in theory but pretty pint-sized in practice. Today's young people are being given better guidance in school by more highly trained personnel than ever before. Now, if we could just persuade more of them to take the advice they're getting. . . .

(4) So-called extracurricular activities a few years back used to be largely confined to football, basketball, and the junior prom. Now a typical afterschool program for high-schoolers will run the gamut from the Audubon Society clear to the Rocketry| Association, with a lot of extra stops in between for groups like the Cybernetics Club. Sometimes the youngsters will learn more after school than they do in class, and I'm not talking about a slow stroll home down Lovers' Lane, either.

(5) Perhaps the most spectacular work the schools are doing now lies in areas that were unknown territory just a short time ago. Subjects like electronics, the Great Books, psychology, philosophy, and sociology are being offered in high schools.

So we can produce results if we really want to. Where, then, has education come a-cropper?

Exactly where our society as a whole has come a-cropper. The Great Hiatus between where we are and where we should be has its roots in the Sick Sixties themselves. The times we live in demand from education immediate answers to unprecedented questions.

For instance:

There's a grand scene in the recent cinema version of H. G. Wells's *The Time Machine*. In it, the bemused time traveler watches a clothing display in a shop window across the street while time speeds up and he is whirled into the future. First the seasons, then whole years and decades flit by, and as they do the strange and somehow terrifying transformations wrought by time are mirrored in the kaleidoscopic costume changes that successively drape the mannequin in the shop window.

In a sense, we all share in grim reality today that which was only fantasy to Wells in the calm and closing years of the 1800s. For after eons of leisurely and unchanging sand-droppings and clock-tickings, time is obviously accelerating. We are all time travelers now, watching our children's century rushing upon us before we have been given grace and scope to die out decently and leave the world to those who tread so eagerly upon our heels.

This is the secret of the newly discovered and widely trumpeted "generation gap" that to date we educators have failed signally to bridge. Until our own time, things changed slowly enough so that a man—unless he shared the incredible longevity of a Bernard Shaw or a Winston Churchill—did not usually outlive the manners and morals of his own generation. But now we are caught in a speedup, and we find ourselves increasingly alienated by the radically different customs of our descendants before we ourselves have had even half a chance to shuffle offstage into the wings of eternity.

Always before, there had been something called a "decent interval of change" to cushion the shock of clashing mores. The staid burgher of the Middle Ages, for example, would have been horrified right down to his pointed shoes at the art of the Renaissance—the heroic nudes of Michelangelo and the lush ladies of Raphael. But these shockers came along only after a century or two of transition artists like Giotto and Gimabue, who provided an acceptable bridge between the pious draperies of medieval art and the complete lack of any draperies at all that characterized much of the Renaissance. So our friend the burgher never knew what was coming, and what he didn't know didn't hurt him.

Today the great public which throughout history has supported and subsidized art because it was able to relate to what the artist was saying is out of touch completely. In past ages, art was the only universal communication medium. Now it has virtually ceased to communicate at all. Art today is only what the artist says it is, and thus it has become part idiosyncrasy, part irrelevance.

Much of the reason for this preemption of one generation's prime time by the following generation is the freakish imbalance currently existing between youth and maturity. For the first time on record, youngsters are the majority age group. And since youth has never been noted either for its tact or its patience, sparks are flying from the whole surface of the American anvil as the hammer of accelerating time beats upon it with ever-increasing brashness and insistency.

Obviously the puzzle carries within it the seeds of its own solution. Everything and everyone pays a common toll to time. Even Teddy Kennedy grows older every day. Today's long-haired hippie is tomorrow's meek and balding clock-puncher. And Peter Pan lives only in Never-Never Land.

I'm more than a little worried, however, about the Wells Syndrome. If time continues to collapse upon itself increasingly, we may all wind up in a world in which there are no recognizable points of reference for anyone over twenty. And since the classic definition of insanity is inability on the part of the individual to relate coherently to his environment, the implications of such a speedup of the Time Machine are too horrendous even to contemplate.

This syndrome may well explain many of the miseries of our own profession. I refuse to brood about it, however. After all, if our Victorian great-grandparents could see us now, they would say with grim certainty and some justification that we were all stark, staring crazy, anyhow.

Of late, and to a large extent because the eyes of John Q. Public have been rudely opened by the continuing campus convulsions, a counteroffensive has been mounted against the disciples of permissivism. In California, some of us fighting under the banner of "Education in Depth" clashed shield to shield and helm to helm with Progressive Education a few years back and brought it crashing heavily to earth. Our new philosophy then began to spread east across the country, borne on the wings of its California accomplishments to date: annual statewide reading, mathematics, and English tests for all pupils; new, stiff, subject-matter requirements for the would-be teacher; grammar textbooks as far down as the first grade; geography texts as far down as grade three; the banishment of "social studies" and "language arts" from official terminology on the state level; the final and unregretted demise of "Dick and Jane"; the adoption of state reading texts stressing phonics and the children's classics; new, state-prepared courses in economics.

Still to come and currently in the mill: basic competence tests for new teachers; state-adopted moral and ethical instructional guidelines; a decent, scientific course in human reproduction instead of the raw sex material spread across the land in recent months by S.I.E.C.U.S. like so much malignant margarine. In fact, a program calculated to cause Dr. Dewey to revolve in his grave like an electric fan.

Here for the record are the differences between the two warring philosophies:

Progressive Education is convinced that there are no absolutes, no eternal verities, no positive standards of good or evil. We who uphold the standard of Education in Depth know that there are, and we know too that education exists in part to identify these lasting values and to equip young people to seek after them as long as life itself shall last.

Progressive Education stresses "life adjustment" as the main goal of the instructional process. Education in Depth holds that the teaching of organized, disciplined, and systematic subject matter should be the principal objective of the schools.

Progressive Education feels that the curriculum should depend upon the immediate interests of the individual child. Education in Depth wants a curriculum to provide for the child the tools and skills he will need later on to become a cultured and productive citizen.

Progressive Education believes that schools exist to make the individual popular and accepted by the "group." Education in Depth wants to make him learned.

Progressive Education advocates "experiencing" learning through as many sense avenues as possible. Education in Depth thinks this is pretentious jackassery and regards reading and recitative discussion as the most effective as well as economical method of instruction.

Progressive Education holds that the pupil should be encouraged to compete only with himself, or rather with his own previous best efforts. Education in Depth believes that the success of the individual in later life depends upon how well he is taught in school to hold his own in an increasingly competitive world.

Why does the California philosophy possess such popular appeal that it has Deweyism in nationwide retreat, looking apprehensively back over a once smug shoulder and whistling nervously to itself? Why, because Education in Depth is essentially what nearly all parents have always wanted for their children. Mark this: The schoolman who dares to unfurl the flag of Education in Depth within the boundaries of his state will certainly focus upon himself the malicious enmity of the professional education Establishment, but he will simultaneously gain the strong and even enthusiastic support of just about everybody else in his state.

I know. It happened to me.

Another thing that is happening these days is a frenzied Establishment counterattack: "Why keep knocking Progressive Education? It's dead. Been dead for years. And even when it was alive, it never was very widespread."

There's about as much truth to this claim as there would be to the report that I am to be selected as the A.F.T. candidate for "Educator of the Year."

It's true that Deweyism is on the run. You'll notice, for example, that it doesn't call itself "Progressive Education" anymore. The national organization operating under that name disbanded some years back. "Bad notices," as *Variety* would phrase it. Far fewer educationists dare to defend "life adjustment" openly, and it's possible now to criticize at least a few of its further-out aberrations at an educational conference without being relegated automatically to a particularly icy version of Coventry by the horrified delegates.

But to say that Progressive Education is dead just because it has changed its name and hidden behind various aliases is as unwarranted as it would have been for our grandparents to assume that Jesse James was dead because he had changed his name to Mr. Howard and was pretending to be a respectable family man.

As a sort of Grand Guignol windup to my case against today's version of Progressive Education, let me describe a couple of its practitioners. The first is Dr. James Craig, assistant superintendent of Montgomery County, Maryland, schools, and he wants to let pupils do as they please.

"In seventh and eighth grades, why not let students study anything of their choice?" asks Dr. Craig. "What they study is not nearly as important as getting into something they're interested in."

Sound familiar? This is where a lot of us came in.

This bland, infuriating assumption that the curriculum should be prescribed by the kids is as old as John Dewey. Junior high youngsters are interested in rock combos, motor bikes, and baton-twirling, roughly in that order. Apparently Dr. Craig feels that letting the students concentrate on these lastingly rewarding subjects will be more beneficial than imposing upon them such irrelevant and stuffy courses as English, science, and mathematics.

What's taught is unimportant.

No body of knowledge is essential.

The curriculum should be shaped by the immediate interests of the immature.

And I am the Sultan of Sulu.

Nowhere in the progressive philosophy does there seem to be the merest hint that children should learn to think and act in an orderly, disciplined manner. Nowhere is there even the insinuation that in this life, this world, this universe, there are some things that are important to be learned, simply because they are there. If a child is to grow up saying and doing just as he pleases, there is precious little use in spending money on his tuition. He can do this sort of thing at home, free.

A school is neither a health resort, a recreation center, nor a psychiatric clinic. It's a place where the massed wisdom of the ages is passed from one generation to the next, and where youngsters are taught to think in a logical and systematic fashion. A school where subject disciplines are unimportant is a school where education itself has become irrelevant.

But there's more from Dr. Craig: "What a student does in high school has little relevance to his success in college. Let the ninth-grader plan his own next four years. It might be school, a job, travel."

Or maybe discotheques, pool halls, or drag-racing.

I wonder how the good doctor proposes to find out which students should go to college if their high school work is as gloriously irrelevant as he thinks it is. By entrance exams? But that's the way we used to do it, back in the antediluvian days of mustache cups, Teddy Roosevelt, and decent spelling. Surely the heralds of this brave new world of comfy togetherness, cozy in-groupness, and bloody campus riots are not planning to take us back to the corny old nineteenth century.

Here, and parenthetically, I am beset by the horrid fear that the Progressive Educationists, who hate history, don't really know how things were in the nineteenth century. Judging by some of their brasher manifestoes, they seem to think that life on this planet began approximately on their own respective birth dates.

Another quote from our muddled Maryland mentor: "Grading is socially and emotionally damaging to children. It rewards the bright and rejects the not-so-bright. Why not evaluate instead the student's interest in learning, his progress, his willingness to go on to more difficult tasks?"

Why not? Because life doesn't do this, and we teachers are supposed to prepare children for life. As long as we live, we're graded on what we know, how well we get results, and how successfully we can compete. No one is rewarded on the basis of how interested he is in what he's doing, only on how good he is at doing it. A school that kids the kids into thinking that life is going to be all Roman candles is not a school. It's a dream factory. Some things in this world have to be learned because they're important, not because they're groovy.

My case is virtually complete. If Progressive Education is indeed moribund, then Dr. Craig just has to be the best reviver of potential corpses since the discoverer of the heart transplant.

Finally there is the principal of Bedford Junior High School, in Westport, Connecticut, who is acting as midwife to a dubious new specimen of educational tomfoolery called the "Bedford Plan." Here's what it embodies:

(1) *Mad* magazine is required reading for the kiddies. Rock records are required listening.

(2) A popular course called "Boob Tube" involves that most challenging of all scholarly disciplines, watching television.

(3) Another course apparently designed for the junior ghoul set is titled "Vampires Unlimited" and consists of nothing but horror stories.

(4) There's a class in dieting called "Whittle Your Way to a Bikini" and another one in "How to Play in a Steel Band."

(5) The parents of Westport fork over $1,000 per student per year to perpetuate this fraud on the public, as compared with the national average of $750 for less psychedelic schooling.

(6) The turned-on thirteen-year-olds who populate the expensive bedlam that is Bedford select any courses they like, presumably on the theory that they know better than the teachers. (Considering the kind of instructor who would be willing to work in this nut house, this may be true.)

(7) Racing cars loom large in the curriculum, as do gourmet cooking and electronic music. I scrutinized the press accounts carefully to see whether bongo drums and bubblegum were listed as course offerings. I didn't find them. But I'm sure the only reason for their absence is that the Bedfordian powers that be just haven't gotten around to them yet.

The Westport principal defends his brainstorm as "turning on" the blasé pre-teeners, assuring their lasting interest in learning by letting them write their own educational ticket, and encouraging them to think of school as a real blast instead of a stretch in Dullsville.

Between spasms of nausea, permit me to differ.

Teen-agers "turn on" too darned much as it is, without the school's aiding and abetting their mind-blowing. What our youngsters need today is more seriousness and less foolery, more study and less electronic rock, more great literature and fewer *Mad* magazines.

What's the matter with having a school that addresses itself to organized, disciplined, systematic teaching of subject matter?

What's wrong with hiring teachers with more wisdom than the pupils, and then letting them get that wisdom into the kids' heads?

Above all, what's wrong with running a school in a no-nonsense atmosphere of scholarly dignity where a child can have his mind expanded, not blown?

If these apostles of the upside-down continue to war against your children via their key role in our educational Establishment, their victims will continue to grow up cultural barbarians, popular illiterates, adrenal rather than cerebral, indoctrinated instead of educated. As their declared and mortal enemy for almost a complete generation, let me tell you how to fight them:

(1) Elect local school-board members who believe that the schools exist not to make pupils popular but to make them learned.

(2) See that your school board adopts written policies setting forth a detailed philosophy of Education in Depth.

(3) Hire only administrators and teachers who agree before signing their contracts to follow the policies in spirit as well as in practice.

(4) Set standards of achievement for each grade level, and conduct yearly tests to be sure those standards are being met.

(5) See that a code of basic morality is set up for all the schools in your community, and that the children are taught the differences between right and wrong.

(6) Remember that there are tens of thousands of good teachers who never bought the doctrine of "life adjustment." Identify them, cherish them, and reward them accordingly.

None of these actions by themselves, nor indeed all of them together, will insure your children a victory in the education sector of the war against them. But they will at least insure the kids an even break. Which is more than they're getting now in many places.

Of all the children's enemies, the Progressive Educationists are the ones I feel most strongly about. Because they have miseducated so many millions. Because like the Bourbons of old, they have learned nothing and forgotten nothing. Because they are so damnably self-righteous.

And lastly, because they are mine own people, long gone wrong.

CROSSROAD #3

The Establishment Roadblock

No ANALYSIS OF education at the crossroads can be made without posing the subject before its proper backdrop. Progressivism under a whole series of masks and disguises has mutated and proliferated all over the block. In so doing, it has taken on some strange dimensions and has gone into areas that would have raised even Dr. Dewey's eyebrows. The backdrop has become a kaleidoscope, with each frame representing a logical if seemingly unrelated facet of the glass life-adjustment diamond.

FACET NO. 1—STATISM IN EDUCATION

In 1966 a regional conference was held by the National Education Association at which its educational-policies-commission chairman complained that the job of teaching youngsters to think cannot be accomplished if the schools continue to be subject to local control.

His name is James E. Russell. The Spokane newspapers

quoted him as saying that the country is suffering from the outmoded concept that the effectiveness of any educational program can be measured in terms of its impact on human behavior.

"This condition exists," continued Big Brother Russell, "because the conduct of education in this country is dominated by the populace, which sets the main goals."

What a shame that public education should be dominated by the public. And that outmoded old chestnut about measuring the effects of schooling by its impact on human behavior!

Everybody knows that our great educational professional hierarchies don't want educational effectiveness measured at all. To do so opens all sorts of horrid doors, from comparative-achievement rates in different schools to merit rating for individual teachers. Chaos thrice confounded! It's much safer, after all, to talk about educational goals in purely subjective terms that don't lend themselves to any kind of objective measurement.

How do we measure the success of "relevance"? Or democratic socializing with one's peer group? Or plain old togetherness, for that matter?

Answer: We don't. And that's what we like about them.

Whereas such high-button-shoe educational items as spelling and the multiplication tables and history and geography lend themselves very easily and readily to simple achievement testing, thank you, and thus enable the uninitiated lay public to figure out how well or how poorly some of us are teaching these things as compared with others. And that's what we don't like about *them*.

If we educationists could just connive or cajole or coerce old John Q. Public into changing his stubborn ideas about the primacy of measurable mastery of subject matter in determining educational goals, then the great hierarchies with their trailing clouds of well-paid executive secretaries, consultants, and press agents could sleep much more soundly. But old John persists in his benighted ways, so the only thing left to do is to turf him out of the school picture altogether.

I really think we owe Mr. Russell a vote of thanks. A condemned man always deserves a word of warning from the warden as to the date and hour set for the execution. And when the banker is getting ready to foreclose the mortgage on the old homestead and boot me out into the snow, I appreciate the twenty-four hour notice so I can don my thermal underwear in preparation for life in the great out-of-doors.

So it is that Mr. Russell has done us a favor. He has put us on notice that the bell we hear is tolling for you-know-whom. The process of ejecting the American people from their own school system is, of course, already far advanced. Ask any local school-board member who has served a long term if he had more or less say over school policy fifteen years ago than he has today. I'll bet $5, sight unseen, that he tells you the rights and powers of local school boards have been so cramped and cribbed and circumscribed that today they are markedly and frighteningly fewer than they were a decade and a half ago.

The Establishment is always opposed to local control, whether that Establishment be educational or political, reactionary or radical, Communist or Fascist. It wants more boards and commissions, more appointive officials, fewer elected ones. It bends its every effort toward removing itself from a position of accountability to anyone on God's earth except itself. It's the closest thing in nature to perpetual motion—self-energizing, self-evaluating, self-reproducing.

One slight exception: It can always be persuaded to let the general public foot the bills.

In fact, it's amazing how all of a sudden grassroots control of education has become atrophied, palsied, and positively immoral.

Over the generations, our thousands of local American school boards managed to do a pretty fair job. They turned out men like Lincoln, Edison, and Eisenhower. Even Lyndon Johnson and Richard Nixon.

They saw us safely through seven big wars and a whole clutch of little ones. They educated the men and women who tamed a raw and savage continent and in so doing built a nation that became in due course the wonder and the envy of the human race.

To their eternal credit they stayed local in every sense of that word. They concentrated on giving their constituents the kind of schooling they wanted for their children, not necessarily what some Columbia University philosopher thought the children ought to have.

Through the years, too, both urban and rural boards of education have concentrated on buying the best possible instruction the taxpayer could afford. Elected school-board members, incidentally, are a taxpayers' bargain. Almost none of them gets paid a cent.

Most importantly, perhaps, they sturdily resisted any and all attempts to introduce statism and centralized bureaucracy into the highly individualized process of instructing children. They were one of the last big bulwarks shoring up grassroots control by John Q. Public of his own affairs.

Maybe this is why local school boards are catching hell these days.

In a Washington effusion, just a few years back, our national secretary of Health, Education and Welfare called for wholesale change. He frowned officially on "most school boards in this country," charging that they are "inadequately organized to do their jobs."

"They need to be improved," John W. Gardner announced portentously.

I think the word "improved" wasn't quite the term he had in mind. One of the following would seem considerably closer: "consolidated," "emasculated," or plain "plowed under."

Almost five years ago, one of the biggest political wheels in California at that time said to me, "Doctor, isn't it true that all these local school districts are useless, and that it would be a lot cheaper and more efficient to do away with them and let the state and federal government do the job?"

I disagreed most strenuously. The day American education ceases to be local in nature and becomes statist or federalist, it will cease to be education as we and our ancestors have known it.

There are quite a few so-called leaders in extremely high places in government who would like very much to deprive you of the right to run your own local schools and to determine the educational destiny of your children.

In California not long ago we came breathtakingly close to wiping out 95 percent of all local school districts by mandate from Sacramento without so much as giving the residents and taxpayers of those districts a chance to say "Boo!" about it. Other states are moving in the same direction.

The whole trend, in fact, seems to be running in favor of letting some anonymous Big Brother make decisions for us because, it is said, we the people are too easily swayed by our emotions and can't be trusted even to come in out of the rain, much less decide the final format of our own school systems and the educational destiny of our own children.

I can't buy this. I can't buy it in education, and I can't

buy it in anything else. This is the sort of thing that would have made the Founding Fathers' hair stand on end, right under their wigs.

As far as federal "aid" to education is concerned, let's look at what happened in Chicago. The city found out several years ago what it means to tell the federal government to mind its own business when that same federal government controls the pursestrings. You'll recall that some $40 million was suddenly withheld because Washington was annoyed with some of the policies of the Chicago school board. Later, due to Senator Dirksen and Mayor Daley, the money was restored as suddenly and arbitrarily as it had been withheld. Politics took it away, and politics returned it. This is what federal aid to education on a grand scale really means.

Every indication I have is that people don't mind combining their school districts or revising their curriculum, or even de-emphasizing football as long as it's of their own free will. But they hate to have it shoved down their throats by some bland but browbeating bureaucrats from hundreds of miles away. Yet this is the trend, and it's running strongly.

The clincher for me lies in Gardner's concluding statement: "The way education is organized determines its effectiveness, so critics of the system must sooner or later come to grips with it."

Yep. And if we can just "reorganize" local school government out of existence we can move on to take an equally critical look at the rest of local government, can't we?

After all, the advocates of neighborhood self-government are too parochial in their outlook, too narrow in their interests, and quite often too downright belligerent in their attitude to be allowed to run their own affairs, aren't they?

Odd, isn't it?

That's exactly what the British said about those stubborn, narrow-minded, belligerent farmers who stood up to them at Lexington and Concord.

Crossroads, in fact, are to be found in almost every element of education today, especially in the crucial area of who is going to run the show.

When I hear teacher unions say, "The school board won't pay us what we think we ought to be making, so we're going out on strike," my answer is: "If the people in your present school district won't pay you what you think you're worth, then look around for another bunch of people who will. You have the ancient and unalienable right of every professional since mankind crawled out of caves to take your services and your talents to more appreciative customers."

And when I read statements urging teachers to apply "sanctions" against entire sovereign states that refuse for one reason or another to vote more money for public education, I'm inclined to say: "Lay citizens in a free country are entitled to make their own decisions, and even from time to time their own mistakes. We educators can reason and argue and persuade, but nothing in our calling or its ethics gives us any right to threaten and to intimidate and to coerce. After all, we teachers ought to be able to *educate* folks into doing what's right. If we can't, who can?"

We've been hearing a lot recently about various fringe groups throwing their weight around and trying to dictate what goes on in the classroom, but have we stopped viewing with alarm long enough to ask why this sort of thing is happening? It's happening because of some of *us*. Whether we like it or not, the great public that supports and populates the schools is becoming increasingly concerned about the antics of some schoolmen who have become of late so out of step with the great parade of public opinion that they wound up on another street entirely from the rest of the marchers.

Just a short time ago, the chairman of the board of trustees of one of our largest state-college systems ventured to tell a Commencement Day crowd that Communist speakers on campus should be rebutted, in his opinion, by speakers of equal importance and persuasiveness from the other end of the political and economic spectrum.

The result was predictable: a rash of resolutions from horrified faculty associations demanding that the chairman resign, on the grounds that he was infringing upon academic freedom. I'm sure that if the *chairman* had suggested that one of the *professors* resign, there would have been anguished breastbeatings and Macedonian outcries from every professional group in the country, from the American Association of University Professors on down. But the professors had no scruples whatever about trying to get the president's job, did they? And without even attempting to argue the merits of the case he was endeavoring to make.

Academic freedom cuts both ways. I've always believed that a teacher, operating within the scope of his special competence, lecturing on his assigned subject, clearly identifying his personal beliefs and hobbies as such to his students, giving the pros and cons of controversial issues fairly, should be protected to the utmost by the institution that employs him. His superiors have an obligation to defend him against cranks and pressure groups and crusaders in behalf of personal causes.

On the other hand, an instructor who is more interested in promoting a certain ideology than he is in seeking truth, who parades a train of whimsical crotchets and beliefs in the guise of facts, who neglects or ridicules all facets of argumentative issues except the one to which he is personally committed, is *not* entitled to the protection of academic freedom.

Indeed, he is not an educator at all, but a promoter. And who ever heard of a promoter being entitled to academic freedom? Anyone who deliberately places himself beyond the pale of his own profession's ethics can hardly expect that same profession to spring to his defense when he runs into trouble. If the profession does so spring, it is laying up a store of potential mischief for itself.

The proper thing for us schoolmen to do is to deal with abuses of academic freedom ourselves, and so effectively that it will be unnecessary for outsiders to come in and do it for us. This is the way medicine and the law and the other learned professions handle their occasional mavericks. If we refuse to follow their example, and if the outsiders do eventually come in to fill the vacuum thus created, this will not constitute a violation of academic freedom; it will be an abdication of academic responsibility.

The purpose of an educational institution is not to bring about a new social or political order, nor to preach the gospel according to Saint Anybody, nor to serve as a haven for hippies. Its purposes is to instill in young people a reverence for accurate and logical thinking, to share with them the intellectual artifacts of the past that combine to form the firm foundation of our cultural present, and above all to inspire within them an insatiable curiosity about life and learning.

The graduate who leaves the hallowed halls of academe convinced that his teachers have found the answers for him and have shared those answers with him has failed to get an education, regardless of what those answers may have been or how feverishly they may have been promulgated.

If we insist upon indoctrinating kids with certain points of view that we believe to be right, we have opened wide the door to every way-out outfit that has a doctrine to put over and the votes to take over. The schools do not exist to pander to a certain point of view—even ours.

If we schoolmen will only concentrate on teaching instead of promoting, the schools will continue to be controlled by the only group that *ought* to control them—the general public.

FACET NO. 2—GIMMICKRY IN EDUCATION

Education has long been a fertile breeding ground for gimmicks, every one of which was originally and ecstatically hailed as Revealed Certainty by some of my starrier-eyed and fuzzier-minded colleagues.

Back in the nineteenth century, the "Lancastrian system" of instruction was developed to meet the urgent need of the Industrial Revolution for a proletariat at least minimally literate. Certain of the brighter children were taught to read quickly and then were set to work at no cost to the state to help their slower classmates learn their letters. Today the same principle brings college students into the slums to tutor the culturally impoverished.

The Roaring Twenties saw the birth of the so-called platoon system, which was widely heralded as the definitive answer to the problem of the overcrowded high schools. It embodied the ingenious scheduling of pupils by brigades and squadrons into the various academic and vocational divisions of the school plant, utilizing split-second timing and resembling to a certain extent the Notre Dame shift, a more lastingly rewarding innovation with which it was incidentally contemporaneous.

In my own salad days, something called "fusion" was dreamed up as the answer to any and all questions involving curriculum. All sorts of formerly respectable and highly individualized subject disciplines such as history, geography, civics, economics, and even English were homogenized with one another and served up confusingly to the children in one three-hour-long mishmash each day. "Fusion" was the Final Answer of the Forties. Today nobody except a few of us old-timers has ever heard of it.

The 1950s fathered a whole gaggle of gimmicks, one of which was "group dynamics." With its comet tail of "resource persons," "interrogators" and "discussion leaders," this glamorized version of the venerable seminar panel swept the land, doubled the average time needed to conduct an efficient faculty meeting, and generally wreaked the usual amount of havoc common to most educational freaks and foibles. Once again, "group dynamics" is long forgotten save by the scholarly historians of my profession.

Now we have Sensitivity Training, Programmed Instruction, and the Audiolingual Method. Next year it will be something else again, no doubt. The trouble with all this froth is that it sidetracks a lot of valuable time, money, and energy from the main job of education, which has always been, is now, and shall ever be the equipping of young people with enough organized, disciplined, systematic subject matter to become truly learned.

Every decade spawns its own particular scholastic salvation, yet every subsequent decade either rejects that same ultimate salvation or forgets it and sets forth upon an equally infatuated quest for its own guaranteed and patented brand of educational snake-oil.

The most popular labels to be found on today's nostrums are "teaching machines" and "team teaching." The first is misnamed, the second usually misapplied.

There is no such thing as a teaching machine, because no machine can really teach. The one thing that all teaching has in common is the impact of the personality of the instructor upon the personality of the child. A machine, no matter how intricate or ingenious, has no more personality than an alarm clock.

There are indeed modern mechanisms that help the teacher, and they can be put to very good use, as were certain older teaching aids such as books, maps, globes, slides, and 16-mm. films. But a machine that embodies the inspiration and the spirit of true teaching is a contradiction in terms.

Team teaching is simply a method of permitting the diverse talents of several instructors to play upon large numbers of pupils simultaneously. The theory is a sound one, but in actual practice team teaching is severely limited by the chronic lack of both the big, hundred-pupil classrooms and the small cubicles upon which the new method ideally depends. In most of our overcrowded schools, too, team teaching is hard to implement because of scheduling problems involving hundreds of pupils.

To sum up: Both teaching machines and team teaching are valuable instructional tools—when used sensibly.

But the best and most durable setup is a dedicated, inspirational teacher with twenty-five youngsters in a well-equipped classroom supplied with interesting, subject matter–oriented textbooks.

Just the same, the advocates of mechanized learning are dedicated and articulate. Many of them use the "wave of the future" technique in letters like this one:

"We're entering a new world where each child will shortly be educating himself. The benignly fascinating computer will enable Junior henceforth to move at his own pace instead of being manacled into an arbitary grade based on chronological age. You, sir, are a relic of the Dark Ages."

So I'm a heretic. *"Eppur si muove!"* as old Galileo said.

Machines are fine as teaching aids. But they are not teachers. And neither is Junior, even of himself. A kid left to his own devices with a fancy electronic gadget is just as apt to dismantle it with a pocketknife as he is to learn anything from it. More so, in fact.

Note the assumption implicit in the Gadget Syllogism:

(1) A child has an innate love of learning that is too often burned out and frustrated by poor teaching.

(2) A machine is more efficient, more patient, more stimulating than any teacher. It also lights up, whirs, and clicks, none of which a teacher can do without considerable difficulty.

(3) Therefore, since a machine permits the natural love of learning to blossom in each child by enabling him to compete only with himself at his own natural rate of speed, the machine is the final answer to the educational Riddle of the Ages.

In my role of heretic, let me now torpedo this all-too-blithe assumption:

(1) A machine is not efficient at all. Its efficiency depends upon its user. More, its memory banks are necessarily restricted to one narrow subject field. But every teacher knows that a mathematics class on any given day is apt to elicit questions from Junior on everything from Greek columns to the hypothetical planetary system surrounding far Centaurus. A machine programmed to answer everything a normally inquisitive child can dream up in the course of a half-hour class would displace the Pentagon.

(2) A machine is too darned patient. Every educator should lose his temper once in a while, if only to show his pupils that he cares deeply about them. A computer

can do many things. Losing its temper is not one of them.

(3) All Americans do *not* share a love of gadgets. Personally, I hate the things.

(4) Finally, to say that children have an innate love of learning is as muddle-headed as to say that children have an innate love of baseball. Some do, some don't. Left to themselves, a large percentage of the small fry will go fishing, pick a fight, tease the girls, or watch Superman on the boob tube. Even as you and I.

Yet humanity must learn, whether it wants to or not. So long ago, before Plato, before Homer, our forebears taught with floggings and with rods, for sheer survival's sake, knowing that reliance upon mere eagerness to learn was not enough, knowing that even the stubbornly resistant must absorb the rudiments of civilization if that same civilization were not to reel back into the ape.

The key word here is "motivation." Some youngsters are motivated to learn through rewards, some through fear, some through love of notice, a very few through sheer love of learning for its own sake. And no one through all the ages has found a better motivating agent than a vibrant, dedicated teacher.

A machine does what it's told. But a child needs someone to tell *him* what to do. This has been the function of the teacher since time began, and it's one reason why a machine can't really teach.

There are a few children in every generation who have the drive and the will to teach themselves. For them, almost any system of instruction will do. For the millions of others who need a pat on the back or a friendly swat in the rear to spur them on to knowledge, I think we'd better keep our teachers warm and breathing.

In this connection, certainly, and quite recently, the

veil of the Progressive Education temple hath been rent asunder yet once again, and there are weepings, wailings, and gnashings of teeth in the ranks of the Philistines. For out of Pennsylvania have come dire tidings to the ears of the children of Baal. Babel, it appears, is having a rerun, this time minus the Tower.

It seems the modern "audiolingual" method of teaching foreign languages to children doesn't work one whit better than the corny, condemned old technique of "Teach-'em-the-rules-and-let-'em-practice." At least it doesn't in Pennsylvania, where for two years now a federally funded project has been experimenting with the two ways of teaching French and German.

Part of the kids were taught by the traditional approach, which involves grammar, vocabulary drills, and conjugations. The other pupils learned via the new audiolingual method, which emphasizes their speaking the language any old way no matter what, and discovering the correct rules on their own later on, if ever.

Result: The traditional classes "exceeded or equaled" the audiolingual classes all the way down the line.

Authority: The Pennsylvania Department of Public Instruction.

Conclusion (mine own): Another educational gimmick, this time with a Franco-German accent, has gone down the tube.

Sacrebleu! Or even *Donnerwetter!*

The fatal fallacy underlying the flop of the audiolingual approach to mastery of a foreign language is the obvious fact that many people who can speak, as it were, in tongues do so abysmally badly. Many Americans can be said to speak even English only if we describe their efforts with maximum compassion and minimum veracity. They need explicit instruction in the principles of the language they are so barbarously abusing, and this means grammar, sentence structure, punctuation, and all the rest of it.

A comma fault is not irrelevant to the learning of a language, no matter what we have been so confidently told. Neither is a dangling participle, nor an improper use of the subjunctive mood, for that matter. And spare me the old cry that such mastery of the essential building blocks of a language "stultifies" the subject and mummifies the students in musty wrappings of dead grammar. This is about as sensible as to claim that it's just too, too stuffy to expect a physician to memorize the bones of the human anatomy.

And please, gentle reader, don't write pityingly to tell me that the important thing in learning a language, after all, is to make oneself understood. That's important, all right. But for schoolchildren it's far more important to learn to do a complex thing correctly and to know precisely why it's correct.

FACET NO. 3—SEX AND SENSITIVITY IN EDUCATION

Back in my unregenerate undergraduate days, my college fraternity had a perfectly horrid custom called the "critique meeting." Once or twice a year, whenever the brothers of old Sigma Pi were feeling more than usually antsy and antipathetic toward one another, our officers would hold one of these little slam sessions as a means of letting off steam.

The object of the critique meeting, as I look back at it through the encroaching mists of time, was to permit each brother to know just exactly what all the other brothers thought of him, presumably in order that he might bethink himself of his fraternal image and forthwith mend his wicked ways. The procedure was simplicity itself. We all sat around a big table and took turns giving each other hell.

The house president, by virtue of his eminence, was Target No. 1, so when it was finally my time to be prexy, for obvious reasons, I quietly did away with the pernicious practice. Besides, the last two or three blast sessions had broken up in considerable disorder, with several of the brothers sporting black eyes and assorted contusions. This, I felt, was not exactly the spectacle of fraternal accord we were trying to project to the campus at large.

I wouldn't say the critique meeting was a total loss. It added considerably to our vocabulary, raised our resentment potential, and lowered our boiling point. In addition, I managed to make several devoted and lifelong enemies, some of whom I retain to this very day.

I had long been under the impression that the critique meeting was dead and that I had helped to kill it, when, lo! just last year I heard of the new phenomenon called "sensitivity training," which is apparently either the reincarnation or at least the lineal descendant of our old college custom. From all accounts, it involves the getting together of various persons with the common goal of understanding themselves through group dialogue and mutual soul-searching. Goal: a better knowledge of what makes each person tick.

For some reason that eludes me, sensitivity training seems especially popular among schoolteachers. I can't imagine why, inasmuch as any teacher can get a highly accurate and sometimes devastating picture of himself merely by asking any one of his pupils to really level with him.

"*Gnotho seauton*," old Socrates used to say. "Know thyself." And I guess this is the goal of sensitivity training. Nothing wrong with this. It's just that you don't get to know yourself better by asking what other people think of you. You ascend to this valuable knowledge, if you ever do, only through self-study combined with self-discipline, and this doesn't require anybody else around at all.

Others, you see, have even a more distorted picture of you than you have. After all, they don't look into the same bathroom mirror at your reflection every morning. More importantly, they can't possibly distinguish between the real you and that phony front you put on half as well as you can.

I guess I just don't care much for the idea of a bunch of folks sitting around in a circle and analyzing each other, whether they are using praise as a balm or criticism as an irritant. For what it's worth, I think it's a lot more important these clamorous days to forget ourselves and to think of others than to spend our valuable time massaging our own egos through group therapy and worrying about whether we're sufficiently sensitive.

In the long run, "Forget thyself!" may turn out to be a better motto for the final third of the twentieth century than "Know thyself."

Insofar as the fundamentals of sex are concerned, there's no question that adolescents need to know the facts of life. These, incidentally, can be learned by every kid above the low-grade-moron level in something less than half an hour.

There's also no question that children need to be informed about the facts of personal hygiene. Such personal and humdrum matters as toothbrushing, shampooing, and deodorizing obviously must be part of every child's learning experience—unless, of course, he's preparing to grow up as a hippie.

But saying that youngsters need to know such necessary things is a far cry from the *non sequitur* assumption that America's far-flung public school system should therefore set up special courses in them, which all pupils would be compelled to attend. For that matter, I suppose a case could be made for offering a class in beginning shaving for teenage boys whose fathers were too busy or too bashful to teach them how to load a safety razor, apply lather, and so on.

A school exists to teach things that experience has shown are essential weapons in the individual's intellectual, vocational, or aesthetic arsenal. Further, a school teaches things that the individual cannot reasonably be expected to pick up elsewhere. Now, if anyone can show me how universal and compulsory instruction in the mechanics of sexual intercourse can meet anybody's intellectual, vocational, or aesthetic needs, I will reconsider my objections.

It's fashionable to point to the mushrooming incidence of premarital pregnancies, venereal disease, and sex crimes as an overriding rationale for universal sex education. But what is needed to combat existing evil is not an encyclopedic knowledge of its techniques; it is the conviction that evil is indeed evil. Some of today's kids have never even heard the word.

Some things schools cannot do. Making young people want to do what they know is right is one of those things. We Californians for years have taught teen-agers in organized classes how to drive. Unfortunately, this has not noticeably diminished the percentage of adolescent dimwits who despite their knowledge of techniques drag-race on the county highway and end up on a slab with tags on their toes.

And teaching everybody in school about the horrendous effects of cigarette-smoking hasn't reduced the rocketing rate of lung cancer, either.

All this is not to say that there should be no sex education in the nation's schools. There should indeed, but only for those pupils whose parents confess their inability to instruct their own children by asking others to do it for them. Similarly, I suppose, we might set up seminars in "How to Tie Shoelaces and Bow Ties" for youthful unfortunates whose parents didn't quite get around to showing them.

I'm by nature a kindly, compassionate fellow. I hate to see kids grow up uninformed. It's just that I ache a little inside whenever I have to take teaching time away from Newton and Keats to spend on the kind of instruction any reasonably competent gorilla could give its offspring in a couple of hours.

FACET NO. 4—DISCIPLINE IN EDUCATION

Here's one crime to which educators can properly plead "Not Guilty." Discipline has been broken down, all right, but not by us. By the courts.

American education is in trouble these days, and the courts are not helping one bit. In fact, some of their weird and way-out decisions may prove the straw that finally breaks the overloaded educational camel's back.

Here, for the record, are a few examples of what I'm talking about:

(1) I'd have sworn it was impossible for the U.S. Supreme Court to top the record of jackassery it has so effortlessly set over the past ten years, but I would have been wrong.

Their 1969 fiat affirming the right of children to stage protest demonstrations in classrooms is really an unexampled tour de force. Justice Abe Fortas was chosen to voice this deathless decision, and it must be admitted that he was an appropriate choice to evaluate demonstrations. After all, it was the sensational demonstration of a certain stag movie a few months earlier that terminated Mr. Fortas' brief career as a candidate for the post of chief justice and which first turned the spotlight of public attention on his interesting financial connections in such a way as to hasten his departure from the High Court altogether.

Briefly, the Court held that from now on it will be perfectly all right for the kids to come to school wearing "protest" armbands, and to enjoy "freedom of speech and of expression" inside the schoolhouse.

The premise here is that school is a place that society subsidizes so that every kid can "turn on," "blow his mind," and "do his own thing." It isn't. And society doesn't. School is a place where teachers try to establish a climate conducive to organized, systematic, and disciplined learning. Anything that interferes with a scholarly atmosphere is inimical to good education and should be tossed out on its exhibitionistic ear. Hence school dress codes. And personal appearance standards. And disciplinary rules. And a lot of other things.

Anyone who has ever taught children knows perfectly well that a school where pupils employ their constitutional right of free speech ceases with remarkable speed to be a school at all and instead degenerates into something resembling a cross between a rock festival and a lunatic asylum. The same principle, incidentally, applies to the faculty. A teacher certainly has all the rights to free speech guaranteed every American citizen, but this doesn't mean that he can exercise them in his classroom. If he did, we would be regaled with the dubious spectacle of the geometry teacher holding forth on Black Power and the chemistry instructor lecturing on Etruscan tomb carvings. As citizens, they have the right to talk about these things any time they feel like it; as teachers, they do not.

So it is with students. A school is not a microcosm of the United States of America. It is a highly artificial entity engaged on the one hand in an activity essential to society, and on the other unwelcome to many of its participants. No one will question the fact that a considerable percentage of small boys don't like to go to school; this has been a truism ever since schools were invented. By the same token, no one will question the fact that small boys have to go to school if civilization is to endure.

Now, if these premises are valid, two conclusions follow:

(a) If pupils can be legally required to attend school against their will, they can also be legally required to shut up against their will, to leave their armbands and similar noneducational distractions at home against their will, and to listen to the teacher against their will in order that they may learn.

(b) Therefore the Supreme Court is guilty of jackassery, which is what I said in the first place.

What annoys me most about this decision is its detestable hypocrisy. The High Court would give short shrift, I'm sure, to any members of its Washington audiences who dared to interrupt its august proceedings with courtroom demonstrations or indeed with any audible exercise of free speech whatever. The Court apparently expects schoolteachers to put up with the same things they themselves wouldn't tolerate for five seconds.

(2) Then there's the American Civil Liberties Union, which has taken another giant stride in its current campaign to turn our high schools into hippie pads. An eastern court recently decided to permit two male students to let their hair grow down to their knees despite frantic efforts by the school authorities to enforce some kind of personal grooming standards on campus.

It was that stalwart friend of public education, the A.C.L.U., which furnished the time, the money, and the high-priced lawyers to push this crummy case through the courts.

At this juncture, a plaintive plea to my readers. Please friends, no indignant statements citing the sacred right of every citizen to go around looking like an unmade bed. No comments reminding me that the Twelve Apostles grew their hair long. And for the sake of my secretary's sanity don't send me any pictures of Zachary Taylor with his ringlets caressing his shoulders.

Such observations miss the point completely.

Neither the Apostles nor old Zach were trying to show off, to appear conspicuous, and to break down school discipline. They dressed and barbered in a manner appropriate to their day and age. They did not deliberately set out each day to introduce a hilariously disruptive element into classrooms where a hard-working teacher was doing his best to get a little attention from an all-too-easily distracted audience.

Distractions of any kind simultaneously and sharply reduce (a) the teacher's limited store of nervous energy and (b) his ability to get his students to listen to what he's saying. It's absolutely addle-headed for the school to supply those distractions gratis.

The question is often asked: "But does long hair really distract?"

You're darned right it distracts. A few of its immediate classroom byproducts are snide jokes about the hairy ones' sex, phony protests from the local Barbers' Union, assorted lewd whistles and wolf-calls, and a positive need to supply hairnets if the class happens to be swimming, shop, or lab science.

Anything that draws attention to itself because of its deliberate cultivation is as out of place in a serious classroom as Milton Berle in the College of Cardinals. A school is an institution where young people go in order to learn important things, and it's a little hard to do this except in a profoundly pejorative sense when the school has been transformed into a psychedelic cross between Haight-Ashbury and the Sunset Strip. Some parents baffle me. They complain bitterly about the various ways the school wastes their hard-earned tax dollars, but they let their kids attend school looking like Skid Row bums—and acting the same way. What else can they expect but a glorious waste of money when school people are prevented from maintaining an atmosphere of scholarly learning?

(3) Lastly in our brief discussion of the law's shortcomings, here's a question directed ostensibly to me but actually to all of us.

A civics student asked me the other day, in all innocence, "How do we tell what laws should be obeyed?" As the French say, it gave me furiously to think.

The do-it-yourself craze began back in the Fifties with carpentry and linoleum-laying, escalated to homebuilding around the turn of the decade, and in the Sick Sixties has spread at last to legislation. I sympathize with the fellow who enjoys baking his own bricks down in the cellar, or who installs a fancy birdbath in his own frontyard; but I'm beginning to wonder about this "every-man-his-own-Supreme-Court" syndrome we're seeing so much of these days.

Everytime our youngsters open a campus newspaper, they are regaled with illustrated anecdotes usually written in four-letter words about starry-eyed amateur Galahads who are demonstrating their invincible idealism by breaking into buildings, assaulting passers-by, and lying down in front of trains, all in the holy name of deeply held personal convictions.

I used to tell my classes in American government that a democratic society can exist only on the premise that the majority is usually right, and that the minority that disagrees has its only recourse in trying to change the majority's mind through logic, reasoning, and persuasion.

In individual instances, of course, this is a gross oversimplification. The majority has been wrong a lot of times in our history. I think we Americans were domestically wrong, for example, when we overwhelmingly elected Warren G. Harding as President, internationally wrong when we confused Charles de Gaulle with Joan of Arc, meteorologically wrong when we poisoned our air and polluted our water supply.

But still my thesis holds up. Over the long haul, a democratic society simply has to operate on the principle that the majority is right, if only because the alternative principle is that the majority is wrong. And this is precisely the premise that every Fascist elite in history has adopted in justifying its rise to power.

As I said at the beginning, education in this year 1970 is in bad trouble, only part of which is due to the inadequacies or inanities of educators. In the light of the legal profession's recent peculiar decisions in such key areas as patriotism, prayers, and protests—to say nothing of one humdinger back east where a judge actually outlawed a distinguished educator's life-work in the field of ability grouping—teachers can't be held solely responsible for the current mess in education.

But we can't blame everything on others. Much classroom misconduct, for instance, is due to our own bubble-headed educational psychology. Consider if you will the following effusion by Bruno Bettelheim:

"Many parents slap their children, or spank them. This is an exercise in force, comparing your size and his. When the Russians do it to the Hungarians, you don't like it, but in the family it's considered all right. If you like a world ruled by force, where whoever's stronger beats down the weaker, then by all means go on spanking your children."

Let's isolate and identify a few logical fallacies:

(1) *"Spanking children is an exercise in force."*

So is yanking them back on the sidewalk when they wander innocently out onto a busy street. Or jerking them away from a hot stove. Or even snatching the pretty, sweet-tasting ant paste out of their eager little mouths. So what?

(2) *"When the Russians do it to the Hungarians, you don't like it."*

No, sir, I do not. And when we American parents start machine-gunning our offspring, smashing them to a jelly with huge steel tanks, and executing the survivors in batches of ten, I won't like that either.

(3) *"In the family it's considered all right."*

In whose family?

(4) *"If you like a world ruled by force . . . then by all means go on spanking your children."*

Let's carry logic according to Dr. Bettelheim a little further.

How about: "If you like a world that isn't housebroken, then by all means go on putting diapers on your children."

Or: "If you like a world with bands on its teeth, then by all means go on taking your kids to the orthodontist."

Or even: "If you like a world that sleeps half the time, then by all means go on putting Junior to bed at eight every night."

What about the doctor's principal pitch? He's really asking us to believe that children and adults should be equated—that they are exactly alike—that a child is actually a miniature adult, with all of an adult's judgment and discretion, instead of that most different, maverick and completely individualistic of all organisms: a child.

Even if this whopping premise should happen to be true, and if children were genuine midgets with a certain growth potential instead of the precious, unique things they really are, it still wouldn't necessarily follow that spanking should be completely ruled out.

Some adults I'm acquainted with should be spanked resoundingly now and then, and we all know a few who ought to be beaten regularly, like gongs.

But the premise *isn't* true. Kids are raw material, not the finished product. Like all raw material, they have to be shaped and molded and refined. In human affairs, this process is called education. And a good, swift smack on the childish gluteus maximus is occasionally the most effective and the most sensible way to make a long-remembered point.

Certainly there are better long-run teaching techniques than the stupid, often brutal hickory-stick floggings of some of yesterday's homes and schools. But I greatly doubt that Dr. Bettelheim's comparison of mother's willow switch with Stalin's steel tanks, or Junior's naughtiness with the revolt of the Hungarian Freedom Fighters, is going to help very much in arriving at a more widespread use of those superior techniques.

After all, the gentlest people in all history, from the early Christians to the placid Polynesians, have spanked their children. And Armageddon, praise be, is not yet upon us.

FACET NO. 5—JARGON IN EDUCATION

I love words. Since the age of four, I've had a perpetual love affair with the English language. That's why I'm a little concerned about it today.

Language, you know, is supposed to evolve—much like a biological genus. Over the centuries, English has. But better than just developing from the simple to the complex, English words became happier, nobler, more hopeful.

Back in Shakespeare's day, for instance, "cute" meant merely "clever" or "sharp," not "attractive," as it does today. And it took the little word "nice" several centuries to do a complete flip-flop from its somewhat unfavorable meaning of "overparticular" and "fastidious" to its current upbeat definition of "pleasantly agreeable."

Note that these homely, familiar adjectives, in company with unnumbered others, tended over the years to get better and better, very much as did the great English-speaking world in which they played a humble but useful part.

Contrariwise, our language today seems to be rapidly

devolving. Fine old expressions are currently undergoing the same insidious sea change that is turning modern
painting into chimpanzee-squiggling, sculpture into
junk-collecting, and even humdrum, utilitarian bathing
into a sometime thing in certain avant-garde circles.

"Discipline," both as a word and as a practice, is increasingly a dead letter in our institutions of higher
learning.

"Punishment" is equally unfashionable, both in the
writings of our child psychologists and in the decisions
of our courts.

Even the lovely and anciently venerated word "virginity" stands today at the wall of in-group ridicule and
bows to the sticks and stones of sophisticated sarcasm.

And so it goes. Words dear to our forebears, phrases
that have walked familiarly down the centuries hand-
in-hand with whole generations of Americans, now
seem headed for the scrap-heap or, worse yet, are dwin-
dling and degenerating in their meaning for all the
world like handsome fairy-tale princes transformed into
loathsome toads.

If there is a common thread running through the bizarre, violent, and sometimes frightening tapestry the
twentieth century has so far flung upon the wall of history, it has to be the use of the weasel word. Even the
Victorian Age, long celebrated as the heyday of hypocrisy, can't touch us in the dubious art of using fuzzy
phrases to disguise our real meaning.

We simply can't bring ourselves to call things by
their right names, it seems, and I'm not merely referring
to our currently regrettable habit of labeling a public
toilet a "powder room," either.

Back in the Gay Nineties, when Abdul the Damned
was slaughtering Armenians right and left in the name
of the Ottoman Empire, the butchery was called by its

correct title: "massacre." And when the Cossacks of Czar Nicholas used the Jews for saber practice, the short and ugly word was "pogrom." But when Nicholas' lovable successor Nikita Khrushchev killed off millions of small Russian farmers in our own time, he referred to it blandly as "liquidation of the kulak problem," and we let him get away with it.

It's not just political palaver that is all semantically gussied up. It's just about everything.

Not so long ago, undertakers embalmed corpses. Today, morticians preserve the departed from the ravages of time.

Doctors once came right out into the hospital corridor and told the grieving and/or anticipatory family that a rich relative was dying. Now no medico worthy of his shingle would speak so crudely about poor Uncle John. No, he has become of late something much more gratifying: a "terminal case."

The hippies, too, have gotten in on the act. They don't take dope. Perish the thought. They "turn on." And so it goes. If we don't like to face an unpleasant fact, we hang a pretty mask on it.

The mutations of the spoken language usually mirror pretty faithfully the state of mind of the people who speak it. When good words go bad, the cause should commonly be sought in the speakers, not in the spoken.

Surely the nation's schools should do what is necessary to reclaim the nation's language. It is, after all, our most precious cultural inheritance.

Perhaps in so doing, our schools can help to return joy and serenity—yes, and simple decency—to an increasingly vexed and fretted generation.

Education, however, which should be helping in this matter, simply isn't.

Did you ever hear of something called "pedagese"? It's

the jargon of the educational Establishment. Here's an example:

"With the proliferation of allegations promulgating an either/or attitude toward the use of textbooks in elementary school social studies, it is well to ponder both the pros and cons of propensities to vindicate the one contention while repudiating the other. To asseverate a denial of value for either orientation is not the point. To relate the utility and soundness in the use of multifarious resources is the intent."

Translation by your kindly interpreter: "A good teacher does not depend solely upon a textbook."

The "big words" of the past two years have been "relevant" and "relevancy." Their popularity apparently stemmed from education's current obsession with immediacy, a fixation that if allowed to burgeon unchallenged will eventually eliminate from the curriculum everything that happened more than five years ago.

Here are a few more flawed gems from education's semantic diamond mine, with my own somewhat jaundiced definitions appended:

"Paraprofessional"—a mom who helps teacher collect the lunch money.

"Resource center"—a library with a film projector.

"Media coordinator"—anybody who can work a tape recorder.

My own research recently turned up the perfectly ghastly word "descriptor," and I refuse to define it because I just ate lunch.

A few years back, the jargon was different, but just as bad: "togetherness"; "routinizing" a practice; "overviewing" its results; "auditing" a recitation instead of listening to it.

Why do we teachers indulge in such unspeakable terminological orgies? Are we doomed by the very nature of our ancient calling to go through life babbling about "learner-center merged curricula" and "empirically validated learning packages"?

I think not.

We talk this way largely because we have a feeling of occupational inadequacy. We build ourselves up at the expense of the unwashed non-in-group by inventing our own brand of Pig Latin, which nobody can understand except us.

Unconsciously, we rationalize this way: "We don't get paid much. In some places, we lack prestige. Doctors and lawyers, on the other hand, are paid plenty, and they have prestige coming out of their ears. Notably, too, these prestigious practitioners have their own professional jargon. *Ergo,* if we teachers can develop a sufficiently exotic terminology, we, too, will be well paid and well thought of."

Sorry, fellow pedagogues. It won't work. Other professions may hide behind the incense fumes and the temple chants of gobbledygook because they do not have the solemn charge laid upon them by the very nature of their calling to make themselves clear at any cost.

We do.

Indeed, if a teacher doesn't make himself understood above and beyond everything else he tries to do, he's in the wrong profession, as out of place as Barry Goldwater in a hippie pad. So, as the campus activists so earnestly and so ungrammatically say, let's "tell it like it is." And this means telling it as simple and as clearly and as understandably as we possibly can.

In education, however, we go the other way. Even when something isn't particularly disagreeable, we educators have an apparently irresistible itch to dream up new and outlandish terminology with which to describe it.

"Meaningful relationship," for example. In any school-guidance get-together nowadays, this ubiquitous little phrase positively sparkles. Fagin had a meaningful relationship with Oliver Twist, as I recall, but I wouldn't recommend it to guidance counselors.

"Relationship," in one form or another, in fact, is quite the rage in educational dialogue. Indeed the computer age has recently spawned the bastard bromide "interdigitated relationship."

We teachers seem to have remarkably little respect for the civil rights of nouns, either. We're always trying to make verbs out of them. Hence the proliferation of such rococo grammatical abominations as "quantify" and "conceptionalize."

William Clark, in a recent article, reported a new and horrid linguistic love-child apparently procreated in a reading supervisors' conference: "directionality." When I contemplate the tortuous racking and stretching that the poor little word "direction" had to undergo in order to attain this new and ghastly incarnation, my head aches in sympathy, and like Scarlett O'Hara, I prefer to think about it tomorrow.

Some years ago, I stirred up a modest storm by quoting a definition written by a West Coast educator:

"*READING:* An audiovisual verbal processing skill of symbolic reasoning, sustained by the interfacilities of an intricate hierarchy of substrata factors."

Now, at the time I thought this was a classic example of pedagese, and the passage of the years has only served to confirm my reverent admiration. The definition has everything: big words, fuzzy words, mysterious words, pseudoscientific words. Moreover, I can't figure out what the devil it means, nobody I've shown it to can figure it out, and I strongly suspect the author couldn't figure it out either. In short, it was perfect pedagese, and I paid tribute to it as well as I was able, in standard English, that is.

But to hear some of my colleagues react to my gentle raillery, you would have thought I had stabbed their mothers. I was accused of (a) unprofessionalism, (b) character assassination, (c) gross ignorance, and (d) green-eyed jealousy of anyone gifted enough to dream up this kind of gobbledygook. I had to confess that my critics were probably right, and I'm going to compound my abasement right now by admitting I feel the same way about the 1970 crop of semantic corn, most of which has grown up around the thorny topic of ghetto education.

For instance, I'm informed that words like "poverty," "ignorance," "segregation," and just plain old "bad luck" can no longer be used to describe the problem of the slum-dweller. The "in" word now is "disadvantageness," and it's such a gem of what even our Victorian ancestors called a bastard etymology that I suspect its parents not only didn't know each other at all but were in fact ill-met by moonlight while wearing masks.

Along the same line, there is the currently popular phrase "developmental deprivation," which is less effective precisely to the extent that it's a little more understandable, and which must therefore yield to the triple-headed monster of a term, "cumulative-deficit phenomenon."

The ability to communicate ideas has always been the acid test of the good teacher. He may be a brilliant scholar, a formidable researcher, and a greater lover of children than Santa Claus, but a teacher who can't communicate is no more a real teacher than I am St. Francis of Assisi.

I was put neatly in my place the other day when I came across the word "crescive" in an educational journal describing a certain instructional problem. Stirred to my depths, I took pen in hand and wrote the author: "Doesn't 'crescive' mean the same as 'increasing'? And if so, why not say so?"

I should have known better.

In due time, the answer came back, weighted with pity for my crassness.

"Utilized in the context of the paper," it said icily, " 'crescive' is used synonymously with 'accreted.' "

Now, why hadn't I thought of that?

People don't listen to us teachers in order to become even more confused than they already are. They rely on educators to clear up confusion, not to foul up the atmosphere with more high-sounding smog, like so many educational smudge pots.

But what about you, oh plain-thinking, straight-speaking, no-nonsense lay public? Are you giving aid and comfort to the tide of jargon presently overspreading the land?

Didn't you grin weakly and go along with the Pentagon when it labored like a mountain to produce the mouse "escalation" as a euphemism for killing more Communists? And who is it right now who is busily and importantly savoring the sound of that badly overworked word "thrust" as a substitute for everything from "trend" to "point"?

You, that's who. And I think you should cut it out, if only for the sake of future "intergenerational communication," to use the corrosive cant of the moment.

After all, we educators have our own shabby reason for being unintelligible. Let Mom and Pop really understand what we're saying, and all is lost, we tell ourselves.

But what's your excuse?

CROSSROAD #4

The Need for Standards

In these days when so many swingers in clerical collars are telling us that God is dead, it might be a good idea to consider for a few moments the somewhat different point of view held by the ancient Greeks. Their gods were not only very much alive; they were extremely reproductive. As a result, if there wasn't one god for every Greek, there was at least one god for every activity the Greeks had a word for. Mt. Olympus had its faults, but a high unemployment rate among its occupants certainly wasn't one of them. They kept busy!

Maybe we should resurrect for our own present-day purposes the old Olympian deities. We should be able to keep them even busier than the Greeks did.

Aphrodite, Goddess of Love, for instance, would be the busiest of all. Richard Burton and Liz Taylor would take up most of her time all by themselves. But she could always call on Justice Douglas for professional advice and even for part-time help.

Mars, as usual, would be busy supervising the combat zones: Vietnam, Cleveland, Chicago, Watts . . .

There'd be a full-time job for Mercury, god of Business-as-Usual. Vulcan, god of heavy industry, would feel right at home in Pittsburgh and Detroit; in fact, they've already put up a statue to him in Birmingham, where I saw it not too long ago. And if Pluto had any recruiting problems, I could give him a long list of names I've personally been compiling for the past eight years.

I'm a little puzzled about us educators, though. The old Greeks didn't seem to have a god for us. The doctors would have Aesculapius, and the lawyers Hermes. But I'm afraid we'd have to create a special god for education.

When that time comes, and when the new deity sits enthroned upon an Olympus of slate, chalk, and old N.E.A. bulletins, I have a professional decalogue, modern education's Ten Commandments, which I plan to submit for his consideration:

(1) THOU SHALT NOT PREACH ADJUSTMENT TO ENVIRONMENT

We're in a proliferating crisis these days. Around us on every hand we see wars and hear rumors of wars, racial hatreds, strikes against the public interest, crime run wild, pornography puffed into big business, insane mass murders, and public officials so crooked they make Boss Tweed look like Billy Graham.

In the face of a crying need to make basic and far-reaching changes in almost every aspect of our environment, we Americans until quite recently were happy and content with an educational philosophy that openly bragged that its main objective was to adjust kids happily and easily and comfortably to what was going on around them.

Education doesn't exist to adjust anybody to anything. Its purpose is to supply the individual with the intellectual tools and weapons he needs in order to adjust his environment to himself. I can't think of anything worse, or of a greater crime we could have committed against our children, than to have adjusted them to the Sick Sixties. To adjust to what we read in the newspapers, see on television, and hear on every side these days would be to come to terms with madness.

(2) THOU SHALT HONOR SUBJECT MATTER

Here's what a small businessman told me the other day:

"I hire a lot of kids fresh out of high school, and I fire a lot of 'em too. Not because of race or color or what side of the tracks they come from. I couldn't care less.

"Want to know what they need to hold a job with me, and what darned few of 'em have?

(1) "Ability to read simple instructions without moving their lips and letting their eyeballs glaze over whenever a word of more than two syllables comes along.

(2) "Ability to make ordinary change from a cash register, which in turn requires certain minimum essentials in adding and subtracting.

(3) "Ability to conduct an ordinary conversation with relatively few gross grammatical errors and without having to rely constantly on such ineffable verbal crutches as 'Cool it man!' and 'Blast off, weirdo!' "

That's what the man said. I believe him, too. Seems simple, you say? Surely any kid above the imbecile level can learn these three simple things.

I've got news for you. A lot of them don't—including practically every one of the teen-agers currently being caught up in these moronic, useless street riots.

They could, though—if your local school insisted upon these things as minimum essentials. It's up to you to see that the school district you're supporting with your tax dollars has gotten the word. If it hasn't, see that your school people get with it. Like maybe next election day.

(3) THOU SHALT TEACH THINGS AS THEY ACTUALLY ARE

George Orwell, that mordant chronicler of the mysterious future, foresaw a day when history would be written up as it should have happened, not as it actually did.

"After all, what is really important is what people *think* took place," one of his characters soliloquized.

So just see to it that the relatively few writers of history in any generation put down only those past events that tend to justify the current "in" point of view—and presto! we have a built-in apologia for anything we are doing or may wish to do—from abolishing the gold standard to drafting doctors for Medicare. Our antics are automatically justified by antiquity.

Mr. Orwell put the tentative date for such organized revising of the past at around 1984, but if you ask me, things are moving much more rapidly than he anticipated.

For instance:

I sit on the commission that screens textbooks for the biggest state in the union. Not too long ago, an American history textbook was offered for adoption that described General Eisenhower as skillfully leading United Nations forces into North Africa in 1943. Inasmuch as the United Nations was not permanently chartered until the year 1945, in San Francisco, this blithe juggling with chronology required the reader either to develop convenient amnesia or hop aboard the old time machine.

More recently, writers of schoolbooks have tended to take an increasingly dim view of the 1920–1930 decade. Far from ascribing any roaring qualities to the Twenties, our contemporary breed of authors tends to describe them as a sort of historical Slough of Despond, during which all progress came to a standstill and the nation wallowed in sterile reaction. Stock-market gambling and organized racketeering are stressed; the doubling and redoubling of our gross national product is glossed over. So are Lindbergh and radio and talking pictures and the Washington Disarmament Conference and a thousand other evidences of yeasty, vital achievement.

Then came the Hungry Thirties, and of this era I have plenty of personal recollections. But when I read some of the latest textbooks submitted for my consideration, I have to pinch myself at regular intervals to be sure I'm not reading about some other century.

F.D.R., it seems, cured the Great Depression all by himself. I could have sworn that when I got out of college in 1938, Old Man Depression was still very much with us. As I recall, there were just about as many unemployed then as there had been when Mr. Roosevelt took over from Mr. Hoover 'way back in 1933. I know. I was one of them.

In fact, it took World War II with its endless demands upon our factories and our granaries to dust the cobwebs off the wheels of industry and set them humming once again. One tragedy was ended by another, greater one. But the politicians had little to do with it, though you'd never guess it by reading some of the latest manuscripts that come across my desk. I guess I'm getting tired of today's historians second-guessing the past instead of just telling us what happened.

California recently adopted another history textbook that managed to kick up quite a storm. It was upbeat in the attention it properly paid to the role of America's racial minorities. Unfortunately, it was downbeat in a lot of other ways.

I opposed the book when it first came out, not because it was pro-Communist as some folks wrongly alleged, but because it was negative when it should have been positive. It was the first really pessimistic book on American history I had ever seen, and I couldn't help but wonder why. A look at the record doesn't exactly call for the crying towel.

We did enslave Negroes, which everybody knows, and quite a few whites as well, which almost nobody knows. We also set them free. Both colors.

We had a mild case of colonialism around the turn of the century, but we got over it in a bigger hurry than did any other major power. Russia and China, for example, haven't got over theirs yet.

We managed to fight quite a few wars over the years, but most of them were fought either to set or to keep men free.

We gave some of our immigrants a bad time for a while, but we also gave them opportunities unheard of in the lands of their birth.

Not just history books, though, are suffering from the gloom-and-doom syndrome these days. Newspaper headlines are not only apoplectic; they're apocalyptic. Television shows us so many hate-filled, contorted close-ups that I have learned more about Rap Brown's bridgework than I care to know. And our magazines run articles with such jolly titles as "The Death of Our Cities," "America the Product of Racism," and even, "Drug addiction: Protest Against the Intolerable."

I suppose this kind of stuff, by appealing to the masochistic minority, helps sell magazines. But as Gigi said: "There must be something more to life than this."

There is.

I've had occasion myself from time to time to refer to the Sick Sixties and to join in the chorus of sobs, but there's another side, and a bright one. Let's take a quick look at it:

(1) The ghettos are still with us. But we have so many more Negro millionaires, legislators, government officials and television stars than we did just fifteen years ago that it's almost unbelievable.

(2) People-to-people violence is increasing. But so is humane treatment of animals. The recent mass rescue of flood-periled African wildlife has no parallel in history.

(3) Our youngsters supposedly repudiate the past. Yet, what other generation would have salvaged Abu Simbel? Or worked like dogs to preserve the priceless treasures of antiquity endangered by the disaster in Florence?

(4) Riots increase in the cities. But the lynch mob with its ghastly appurtenances of the lash, the gelding knife, and gasoline can has apparently gone down into the same limbo with the Inquisition and the black-hooded hangers, drawers and quarterers who helped make England merrie under bluff King Hal.

(5) The hippies multiply odorously among us, causing considerable incidental soul-searching as to the ultimate destination of the next generation. But the flower children are outnumbered ten to one by the members of

such comparatively scrubbed and shorn youth groups as Moral Rearmament and Young Americans for Freedom.

And so it goes. For every minus sign, there's a corresponding plus. 'Twas ever thus.

So we declared war on Spain in 1898. Don't tell us how bloodily imperialistic we were. Let us figure it out.

So we sent Marines to Haiti forty years ago to keep the voodooistic islanders from butchering one another, just as we may have to do again in the Seventies to rid that unhappy land of the unspeakable Duvalier and his bully boys. You don't have to tut-tut loftily about gunboat diplomacy. The kids will interpret straight history—if you'll just give it to them straight.

The Tories obstructed Washington, but the Patriots won the Revolution. The Copperheads plotted against Lincoln, but the Union men rallied around the old flag. The slackers sang, "I didn't raise my boy to be a soldier," but Wilson beat the Kaiser.

As Sergeant Friday was wont to say: "All I want are the facts, Ma'am."

And, confound it! When I read a history of the United States, I want to know exactly what went on, not what the author in his infinite wisdom thinks should have been going on.

If the present trend continues, our grandchildren are liable to be reading in school about how Eldridge Cleaver emancipated the slaves.

America has always had her dark side. She still does. But the radiance and the hope and the promise that Miss Liberty sheds across the oceans and over the continents have augmented, not diminished, with the ebb and flow of time.

(4) THOU SHALT NOT PROPAGANDIZE

One of our biggest problems in education today is teachers with a message. Seemingly the more half-baked, the more poorly grounded in his field, and the more steamingly intolerant an instructor is, the more apt he is to be a promoter instead of a teacher.

Any attempt to stop a physics prof from reading aloud to his class the Meditations of Mao will evoke automatically the tired old knee-jerk reflex yell of "Academic freedom!" Any effort to prevent school facilities from being used to promote a partisan political candidacy will bring forth myriads of ACLU attorneys.

Yet the schools are built and maintained to pursue the truth, not to indoctrinate the immature. The thing that has "turned off" so many lay citizens at the expense of education is the widespread conviction that only one point of view is being taught their children, whether in regard to civil rights, the Vietnam War, or the setting of policy for higher education.

Education does not exist to push one point of view, and especially not mine. It exists to pursue the truth. This is why so many of our colleges and universities are out of line these days. Some years ago, I addressed a student meeting in San Diego. A charming lady faculty member walked by and my student escort nudged me.

"I certainly admire her," he murmured.

"And I can see why," I responded gallantly.

"No, no," he protested. "It's because she's the only conservative economics professor on the whole campus."

Now, I don't give a tinker's damn whether you're conservative or liberal. This sort of thing is just plain no good. How in the devil is education going to pursue the

truth if its practitioners are all sold beforehand on one
point of view—theirs?

I'd be saying the same thing, incidentally, if the lady
prof had been the only *liberal* economics instructor in
the college. In that case, I'd have spoken up for more liberals.

(5) THOU SHALT CONCERN THYSELF WITH
INDIVIDUALS

I can remember when the education of the individual
used to be the be-all and the end-all of my profession. Not
anymore. Now we hear interminably and unceasingly
about "group psychology" and "peer-group adjustment"
and "group recreation" and more recently "group therapy"
until I'm beginning to wonder what happened to the poor
unfortunate individual.

I'll be hanged if I want to be considered just a member of some group, especially by school people. There's
a very real danger that as our already fantastic population total heads for greater and greater peaks, the American as an individual is going to be a dead duck.

A beehive, you know, is a comfortable place. It's warm,
safe, and stocked with delicious food. Its inhabitants are
disciplined, cooperative, and seemingly happy. They labor unceasingly in highly specialized but relatively
pleasant jobs for the greater good of the hive. In return,
they are cared for by the insect equivalent of the Welfare State from the cradle to the grave, or maybe it
would be more accurate to say from egg to bird's craw,
under the circumstances. They are perfectly adjusted to
their environment. They are born, they eat, they repro-
duce, they die. It's pretty hard for the observer to find any

difference at all in the way most bees look and act.

Such is the life of the social insect, and such it has been, unvarying and unchanging, for about fifty million years. There's just one slight disadvantage connected with this seemingly foolproof system: the disappearance of the individual. Any baby bee that, touched perhaps by some random cosmic ray, showed the slightest sign of becoming an insect Moses, Newton, or Leonardo da Vinci would ring alarm bells all over the hive and alert the guardians of the elaborate structure to perform the insect equivalent of mercy killing upon the unfortunate mutation. In justice to our ancient friends the bees, it should also be pointed out that they would take equally drastic preventive action against any larval Hitler, Stalin, or Genghis Khan.

They have thus achieved the delicate balance sought for by all advanced cultures. It's an efficient, highly developed society, operating for the good of all. It's completely materialistic, absolutely equalitarian, and 100 percent deadly to the individual.

I submit that the bees, who are our seniors on this planet by a good many millions of years, have arrived at this evidently final stage of their development through the pressure of strong evolutionary forces acting upon billions of individuals. It's my further contention that similar forces acting upon the rapidly multiplying hordes of our own species will tend to produce similar results. For good measure, I'll throw in my own theory that too many of us educators unfortunately are currently helping those evolutionary forces along to the very best of our ability.

The individual should be, and until a few years ago always had been, the be-all and the end-all of my profession. This country was founded by individualists. The schools stressed the virtues of individualism, and the churches concerned themselves with the saving of individual souls.

Not anymore. Progressive Education has helped change all this.

The great dogma of Group Adaptation forms the cornerstone of twentieth-century educational theory. As propounded by the disciples of John Dewey—who, paradoxically enough, professed to abhor all dogma—the only eternal verity is that of constant change and flux.

All values are relative. All truths are mutable. All standards are variable. What's good today may be evil tomorrow, and vice-versa. So the only thing worth teaching to young people is the ability to adjust to their environment—to be easily, comfortably, happily accepted by their peer group. This is what the life-adjustment boys really believe. This is what they teach the children. And this is precisely what's wrong with the country.

Let's see how the steady increase in the millions of our population, combined with Progressive Education's glorification of the *group* at the expense of the *individual,* have affected two important segments of the American people.

First, let's look at our college students. The whole world is familiar with the recent demonstrations and current unrest at the University of California. As a member of the university's Board of Regents, it's been one of my jobs to try to bring order out of chaos in this complicated and thankless situation. Things now are at least temporarily under control, but in working with young people it's not enough merely to uphold authority and to put down threats to law and order, necessary though this is. There is something more on the Berkeley campus than just the antics of the bearded exhibitionists and the cynical opportunism of the hard-core activists who sparked the illegal activities there. There is in addition a very real if somewhat incoherent grievance on the part of a great number of sincere and sober students with which all of us should concern ourselves.

This grievance is loss of identity—erosion of self-respect—increasing inability to identify as an individual with an institution numbering more than 27,000 souls. This student feeling may be described as a kind of creeping facelessness—a loss of both individuality and individualism in a university that of necessity concerns itself more and more with great problems of research and with projects vital to the national interest whereas it was once engaged almost exclusively in instructing young people and providing them with the indispensable intellectual tools with which truth is pursued.

One college undergraduate wrote me during the height of the disturbances as follows: "I'm photographed, inoculated, taped, carded, and filed. I have a parking pass and a library pass and a lab pass. I sit in a lecture class with six hundred others, and I'm Number 327. The professor's lecture is piped in electronically; I never see him. The multiple-choice tests I take are corrected and graded automatically. I engage in group activities, group health services, and group recreation. But I came to college to find *myself*—to learn how to become a *person*. Instead, I've become a *number*."

This troubles you, no doubt "This is no good," you are saying to yourselves. And you're right. But don't bother looking around to find the "somebody" responsible. The "somebody" is you.

Why *should* you be surprised at such a letter? What else could you expect? Didn't you permit and even condone over the years an educational way of thinking in our public schools that downgraded competition, upgraded togetherness, stressed the supremacy of the group over the individual, and generally preached the overriding importance of life adjustment as compared with individual mastery of essential fundamentals?

No wonder our colleges are turning into huge factories. When people are conditioned from early childhood to believe that adjustment to one's environment is the supreme goal of life—when they are taught day after day that acceptance by the group is more important than the development of the individual's own abilities—when they are grouped by social age down in the grades and always passed through the school with their peers regardless of whether or not they are able to meet any standards of performance—when all these things have been going on for thirty years and more with your active or passive consent—how else can you expect our colleges and universities to deal with the products of such a system of education?

They have been conditioned to conform. They have been trained to cooperate. They have been educated to adjust. In another generation, they should be ready for the hive—and they will be, unless we change our ways. The kids feel this unconsciously. It's time we realized it consciously. I'm not at all surprised that a lot of our students are protesting. The sad thing about it isn't the fact of the protest, but the fact that it's been taken over and exploited by certain cold-eyed outfits interested in nothing but stirring up trouble and creating chaos.

Here, then, is the way the trend toward the hive is affecting one element of our population. Let's turn to another element—our racial minorities.

I happen to be a member of one of the most discriminated-against groups ever to emigrate to this continent. For centuries the Irish had been dispossessed and jailed and starved and slaughtered in their own land by an alien usurper. A hundred years ago, after a frightful famine had killed off a large percentage of the total population of their little island, the survivors disembarked upon bare survival, and for two generations that was all they found.

Almost immediately, the signs went up: "No Irish allowed"; "No Irish need apply"; "We do not rent to Irish." Business careers were closed to them. The learned professions were barred to them. Their accent was mocked. Their customs were burlesqued in cartoons and on the stage. The men were called "Micks" and "Paddies" and were allowed only to lay bricks and carry hods, or a little later to leave their bones under almost every crosstie of the great Union Pacific Railroad as it fought its long way westward across the continent. Their women were derisively nicknamed "Biddies" and were grudgingly permitted to serve as laundresses, cooks, and housemaids in the homes of the rich. No band of immigrants ever had it tougher.

Yet within five decades, the Irish had broken out of the ghettos and had merged with the general American landscape. Irish names appeared on the roster of every profession and calling. Some of them became wealthy; more of them remained poor; but in neither case was it the result of their Irishness. Within another fifty years, one of them had become President.

How was it done? Not by any special talent or intelligence that the Irish happened to possess. It was just that they managed to get America finally to treat them as *individuals* instead of as members of a group. They persuaded their own children to think of themselves and their fellow Americans to think of them, too, as men and women—tall, short, fat, thin, homely, handsome, stupid, smart—just like the rest of us.

Now mark this well. Had the Irish been conditioned as children to think of themselves primarily as members of a national or religious *group,* or even as members of a broader, blander "peer group," they would have stayed in that group indefinitely. Had they been sold a bill of goods about "adjustment to environment" being the main goal both of education and of life itself, they would have adjusted to those dirty, cheerless ghettos and to those backbreaking, menial jobs, and they would still be working at them today. Had they been told that mastery of subject matter was less important than "democratic sharing," they would never have learned enough to convince their fellow Americans of their ability to get things done. Had they been taught that competition was evil, they would have stayed as low man on the national totem pole, kept there by those who *could* compete better than they could.

But during the historical period when the Irish were breaking out of the permanent-minority-group category, our school system was stressing basic education, the dignity of the individual, and the importance of organized, disciplined, and systematic mastery of subject matter by each pupil. During this same period of time, the Negroes and the Mexican-Americans—presently our greatest ethnic minorities—were in most states and in most cases not getting any education at all. In more recent years, and under universal compulsory education, they began for the first time to be enrolled in schools in large numbers. But it was during those same recent years that the "life adjustment," "Progressive Education" cult took over those same schools, lock, stock, and barrel, and started preaching the gospel of groupism at any cost.

Groupism is not what our racial minorities need. They've had too much of that already. When you react to stimuli only as a member of a group—when you find your self-respect and self-fulfillment only as a member of a group—when you vote only as a member of a

group—then you are just asking to be treated according
to the lowest common denominator of that same group,
whatever it is. You abdicate your right to be treated
as an individual in favor of the right to be treated as
just one more cog in the machine, one more faceless
figure in the crowd, one more bee in the hive.

But you're not a bee, and nobody has the right to regard
you or any other American as simply another member of
a certain swarm. A century ago, my people all had the
same accent, and wore the same costume, and had the
same religion. There was a great temptation, as a result
of this, for other Americans to regard them as "all alike"
and to label them accordingly and to deal with them
in the mass instead of as separate, living, breathing human beings, each with a different personality and a different immortal soul.

It's greatly to the credit of this country that we have
successfully overcome the temptation to fragment our
country into Irish-Americans or German-Americans or
any other kind of "special" Americans. Such terminology
did exist for a time, but happily the climate, the tradition, the genius of our people have been uncongenial in
the long run to most attempts to lure us onto the fatal
path of hyphenated Americanism. The last two relics
of this ancient error—the terms "Negro-American" and
"Mexican-American"—must now be subjected to the
same influences that wiped out the terms "Irish-American" and "German-American."

If I were a member of a current ethnic minority in
this year 1970, I would do these things:

(1) As a parent, I would insist upon an educational
philosophy in my local schools that emphasized the importance of the individual rather than the desirability

of in-groupness—which taught each child to use the wonderful, glittering, sharp-edged sword of subject matter to gain success—which took my youngster where it found him and taught him to read so well and to spell so well and to speak and write English so well that he would be superior to the graduates of other schools as an *individual,* not as a member of a group.

(2) As a breadwinner, I would continually upgrade my own capabilities and potentialities in the occupation of my choice by taking advantage of adult-education night-school classes, and college extension courses wherever and whenever I could find them. If I couldn't read very well, I'd take remedial reading. If I spoke bad English, I'd study good English. If I needed some special skill to enable me to get a better job and to earn more money, you can bet I'd find a school that offered it, and I'd sign up for it.

(3) As a voter, I would join a political party which treated me as an individual, not as a member of a voting bloc. I would support better laws for all, and I would resent efforts to use me as a racial-minority member in order to perpetuate any person or party in power. I would resist with my ballot any attempt to discriminate against me because of my race, whether by the government or by industry.

Even today, about all we hear in politics is how to appeal to the "Negro bloc" or the "Mexican bloc."

When we stop to think about it—which most of us seldom do—all of us know that colors are merely light reflected variously. In itself, a color has no more morality or immorality than a mirror. Yet ever since mankind crawled out of caves and probably long before, colors have been throwing their weight around, flaunting themselves in our collective unconscious and causing more fuss, feuds, duels, and even wars than any self-respecting light waves should.

What triggered this little outpouring of philosophy-cum-optics was a recent report that many American Negroes are disturbed about the generally pejorative connotation attached to the word "black." Our culture looks down on anything black, they say, citing certain instances to prove their point and looking hopefully to the schools for help in what Madison Avenue calls the old "image."

"Black magic," for example, is always bad magic, conjuring up old Lucifer himself by means of somewhat questionable incantations accompanied by bubbling brews of frequently emetic ingredients.

"Black as sin" is a simile that Negroes understandably resent, along with such depressing catch-phrases as "black-despair" and "black-hearted."

"Where is a good word ever said for blackness?" mourns one of the complainants. "Even the world's worst epidemic ended up with the label 'Black Death.'"

He's right. I can understand and sympathize. But when you really go into this color business in any depth, you find out in a hurry that every color is insulting, not just black.

The fellow who has a "yellow streak" doesn't brag about it, any more than does his more bibulous colleague who wakes up bleary-eyed with the well-known "dark brown taste" to face the cold gray light of the morning after.

"Green with envy" is not a complexion recommended in the better cosmetic ads, either. The "parlor pink" label, though marginally redeemed in recent years, is not really one to brag about. Then there is "red," which doesn't owe its current notoriety to the unpopularity of Communism. Long before Lenin and Stalin were depopulating the Russian steppes, phrases like "red ruin" and "red-eye" were being bandied unfavorably about.

Even the fair and virginal adjective "white" has taken its lumps. Who wants to show the white feather, especially in front of his girfriend? Or be called white-livered, for that matter? And as for the obloquy attached to the stygian blackness of bubonic plague during the Middle Ages, what about the dreaded "White Plague" of tuberculosis, which carried off more millions over the centuries than all the "Black Death" in history?

It may be thought by some that only the commoner colors have been subject to semantic tampering of this sort. Disabuse yourself of the notion. The more exotic, Oscar Wildeish shades are not exempt by any means, with negative connotations positively running rampant through their prismatic gradations. As one instance of this, I regret that my own deathless prose has on occasion been referred to as purple, although I can't for the life of me understand why.

And so it goes. Maybe the lower animals have it good after all. They're reputedly colorblind, you know. The effect of the red flag upon the burly bull is purely one of motion, we are told, with the same effect being achieved with a mauve banner. Or even puce. This may explain why most animals are relatively peaceful and tranquil as compared to us humans. No colors around to stir them up and set them at loggerheads with one another.

I really think that my Negro friends should settle for whatever problems may adhere to the color black. After all, it has a lot of redeeming features. None of our oil millionnaires are noticeably apologizing for their "black gold," and a lot of people agree with the songwriter that black is mighty attractive when it's the color of a true love's hair.

To clinch my case triumphantly on the positive side of black, ask yourself this question: "What governor have you ever heard of who wanted his annual budget to wind up in the white?"

Closely allied to the black-white syndrome is the current and mindless campaign against ability grouping. In both cases, the individual is lost sight of in favor of the group.

Unless we school people are careful, one of the innocent casualties of the present Negro fight for better education is liable to be the so-called track system of instruction.

For the uninitiated, the "track system" is simply a method of grouping children according to their ability and present achievement. The theory is that a gifted child is going to be learning more and working harder if he's put with other above-average youngsters than if you let him loaf along in a regular classroom situation where he's so much smarter than anyone else that he ends up bored stiff. Similarly, putting the slow child with others with similar problems enables the teacher to concentrate on his particular needs and weaknesses without neglecting the rest of the class.

The track system, in a highly sophisticated version, was the basis for Carl Hansen's famous "Amidon Plan," which did so much to help the culturally handicapped Negro children of Washington, D.C., and which went down the tube recently under the onslaught of the black-power activists.

Why is tracking currently in the racial doghouse?

Basically, for one reason: In any school with a sizable black enrollment, the so-called slow track is bound to have an outsized proportion of black students. Since this amounts to an apparent resegregation of an otherwise desegregated school, some of our leading civil-rights advocates have recently been looking at the track system with a cold and somewhat jaundiced eye.

Well, they'd better look a little longer.

Of course the slow track is going to be mostly black today. But how about tomorrow?

One of the purposes of the slow track is to meet the special needs of the educationally disadvantaged. The color of the disadvantaged child is gloriously irrelevant to the problem. A century ago, the slow track would have been populated with freckle-faced, full-of-the-devil Irish kids. Fifty years later, it would have resembled Little Italy. Today it's black.

So what?

Here are the characteristics of a good school tracking system, and I only wish my black-activist friends would concentrate on getting these into their local schools instead of trying do the whole valuable program in:

(1) Children should be placed in the several groupings solely because of indicated individual abilities and needs. No one should pay the slightest attention to whether the kids are black, brown, white, or yellow.

(2) Semiannual evaluations should be an important part of the program, with emphasis placed on moving a child from one track to another just as soon as the evidence shows that he can profit from the move. The goal of the low track should be to send its enrollees on to higher tracks.

(3) The teachers of the slow tracks should be every bit as well trained, dedicated, and experienced as are their colleagues who are shepherding the high trackers.

(4) Each track should have its own books, tapes, and other teaching materials carefully chosen to meet the needs of its own youngsters.

Give me an integrated school with this kind of a track system for about three years, and at the end of that time I'll show you high tracks with plenty of black youngsters working in them and doing well. In thirty years, if you let me spread the system all over America, I'll show you low tracks that are no longer disproportionately black.

Why thirty years? Because that's how long it takes for any educational practice to change things.

Too slow?

Education is slow. It has to be, or it's not education. Real schooling moves not like a prairie fire but like a glacier.

In summation, put the child where he will be helped the most as an individual, not where he will act out unwillingly and unhappily some adult's charade of racial equality. To a real teacher, a child is himself and nothing else. Talk about his "peer group" is meaningless.

I take a pretty dim view of such things as "group psychological testing" and "group counseling" in education. Certainly, it costs more to deal directly with the individual than to lump him in a mass and deal with him that way. Your doctor could treat your ailments more cheaply too, no doubt, if he could diagnose and prescribe medicine for a bunch of you at a time. But who wants this kind of medicine?

(6) THOU SHALT STAY OUT OF POLITICS

There are an awful lot of recalls occurring and being threatened against school boards all over the land. Board members have recently been bounced in one part of this country because they were too conservative and in another section because they were too liberal.

If these recalls are occurring because the board members are actually engaging in partisan politics, that's one thing. But if it's because board members go for phonics approaches to reading, or better literary materials in the kids' readers, or honors courses in the high school, and as a result are being branded "liberals" or "conservatives," then that's something else entirely.

Just because a board member may not want certain types of sex education taught in school, this does not automatically make him a charter member of the John Birch Society. And the fact that he might hold out for a history textbook that portrays accurately the role of our racial minorities in American history does not necessarily mean he's a Communist.

By staying out of politics, I mean that teachers and school administrators should never express their own political or partisan preferences in their classrooms or around their pupils. On their own time, fine. On the taxpayers' time, no.

I well remember not too long ago a California election where teachers were actually dunned for campaign contributions for a certain candidate for public office during the school day and on school property. This is dirty pool. So is using class bulletin boards for one-sided displays of campaign materials and utilizing the school mimeograph machine to put out campaign brochures.

Educators are paid by all the people. Therefore they cannot use all the people's money to campaign for or against some of the people.

(7) THOU SHALT BE A PROFESSION

Among the many blurred and fuzzy words that are currently debasing the precious coinage of our common language are the two adjectives "legal" and "proper." Once upon a time they were clear-cut and distinct, with little or no possibility of one becoming confused with the other.

It has always been legal, for instance, for a bishop to frequent taverns at late hours. But it wasn't proper, so the bishop didn't. Similarly, a confirmed pacifist enjoys the legal right to enlist in the Marine Corps, but it would be neither proper not intelligent for him to try to do so.

Of late, however, there is a great spate of verbiage cascading throughout the education profession involving the right of teachers to go out on strike and to boycott their employers, and those small but important words "legal" and "proper" seem to be in mortal danger of complete confusion.

No one of any standing denies the right of organized labor to use the appropriate weapons of organized labor: the strike, the boycott, collective bargaining. There is a serious question, on the other hand, as to the propriety of a learned profession utilizing these same weapons.

Teachers are artists, and what is good and right and proper for skilled labor is not necessarily good and right and proper for creative artists. In fact, it's all wrong.

Teachers have every legal right in the world to organize themselves into unions, and I'll help safeguard them in the exercise of this right, if necessary. But candor compels me to say that I consider such unionization unwise, unsound, and unprofessional. We educators have worked a long, long time to build up our calling to the status of a profession, fit and worthy partner to medicine and the law. Let's not chuck all that work down the drain now, particularly at a time when teacher salaries are at an all-time high.

We schoolmen have paid lip-service all our lives to the ideal of professionialization. We've reacted with expressions of outraged indignation whenever anyone has ventured to suggest that education is not a learned profession. We've fought for "professional salaries" and "professional status," and we've drawn up elaborate codes of "professional ethics." I only wish I had the money represented by the countless man hours we've spent trying to build up the image of education as a profession in the mind of the public.

Yet today, quite a few of us seem to be working just as busily and just as diligently trying to tear the image down. In New York they don't beat around the bush at all. They're a craft union, they say, and they go out on strike whenever they feel like it, leaving the classrooms unsupervised and the children uninstructed.

Out in my state, some of us are demanding "collective bargaining" and the rest of us look on complacently while "sanctions" are enforced against school districts whose duly elected boards of education may happen to disagree with us in some particular. We educators, who went into this demanding and highly complex calling in order to help children, now find ourselves in the impossible position of boycotting those same children, urging teachers to refuse to teach, and trying to prevent other teachers from taking their places in the classrooms.

Who suffers when we do anything that hinders the instructional program in a given school? Not the board members, nor the voters, nor the parents. They've already gotten their education. It's always the children who suffer. How can we possibly expect anyone to take seriously our protestations that we are indeed a profession when we insist upon using such unprofessional methods to achieve our objectives?

To each his own: to labor, the proper and legitimate weapons of labor, to a profession, the proper and legitimate weapons of a profession—logic, reasoning, and persuasion. If we educators can't *educate* the public into doing the things we want them to do, then maybe we're in the wrong occupation. Perhaps if we've given up on the whole idea of education as a learned profession, we *should* make no bones about calling ourselves skilled labor and feel free to adopt all the methods of labor to achieve our ends. But I don't believe this for one moment.

We are public employees. We work for the people. We are specialized experts, true enough, and as experts we have the right and the obligation to request and to receive the treatment and consideration due us. If we don't get it in one school district, we have the ancient right of every professional to take our services elsewhere. We have the further right of every American citizen to petition to remonstrate and to engage in attempts through the ballot to change policy in the communities in which we live and work. But we have *no* right to threaten and to intimidate and to coerce.

Nonprofessionalism shows up in a lot of ways besides teacher strikes, of course. Getting rid of poor teachers is one of these ways.

Even in our brave new world of dropped-out and drugged disinhibition, there are certain things that just aren't done.

Chet simply doesn't argue with David. Liz simply doesn't two-time Richard. Eldridge simply doesn't pay for his own bail bonds. Uncle Sam simply doesn't balance the budget. Hollywood simply doesn't censor its own filth. And so on.

But recently a Ford Foundation official has done the unthinkable and has spoken the unspeakable. Dr. Curles Brown has actually dared to suggest that "mediocre" teachers be fired, and that students have a hand in firing them. To render the blasphemy even more hair-raising, he came right out and criticized the nation's teacher associations for "protecting mediocrity."

Brown, formerly a teacher and superintendent and presently the foundation's program officer, blasted his profession for not taking seriously its oft-announced intention to control its own quality: "As evidence, I offer the situation in New York City, where out of a teaching staff of about fifty thousand men and women, one almost never hears of a teacher being dismissed because he is not a good teacher."

He wound up accusing teacher associations of being "much more interested in protecting mediocrity than they are in ridding their ranks of people who simply should not be teaching," and contending that schoolchildren themselves should have a say in whatever firing might occur.

The enormity of this heresy is reflected in the anguished asininity of the profession's reply to Brown's barrage. The counterarguments may be classified roughly as follows:

(1) *Argument Ad Hominem*

The riposte here is the old tried-and-true personal insult. David Selden, president of the AFL-CIO Teachers' Union, answered Brown's charges by attacking Brown: "He spoke like a true school superintendent and a program officer." How's that for a crushing rebuttal?

(2) *Argument Non Sequitur*

"The problem is not with the firing procedures," declaimed Mr. Selden. "It's with the hiring procedures." The assumption here, and it's hardly worth pinpointing, is that if a governmental unit or a private business improves its hiring techniques, it will never have to fire anybody. This has to be one of the most witless, vacuous, and downright mentally defective blatherings I've encountered in a lifetime spent tracking down similar imbecilities.

(3) *Argument Ground-Shifting*

The National Education Association took a somewhat loftier position. It washed its hands while simultaneously wringing them, a neat trick if you've never tried it. "The teaching profession itself does not hire teachers," its spokesman explained oleaginously, "and some states just don't meet our high standards."

These NEA standards, upon examination, boil down to five years of college and three years of teaching experience. Apparently the association believes that every teacher who has served his stint in college and who has been able to get some school to hire him three times is going to be good enough so that he will never need to be fired.

Tommyrot. Consider the case of Mr. Johnson.

He's an eager young teacher, aged twenty-three. He gets his first job in Blank School District teaching Latin and is a success. He's invited back next year, and the next. At the end of the third year his contract renewal brings him the lifelong benefits of permanent tenure under the laws of his state. Now he has maximum security. Blank District can fire him only if he can be proved guilty in court of certain specific sins.

But Johnson is a good teacher. There's no problem. Or is there?

Let's look at the other side of the coin. Over the years, Blank District slowly changes. Instead of a residential area it becomes an industrial slum. Its pupils need more vocational subjects, less academic ones. Solid geometry and ancient history go out the window; so does Latin.

Meanwhile, what of Johnson? In other lines of work

where a man's skill has ceased to be in demand he terminates employment and seeks it elsewhere. But Johnson, though in the prime of life, is not obliged to do anything but sit tight. His teaching credential entitles him to teach any subject offered in high school. He cannot be terminated.

Knowing this, his principal searches through Johnson's old personnel file, seeking some clue that may be of help in reassigning him. He discovers that Johnson as a college boy majored in Latin and minored in philosophy, neither subject promising to be of much help under the circumstances. But away back in his sophomore year Johnson had taken a semester course in drafting.

The problem is solved. Since he won't go elsewhere to teach his specialty, Johnson is given five mechanical drawing classes to teach each day, and this he does, maybe for twenty years.

He doesn't like mechanical drawing. He's not very good at it. The kids aren't learning very much in his classes. But what of it? He's at the top of the salary schedule, and he would sacrifice his tenure if he went somewhere else. So he stays—and stays.

This sort of thing is simply no good. It gets worse fast if Johnson becomes more and more uninterested and careless and crotchety as he grows old teaching a subject in which he has no interest and from which he derives no sense of satisfaction. The school can't do anything about it. His fellow teachers realize the problem but aren't inclined to back the changes in the law that would be needed to solve it.

Maybe if they realized what Johnson is doing to them they would be a little more concerned.

He's costing them money, you see. No school board in its right mind is going to go for an across-the-board salary raise that will result in Johnson getting a fat pay boost when everybody in town knows he's doing a poor job. Result: no pay raise.

Let me stress that tenure teachers are the salt of the earth. But to safeguard against the occasional bad apple in the barrel, here are the basic principles that should underlie any good state tenure plan:

(a) Tenure is a privilege, not a built-in right.

(b) The only tenure plan that is any good is the one that results in the long run in good education for the children.

(c) Tenure should make possible speedy severance of the few teachers who for any reason do not continue to meet the continuing high standards expected of permanent employees.

(d) Tenure should provide for intervention by fellow professionals to protect the teacher from malicious or capricious firing.

(e) No teacher should be placed on tenure until he has met high performance standards and has undergone observation over a period of years by professional experts.

(4) *Argument Filthy Lucre*

Just as Dr. Johnson described patriotism as the last refuge of a scoundrel, so do the teacher organizations seek sanctuary in lack of money every time someone criticizes their output. It's a regular knee-jerk reflex.

Mr. Selden says it with magnificent irrelevance: "As long as teachers are underpaid and overworked, school systems cannot be selective."

In other words, "If we had plenty of money, there would be no problem attached to the firing of teachers."

As I view the battlefield now that the smoke has cleared, Mr. Brown is camped in sole possession of it.

Very, very seldom is it that I agree with the Ford Foundation about anything except the weather. This is one of those times.

And as for letting the kids in on the teacher-evaluation process, why not get their opinions? After all, they're the ones in the best position to know how good a teacher is. Speaking personally, if my pupils had been convinced back in my classroom days that I was a crummy teacher and had said so, I would have found another occupation in a hurry.

(8) THOU SHALT OBEY THE LAW

Teachers used to be the most law-abiding members of society. They still are, but dry-rot is apparently beginning to set in around the edges.

For instance:

The law says teachers shall teach their pupils to avoid profanity. Some of them aren't doing it. Instead, they're deliberately exposing their charges to so-called modern literature replete with profanity and obscenity.

The law says teachers shall lead daily patriotic exercises in their classrooms. Some of them won't. Instead, some of them insist on sulking silently in the back of the class while somebody else leads the Flag Salute, on the grounds that our nation has not yet achieved perfect freedom and justice for all, as it says in the Pledge. Using the same bat-brained logic, they should no doubt have refused to get married on the grounds that they couldn't promise to "honor" their wives because the poor girls hadn't yet won the Congressional Medal.

I'm not going to talk about the rotten minority of our college professors who teach their students to burn their draft cards, take LSD, and lie down in front of troop trains.

In this connection, one of the so-called wise men of my profession, Robert Maynard Hutchins, has been no help at all. The sage of Santa Barbara sounded off as follows: "A citizen cannot be asked to obey a law contrary to the dictates of his own conscience."

Let's look at the implications of his argument. The existence of a democratic society presupposes that each citizen will obey all laws adopted by the majority of his fellows. If certain citizens are to place themselves above the law for any reason under the sun, whether it be personal conscience, vanity, love, hatred—or Divine Revelation, for that matter—then the democratic society cannot function for very long.

A country like ours operates on the indispensable premise that the law is mightier than the man. Fascism operates on the opposite premise that certain men are more important than the law. Thus spoke Hitler.

Conscience is not above the law.

Because conscience compels certain East Indians to practice ritual strangling, shall the United States then tolerate thuggee?

Because some highly religious individuals have at various times felt impelled by their conscience to practice polygamy, are we consequently obliged to legalize multiple marriage in this land?

Because I happen to be conscientiously opposed to the clearly discriminatory features of the present income tax law, am I therefore free unilaterally to disregard it?

Nonsense. Dr. Hutchins knows better than this. He knows that to accept the protection of our laws implies a willingness to obey them. Otherwise he puts himself in the detestably hypocritical posture of saying: "I'll obey only those laws which I personally agree with. I'll be served and protected by all the laws, but I myself will feel free to subvert them at the same time I am benefiting from them."

If Dr. Hutchins is actually serious about breaking laws for reasons of conscience, then he really should renounce all the protections that are afforded by the law.

He should hire his own armed guards to protect his home and give the overworked police a break.

He should give up the right to vote. What good is voting if one is determined in advance to disregard the will of the majority?

Conscience in the past has done strange things. It has led men to burn old ladies over slow fires, massacre whole cities, sacrifice little children to Moloch, and destroy irreplaceable libraries. Conscience is the most unreliable of human guides for two indisputable reasons:

(1) It's notoriously variable, differing widely within the individual himself.

(2) It's based upon emotion, and emotions are obviously unpredictable.

Law, on the other hand, builds upon the rock of reason, not upon the shifting sands of glandular reactions. Law is cerebral, conscience adrenal.

Dr. Hutchins knows that in any rational society law must reign supreme. Why he preaches the contrary is anybody's guess. It's lucky that while the law prescribes penalties for wickedness, it does not set up punishments for tiresome nonsense.

Thanks to voices of destruction like that of

Dr. Hutchins, a regular lawbreaking syndrome has begun to afflict my profession. Teacher strikes are a case in point.

Now that the schoolteachers in Michigan and New York have shown that they *can* keep children from receiving a hefty percentage of their prescribed instructional time by being rough, tough strikers like Walter Reuther, the time may be ripe to take a long look at the educational implications of their 1968 action.

Since I'm the fellow doing the long looking, I reserve the right to restrict the scope of the inquiry rather ruthlessly. For instance, I'm not going to concern myself with the rights or wrongs of the grievances. For all I know, the Gotham pedagogues may have been forced to slave their lives away in sordid blackboard jungles under the lash of sneering and mustachioed administrators.

And I'm going to rule out the sociological significances, too, including the report that Harlem parents bitterly assailed the teacher strike as racially discriminatory because the Negro children had the most to lose by being deprived of all education during the most important three weeks of the whole school year.

No, I'm going to confine myself to the logic of the situation, and to ascertain whether the New York walkout has been good for education. And this means good for children, because children are what education is all about.

First, New York has a state law against teacher strikes. It matters not a whit that the law may possibly be a bad one. What's important is that it's the law. And every teacher in the land knows that the way to deal with a bad law is not to break it but to change it. I'm reasonably sure that every striking teacher in New York has said this to his pupils and has thrown the following in for good measure: "The only glue that holds a democratic society together is mutual respect for and obedience to the laws that our own elected representatives enact for us."

Actually, when we deliberately break our own laws, we're in the same irrational position as the nut who intentionally sets fire to his own house.

But aside from the fraudulence of your words as compared to your deeds, fellow teacher, consider the example you've set to your wide-eyed captive audience. If you tell a child that a law is a lot of eyewash—that something or somebody is more important than the law—and that therefore it's okay to ignore the law in order to bring about what you unilaterally consider to be necessary and beneficial results, then I say to you: That child cannot be greatly blamed if later on in life he decides to break into banks in order to redistribute the national wealth more equitably or even to knock off a few people whom he may decide the world would be better off without.

What are you going to say from now on, my New York colleagues, when one of your pupils deliberately violates one of your own classroom regulations, gives you the old stony stare and says, "I know I broke the rules, but I was just following your example. You showed me how last September."

How are you going to be able to keep a youngster after school from here on in, or send him to the principal, or even give him an "F" in citizenship for disobeying the laws of the school, when you have set an example for him by disobeying the laws of the state?

If you do dare to enforce your own rules of classroom conduct after this sorry spectacle you've made of yourself, you are a hypocrite.

Striking is legal for longshoremen and television actors and autoworkers and airline pilots and lots of people. It happens to be illegal for teachers. You knew this when you decided to become a teacher. If you wanted to strike, why didn't you become a longshoreman or a television actor or an auto worker or an airline pilot? You didn't, though. You chose teaching, with all the self-restraint and self-denial that goes along with the glory and the wonder of being a teacher. When are you going to start acting like one?

But the lawless syndrome doesn't stem from *within* my profession. Its roots are sunk deep into a diseased and distracted body politic. Those of us who work with young people today are scared stiff. Oh, we're proud, too, and happy about the increasing seriousness and studiousness and attention to duty on the part of the great majority. The country, it is safe to say, has just as large a percentage of decent, law-abiding youngsters as it ever had. But the minority who always got into trouble in the past is getting into worse trouble now. Their crimes are more sordid; their attitude is more defiant; their contempt for civilization's moral and legal codes is more outspoken.

Coastside towns are sacked and looted by drunken teenagers every time a great national holiday comes around. Youthful, leather-jacketed, cold-eyed mobsters on motorcycles roar into peaceful villages. Vicious adolescents roam the streets of some of our biggest cities, slashing and maiming innocent passers-by for the sake of "kicks." Every so often they stomp some cripple to death or roar with glee while they slice up a blind man with their switchblades.

Firemen trying to put out a blaze are increasingly subjected to a rain of stones from packs of young punks.

Presumably intelligent college students in one of our most prestigious institutions of higher learning defy the taxpayers who are subsidizing their educations, wreck police cars, and bite the legs of campus cops because they don't happen to agree with regulations established by the legal representatives of the people who support and populate that institution.

Educators confronted with this kind of Frankenstein monster can use a little help.

In my state we are embarking on a vast endeavor to teach the kids to obey laws even when they don't agree with them. We're bringing firemen and policemen right into the classrooms, clear down to the first grade, so that the children will know who they are and the nature of the perilous work they are called upon to perform for us every day. We're stressing the identification and the educational rehabilitation of juvenile hoods before they turn into adult thugs.

In short, we're beginning to do what one profession can to cure the folly and the feebleness of a sick society. But without some assistance from the rest of you, especially some of you judges who seem to be doing your darnedest recently to break down law and order rather than uphold it, it's a mighty tough job. I propose we get to work, all of us—in our own homes, our own schools, our own businesses, and our own churches—to clean up the mess.

(9) THOU SHALT NOT USE THE SCHOOL AS AN ORNITHOLOGICAL SANCTUARY FOR ODD BIRDS

When I stroll across the campus of one of our better-known—or perhaps I should say more notorious—universities these days, I have to keep reminding myself that it's supposed to be an institution of higher learning. It looks more like Skid Row.

In one corner of the quad there may be a well-endowed

topless burlesque queen going through her bumps and grinds, presumably as an extracurricular advertisement for the freshman class in Anatomy 1-A.

In another corner a table is set up doing a thriving business selling dirty magazines and recruiting for the Filthy Speech Movement.

Just across the way will be the "Give-Blood-to-the-Viet-Cong-So-They-Can-Slaughter-More-American-Prisoners" table, and close at hand is the sign-up headquarters for next Saturday night's LSD orgy. I understand, incidentally, that in the future these are to be held only in the ground-floor rooms of the local pads in order to render less fatal the contusions of those student addicts who at the height of the evening's ingestion get themselves confused with Shelley's Skylark and indulge in an impulse to take off from the nearest window and fly around the building.

And all around the place the doggonedest-looking characters you ever saw, bearded and sandaled and long-haired as Peter the Hermit or Old Man Mose, looking like a bunch of Cecil B. DeMille extras made up for a mob scene in "The Crusades," except that Cecil insisted upon certain minimum essentials on the part of his cast. These straggling hedgebirds look as if they hadn't bathed since they were freshmen, and they arouse in the casual onlooker a nervous and uncontrollable impulse to scratch himself thoroughly.

What do they do besides demonstrate on behalf of their country's enemies? They certainly don't do any work, and they never seem to be in class.

Who pays the freight for their four-year course in sex, drugs, and treason? That's much easier to answer. You do. Every nickel of their tuition—worth thousands of dollars on today's academic market—is paid for by *you*. It's nice that you're rich enough to subsidize these creeps. But I hope you're not expecting gratitude. They hate your capitalistic guts, and they don't hesitate to say so in four-letter words.

In case you think I'm exaggerating, I invite you to pay a visit to the Berkeley campus of the University of California and just look around. This is not a university as any sane society has ever known one. It's a caricature out of Li'l Abner, or even Hogarth, showing what happens when you turn an institution over to the inmates.

At Berkeley, these inmates number not more than a thousand out of the total of 27,000 students. But they are destructive and vocal out of all proportion to their numerical percentage.

(10) THOU SHALT SEEK EVEN-HANDEDLY AFTER THE TRUTH

This is the tenth and greatest commandment, and takes in all the rest. For if education would just get on with the tremendous task that only it can do, then all the other nine would follow.

It is the function of education to let in light, not to generate heat—to rely upon reason and logic and persuasion, not to bow low before the false gods of demonstrating and proselytizing and intimidating. We educators simply cannot afford to take sides in the ephemeral and inflammatory issues of the moment, if only because it is our sworn duty to inquire into the truth behind all of them. More, into our hands has been given for good or ill the most precious and the most dangerous duty entrusted by mankind to men—the schooling of the young. Someone must remain primarily concerned with the days beyond tomorrow, not embroiled in every ugly street fight and entangled personally in every transient ism that may raise its head to further vex an already sadly distressed and fretted generation.

I can think of no one except us educators who can fill this giant-size order, and then only conditionally. The condition is that we cut out the horseplay and get down to work. We have the biggest job of all time right in our laps, and we can do it, too. But not by pamphleteering and propagandizing and picketing. There are plenty of false prophets who specialize in emotionalizing. There are darned few of us in any age who can teach a rising generation to think—calmly, coolly, coherently.

The Commandments are there to follow. But like the great originals, they will have pith and meaning only insofar as they can be taken from sterile stone and perishable paper and engraved in letters of fire upon the minds and hearts of Americans in general, and my own profession in particular.

CROSSROAD #5

The Parent as Dropout

THE OLDEST CLICHÉ in my business is the need for cooperation between the parent and the teacher. The second oldest is that the child is essentially the product of the home, not of the school.

Both clichés are true.

This is why the tendency of parents to "drop out" and to "cop out," in the vernacular of the day, is not going to be compensated for by putting more money into education nor by paying more attention to the schools. Education can help. It can help a lot. But it cannot compensate for rotten homes and indifferent parents.

My contention is that the Dropout Generation isn't the one now coming up at all; it's the one presently in charge of things. The way we oldsters have abandoned the ancient battlements and taken refuge in the cowards' quarters downstairs, there's precious little left of the old castle for the kids to drop out of.

We've been soft when we should have been tough. Permissive when we should have cracked down. Generous when we should have been stingy. Non-involved when we should have been up to our ears.

Result: We, the adult, mature masters and mistresses of our fathers' America, the sons and daughters of the Great Depression, the winners of World War II, have opened the floodgates, let down the drawbridge, hauled down the standards, and in our own time we are trying to leave to our own children a neon-lit, atomic-powered, air-conditioned nuthouse. We did it ourselves.

If you doubt me, endure, with spleen and choler if necessary, a few questions:

(1) Do you give your teen-agers more money than they need for lunch, school supplies, and the Saturday night dance? You know you do. That's why so many of them today own expensive college pads, drive expensive little foreign cars, smoke expensive pot, and go to an expensive hell.

The hippies and the yippies and all their hairy, obscene ilk live from day to turned-on day on Pop's allowance checks. After all, there's hardly a job any of them could hold for more than a day, except maybe that of campus dope-peddler. The college loudmouth is the modern counterpart of the old English remittance man. He's paid to stay away from home so the folks can get a little peace and quiet. And who pays him? Mom and Pop.

(2) Do you know where your high-schoolers are and what they're doing every minute they're out of school and away from home? If not, why not? In this connection, please spare me all the popularly corny rationalizations about Junior needing to learn independence and self-reliance. Independence and self-reliance are the last things in the world our offspring need to learn. They're positively bristling with these sterling qualities, like so many adolescent porcupines.

I think I've heard every argument ever dreamed up about how the "now" generation demands unprecedented trust, confidence, and blank checks. Horse feathers. What every new generation needs is adult concern, supervision, and a good, firm *No!* every once in a while. Every school kid I ever knew who got into trouble did so because his parents didn't know—or possibly didn't care. It's usually as simple as that.

Dear parent, I am loath to push you to the wall, but you don't really know, either. You may care, but you don't really know. Now, do you?

(3) Do you know Junior's friends? Do they look reasonably clean, and talk the same way? Or do they look and talk as though they had crawled out quite recently from under some particularly noisome rock? If the latter description rings the bell, look out for squalls ahead. It's only a question of time until Junior joins them under the same rock.

(4) While we're at it, are you acquainted with the parents of Junior's friends? Have you taken the time to get together with these similarly harassed human beings and plan mutual strategy, if only for sheer self-defense? In case it hasn't occurred to you, it's a lot easier to enforce things like midnight curfews, dress codes, and rules of conduct if Junior's gang is operating under identical home regulations. Or is it just too, too time-consuming for you to do all this?

Your children are being attacked. They're on a battlefield. In this war against the young, it's a jungle strewn with attractive booby-traps. There's a lot of fancy camouflage strung all around, too, to hide the snares and pitfalls. Drive-in swinging churches. All-night discotheques. Avant-garde libraries. Bawdy billboards. Short-order marriage mills. Rockets, robots, rock and roll.

The camouflage is expensively effective. It's intended to be. It dazzles and it daunts. It coats old poisons with now synthetic candy. It invokes the Holy Trinity of the Sick Sixties, whom none may challenge with impurity and before whom all must bend the knee: Youth, Novelty, and Science.

Youth of late has become its own excuse. If one be only young, all things are possible. All doors are open, and all bumps are cushioned. His very Youth confers upon him rare charms and special amulets that will bring him across the battlefield unscathed, immune, amused, with a smile upon his lips and flowers in his hair. So runs the New Dispensation.

If a thing is New, regardless either of its merits or its morality, it is likewise Good and must not be judged in the context of old logic. Its very newness cloaks it in invulnerability, proof against all the slings and arrows of outrageous criticism. This is the "Now" Generation. The past is dead, the future yet unborn. Only the present counts. The critic of the Now, you see, must be by definition Old, and anything Now is intrinsically superior to anything Old. So reads the Gospel according to Madison Avenue.

So speaks today's machine-God, glowing with cold electronic fires, pulsing with myriad tiny, moving parts, mirroring in its steel features the eternal minuet of stimulus and response and the frigid logic of sociological trends, breathing a freezing confidence, an icy certainty in the eternal rightness of its answers.

Such is the nature of the battlefield. What of the combatants?

You have a small son. He's wide-eyed and vulnerable, filled with unguessed promise and potential. You love him more than life itself. For him you have sacrificed much and would give up everything. Yet the battlefield looms ahead, relentless, inexorable, for him as for all his kind. He has certain enemies, you see, of whom more later.

You have a little daughter. Like all such, for you she mingles fairy-dust and violet-essence. She dances through your days and illuminates your dreams. She is dearer to you than all the treasures of King Solomon's Mines.

No matter. She, too, must one day run the gauntlet. How do you want her when grown to womanhood? Joyous, un-sullied, loving, able to look frankly and openly into the eyes of the man who one day will take her to be his wife? I stipulate your assent.

Yet when her enemies have done with her, she may well be what so many of her older sisters have become of late. Haunted and shamed, lank-haired, unwashed, wretched in the knowledge that she has bartered her woman's birthright for a mess of singularly revolting pottage, feverishly pursuing an ideological mirage that if she could ever reach would prove as mockingly empty as the life that has led her up this blindest of all blind alleys.

For she, too, is marked for destruction by the enemies of the children.

Who are they?

They are the Muck-Merchants, who prey upon puberty.

They are the Dope-Pushers, who transplant cancers from the old to the young.

They are the Entertainers, some of whom create an atmosphere for youthful audiences that is an odious cross between a brothel and a gang rumble.

They are the Relativist Preachers, who set such a sterling example for their juvenile parishioners by mouthing "God-is-dead" slogans, supporting homosexual dance clubs, violating democratically enacted laws, and breaking down our entire Judaeo-Christian moral heritage with silent smiles of slow disparagement.

Finally, they are the "Progressive" Educators, who for almost a generation now have been promoting the philosophy of John Dewey, singing the praise of permissiveness, assiduously massaging each other's ego while oleaginously assuring one another that teaching organized, disciplined, systematic subject matter to children is far less important than indoctrinating them in togetherness, in-groupness, life adjustment, and democratic socializing with their peer group.

With this bleating band of permissive pedagogues must be included also the leftist college professors, who throughout the past decade have lip-smackingly encouraged the violent young to become thugs, the unpatriotic to become treasonable, and the obscene to become unspeakable.

I detest these people. For almost thirty years, I've viewed the chaos they have caused, the young lives they have ruined, the hearts they have broken.

Now, let's see what the schools are up against these days when they seek help from Mom and Pop in the current war against your children.

SECTOR #1—PARENTS AND SEX

Let's face it. Americans today are sexually pathological, no matter how you look at it. The evidence:

—A massive rise in the increase of brutish and revolting sex crimes. Everything from the Boston Strangler to the Chicago nurse butchery.

—The puffing of pornography into big, big business.

—The rotting away of our once proud motion pictures

to the sordid status of stag movies. Every vile nuance from lesbianism to fetishism is now deemed acceptable for what has always been a family entertainment medium.

—The decline of the American novel to a mere vehicle for four-letter words and dreary sexual perversions.

—The nauseating material on our neighborhood magazine and pocketbook stands, which more and more resembles the private collection of the late King Farouk.

Now, regardless of how broad-minded you may be, or how healthy and beautiful you may think sex is, you'll have to agree that this kind of leering and lip-smacking preoccupation with a single bodily function is at best bizarre and at worst maniacal. On a more humdrum level, it's somewhat comparable to allocating a completely disproportionate percentage of the nation's resources and attention to the fascinated contemplation of the anatomy and psychology of toothbrushing, shaving, and shampooing.

Who's to blame?

—A good many of our ministers, who organize well-financed and slickly publicized associations like the one in San Francisco, which exists to promote the cause of homosexuality and to persuade a disgusted public that the mincing sodomite is really a misunderstood and noble fighter for the eternal verities.

—Too darned many judges who call hard-core pornography "avant-garde literature" and who assess the mocking muck-merchants such trivial fines that they insult the decent cops who work hard to round up the dirt-mongers and run them in.

—Quite a few psychologists and psychiatrists, who seem dedicated to the uplifting proposition that everybody ought to be able to do his own thing any way he wants to, the nastier the better.

—The news-dissemination media, which grant the same amount of goggle-eyed, respectful attention to some pitiful apologist for pederasty as they would grant to one of the Twelve Apostles.

—And, of course, the smut-salesman, who despises your children even while he bloats and battens upon them. He makes war upon them, and simultaneously he makes big money off them. Without the kids, he would be small potatoes.

My own state of California, I'm sorry to say, is the pornography capital of the country. At the San Francisco airport, you can buy so-called novels in which every vile and perverted act from voyeurism to bestiality is depressingly depicted. In Los Angeles "sex shops" exist where all kinds of dirty pictures, films, and gadgets may be purchased by anyone who has the price. And the slick Hollywood film factories, which once guaranteed family entertainment to the world, now export obscenity to its four corners.

The cheek-by-jowl relationship between pornography and sex crimes is pointed up by police chiefs and county sheriffs all across the land. Whole odorous stacks of this filth are found in the pads of virtually all the youthful sex offenders who are rounded up by the law. And while it's currently popular among some of the more modish psychologists to lift a critical eyebrow at any suggestion of a connection between sex garbage and sex offenses, I ceased believing in this sort of Satanic coincidence at about the age of six.

The muck-merchant relies upon two characteristics of today's youth: its immaturity and its affluence. Mature people find pornography yawningly dull, if only because sheer repetition of its extraordinarily limited

repertoire of words and postures sooner or later pro-
duces boredom unlimited. The immature, on the other
hand, find every elderly nuance and ancient position new
and exciting, thereby affording ample proof of said immaturity.

Moreover, young people today have money to spend on
this sort of offal, which their predecessors didn't have,
to put it mildly. Today's youth market is a multi-
billion-dollar one, capable of changing national clothing styles, revolutionizing the country's record industry,
and even shaking to its foundations that grand old institution, the American barber shop. Lured by such golden
bait as this, the pornography-peddlers circle over the
youth market like vultures over a battlefield.

All such degenerates for profit are enemies of the
children whom they fatten upon. But two groups of these
ghouls deserve singling out, if only because they do more
mischief than their equally festering fellows:

(1) *The Apologists*

Hear the new paeans to pruriency:

"Much of the world's great literature is erotic in
content. It's no longer a question of whether children
should be exposed to such material, but only a question
of when."

and

"Today's 'New Morality' is far franker and healthier
than the old. It's better for the young to be shocked by the
Vietnam War than by a staged simulation of sexual intercourse."

and even

" 'Sexual misconduct' is no longer a relevant term.
There's no such thing anymore."

Every one of these statements is a deliberate lie
aimed straight at your children.

Sexual misconduct is often the cause of the murders

and most of the acts of violence committed in this country. Sexual perversion is a sin as well as a crime. Premarital sex causes thousands of heartbreaks and wrecked lives, if only because of the chilling selfishness that permeates it. And the corruption of the individual to which commercialized obscenity is dedicated has no more to do with the Vietnam War than Hugh Hefner and *Playboy* magazine have to do with General Westmoreland and the Articles of War.

No, the function of the Apologists is to smooth the path of the pornographer, to make his way straight so that he will have a clear shot at your kids. He justifies his filth and simultaneously sows the seeds of doubt among the decent. He talks glibly about "avant-garde literature" and "adult entertainment," and with every word he gnaws away at the moral standards that took centuries to build. His task it is to make putridity the "in" thing, and to tar its critics with the brush of Victorian narrow-mindedness.

The Apologist is an intellectual prostitute. And a two-bit one, at that.

(2) *The Moviemakers*

Of course, there are some healthy exceptions to the rule I'm about to lay down. Yet the premise is universal enough to stand:

"The moviemakers are systematically seducing your children, steeping them in seductive slime in order to make a fast buck."

Want to watch sodomy glamorized? You can see it in the movies.

Like to have adultery portrayed as normal and desirable? You can see it in the movies.

Think lesbianism should be shown sympathetically? You can see it in the movies.

Believe gutter language should become an accepted part of everyday speech? You can hear it in the movies.

So can your children.

I accuse the movie moguls of soullessly and cynically pandering to the basest instincts of the human race.

I accuse the movie producers of filming sordid old sex sagas that past generations scornfully rejected as hardcore pronography.

I accuse the movie directors of staging steamy bedroom scenes that used to be shown only in the gamiest of stag movies.

And I accuse the movie actors and actresses who star in these ill-starred putrescences of debauching the great and ancient art of acting, an art that was beginning at long last to work its way out of an age-old doghouse until they came along to plunge it back.

But the folks most to blame for our present sex syndrome are you, Mom and Pop. Just you.

You let your children grow up thinking that premarital sex is okay so long as nobody gets pregnant, diseased, or jailed. It isn't, you know.

You let your neighborhood moviehouse and newsstand get away with their gradual switchover from family entertainment to filth for profit. You didn't picket them or boycott them or even keep your own kids away from them. Did you?

You let the schools take over your own immemorial job of telling your children the facts of life, and you didn't care that the resulting school sex-education programs were necessarily as devoid of morality and personal dignity as a third-generation computer.

You let the tax-supported colleges abrogate all standards of simple decency. You didn't raise hell, cancel your endowments, or yank your kids out of school. So now we have mixed dormitories, obscene school newspapers, free-love assemblies, dirty movies on campus, and drama-class projects that make the old Minsky burlesque blackouts look by comparison like a Sunday-school pageant. One public college in 1968 prepared an elaborate statuary exhibit that featured sculptured figures engaged in various acts of sexual intercourse. Another produced *The Beard,* a play vile enough to make even Ralph Ginzburg blush. Still another put on a play that portrayed Jesus Christ as a practicing homosexual and, during its last act, pelted the audience with dismembered bodies of animals.

In short, you dropped out. And now you're blaming everybody you can find for the mess we're in—teachers, legislators, Supreme Court justices, movie producers, and magazine publishers.

Stop blaming them. They're like everyone else. They'll do whatever you let them get away with, and they'll stop in a hurry anything you show them you won't stand for. So far, they've been able to find darned little you won't put up with. And so the dry rot spreads. Because of you.

Why did you drop out of this sex push? Why did you consent to exposing your own kids to the sexual Typhoid Marys of the Sick Sixties?

Because you allowed yourselves to be sold a bill of badly damaged goods.

The dirty novelists bellowed "freedom of expression" and you bought it.

The bawdy moviemakers raised their eyebrows, pointed enviously to some odorous films turned out overseas by a few degenerate Swedes and Frenchmen, and brayed "adult entertainment" at the top of their voices. You bought that, too.

The jelly-spined college presidents pontificated solemnly about their institutions not being "custodial" in relation to their inmates, and you bought that. With it, incidentally, you also bought the convenient contraceptives from the campus clinic, the four-letter chants from the student activists, the psychedelic orgies at the Lettermen's Ball, and all the rest of the sorry sex parade that promenades interminably across a hundred college campuses these days and onto the front pages of a thousand newspapers.

Yes, the ax-grinders in our society bellowed and brayed and pontificated, and you got put down, Mom and Pop. You were so hung up over being thought square and Victorian and unmod that you ended up an uneasy vegetable, doing nothing at all about anything controversial —except once in a while viewing with alarm, of course. And even that you did behind dark glasses, for fear someone would think you were guilty of widening the generation gap.

It's not too late to get back in the ballgame, folks. Here are the things you ought to start doing right now about this sex binge we seem to be on:

—Stay away from the morbid movies and the purulent plays, and urge everybody you know to do the same— especially your children.

—Organize neighborhood patrols to inspect, boycott, and picket the obscene magazine stands.

—Elect local judges and civic officials who hate pornography and who guarantee in advance of election to chevy the youth-corrupters relentlessly and ingeniously every day they're in office.

—Tell your state legislators in no uncertain terms to cut off all money to tax-supported colleges that refuse to police their own facilities and student bodies and which decline to adopt definite, hard-boiled standards of sex conduct on their respective campuses.

—Above all, see that your own children know what's right and what's wrong about sex before they blow themselves up with its age-old dynamite.

And don't let anybody box you into that old semantic trap about what's "right" and what's "wrong." The rightness and the wrongness of sex are as old as our Judeo-Christian heritage—as old as the Ten Commandments—almost as old as Adam. So stop trying to justify yourself. Stop dropping out. Adopt a code of behavior you really believe in and stick to it. Eventually, you'll get something from the kids you are certainly not getting now: respect.

Tell them the human body is supposed to be a temple, not a brothel. And make them know it.

You really have only two alternatives in this sector of the war against your children: You can fight back as grimly and as unceasingly as the Enemy is fighting; or you can surrender. Because there is no temporizing with perversion and profit. Either you and your children win, or the Enemy wins. And if he does, may the Almighty grant you an early death so you won't have to look into the Dorian Gray face of ultimate defeat—a face so sickeningly changed from the face that looked up into yours so trustingly, so confidently, so innocently in the days before you chickened out and gave up everything a father or mother ought to be willing to stand up and fight for.

SECTOR #2—PARENTS AND DOPE

Drugs are currently the big hang-up with which the kids are scaring their parents. Mom and Pop increasingly are gumshoeing around, looking under Junior's bed for caches of LSD, surreptitiously eying his forearms for needlemarks. "Pot" is no longer something that calls the kettle black; it has become a parental obsession.

And rightly so. Entirely too many of our offspring are

on the stuff. But America has always been a nation of drug addicts. Remember?

A century ago, patent medicines were the big thing. Millions were "hooked" on potions like "Dr. Herkimer's Happiness Syrup," "Smith's Sure-Fire Cancer Cure," and "Iroquois Herb Tonic for Radiant Health." And I mean really hooked, because most of these dubious brews were heavily laced with laudanum, and laudanum is liquid opium.

Ironically enough, while Grover Cleveland's America was recoiling in horror at lurid tales of opium dens and their creepy denizens, its respectable citizens were the ones who were really keeping the overseas poppy processers in business. I imagine the total percentage of "hard" narcotics-users was considerably larger in the 1880s than in the 1960s. The users didn't know they were users, of course, but that didn't alter the fact. Or the consequences, unfortunately.

Yesterday it was the middle-aged-and-over sobersides who were hooked, all-unknowing, on opium derivatives. Today it's the young wet-behind-the-ears activists who are all wall-eyed on "speed" and "bennies." And since extreme youth occupies a larger band of the population age spectrum than ever before in history, the sins of the children are infinitely more visible—and audible—than were those of the fathers.

Why are more kids taking dope? Here are a few reasons:

(1) They're bored. Conditioned from infancy to a compulsive need for glamour and excitement, they're chagrined to find that adult life in general and school life in particular are not all fun and games but rather a dull grind and plenty of hard work. So they look around for artificial kicks—in capsules.

(2) They're affluent. Dope cost money. Today the kids have plenty.

(3) They're uninhibited. Nobody ever told them dope is evil. Instead, ever since they got out of diapers, everybody's been telling them to live it up and have a ball. And dope knocks down all the barriers to sheer groovyness—for a while.

(4) They're arrogant. Nature's laws have been graciously suspended for them. Through their formative years, they've been protected and coddled and shielded from the normal retributive interaction of cause and effect. Now they're Superman. Nothing can hurt them. So they think.

Who's to blame? Sorry, Mom and Pop, I can't find any other donkeys around to pin this particular tail on except you. The kids are bored because you worried too much about entertaining them and not enough about accustoming them to good hard work. They're affluent because you gave them ridiculous amounts of money to spend and never made them work to earn it. They're uninhibited because you never found or took the time to teach them the meaning of such words as "good," "evil," "honor," "dishonor," "decent," "indecent." They're arrogant because you didn't whale the tar out of them as little ones the first time they disobeyed or talked back or used bad language.

Oversimplification? I think not. In fact, I know not. Show me an adolescent who has been brought up to do reasonable work on a regular schedule before he gets his allowance, who has been sent to church and taught moral principles by precept and by example at home, and who has been promptly and strictly disciplined every time he acted up, and I'll show you a youngster who isn't puffing pot and taking trips on LSD.

What's more, I'll show you a potential adult whose life will be a lot busier and happier and more productive than that of the slack-jawed, bleary-eyed, slovenly drug-addict who grows up whining that society owes him a perpetual handout and an infinite supply of free benzedrine.

One of today's unique problems is that dope has become fashionable. It's no longer considered a disgrace. And, of course, this irresponsible, jug-headed state of mind plays right into the hands of the man who's willing to blast human lives to make a fast and filthy buck for himself.

More masks than a Hallowe'en party, has your friendly neighborhood dope-pusher.

There's the mask of Sophistication, with its gently lifted, painted eyebrows and the small yawn of polite boredom. "Smoke pot," the mask-mouth murmers. "It's the 'in' thing."

Through its brazen mouthpiece, the false-face of Excitement bellows at the kids, "Tune in with marijuana! Turn on with LSD! The only real way to get your kicks!"

And then there's the domino of Rebellion, bitterly sneering, "Get even with your parents. Tear down society. Destroy yourself. That'll teach 'em all a lesson!"

But when the many, masks have been stripped away, there's just one ugly, cynical face underneath: the dollar sign.

The dope-pusher doesn't care whether marijuana is "in" with the jet set. What he does care about is the prevailing price of a stick, and how many he can sell per day at Harrison High.

He's not concerned with the effects of the poison he peddles. If the buyer has a good trip on his brand of acid, okay. If he ends up flying out of a sixth-story window because the stuff has convinced him that he's a swallow going back to Capistrano, that's tough. All things being equal, of course, the pusher prefers his suckers alive;

they can buy more dope from him that way. But if you really think he cares whether you get kicks or a coffin, forget it.

And as far as rebellion against the Establishment is concerned, his only interest is enough chaos and deviltry afoot to keep the police off his back so he can make his daily profit, service his old customers, and infect new clients. He can be compared with the Renaissance *condottiere*, the old-time mercenary soldier who didn't care whom he killed as long as he got paid regularly. The drug-peddler doesn't make war on your children because he hates them but because it's profitable. He's the pimp who introduces kids to Death, for money.

How does he fight his war? Like this:

Your son is out dragging with the gang in the MG you bought him for his birthday. Somebody starts passing around the pot. The scene has been real groovy. Everybody's turned on. Nobody wants to cop out, least of all your boy. So he grabs the grass and lights up. He gets happier and smilier and groovier as the stick burns down to the butt. He floats. He soars. And if he doesn't pile up the MG, he's hooked. Oh, he can kick the habit later on. Lots of people do. But right now he thinks pot's the greatest thing since the Beatles.

Note: The anonymous character who started the stuff going around the car is a pusher, even if he looks like Pat Boone.

Your daughter's at a slumber party with a few of her high school girl friends. They're giggling and playing Tom Jones records and sharing the thousand secrets known only to adolescent girls. Suddenly one of them looks mysterious, lights up something that looks like a cigarette but smells like alfalfa, and rolls her eyes in ecstasy. All the rock singers smoke it, she explains. It makes them relate. Their horizons expand, too. Every-

body's invited to try one. Everybody does. Including your
own pride and joy, who only yesterday was bugging you
for lollipops while you were taking her home from getting her braces tightened.

Note: The eye-rolling little brunette lighter-upper who
started the pot-puffing is a pusher. And I don't care if
she's a minister's daughter and looks like Rebecca of
Sunnybrook Farm.

This is what makes the dope-peddler so damnably
dangerous. He uses the young to make war on their own
kind. The kids not only fill his pockets; they're his front
men. If someone gets busted by the fuzz, it won't be lovable old Uncle Chuckles, the supplier. It will be one of
the kids who pays him half of every dirty dollar he makes
shoving the stuff. He'll have the felony conviction on his
record; Uncle Chuckles will leave town until the heat's
off.

In other words, this is surrogate warfare. The real
Enemy lies back in the weeds and hires kids to spread
the plague and to take the chances. His closest counterpart in the war against the children is the leftist college professor, who urges the bird-brained student activists on to perform deeds of dastardly derring-do which
he's too lily-livered to tackle himself. It's a classic example of the unpalatable malignantly maneuvered by the
unspeakable.

Why don't the local courts protect your children from
this Enemy? For the same reason they don't protect them
from the pornographer. Like Hamlet, the courts are all
sicklied o'er with the pale cast of thought. After all, the
pusher has his constitutional rights, too, one must remember. He didn't really start out to be bad. Society is
as much to blame as he is. And don't forget his parents,
who probably didn't understand him.

So goes the driveling refrain. And the pusher gets

scolded or fined and turned loose, and in a few days he manages to seduce enough children with his devil drugs to pay off the fine and then some.

Tell me, Judge, have you ever seen a kid try to kick the heroin habit cold turkey? Have you heard him scream like a stuck pig? Have you watched him bend double and vomit until you think he'll never stop? Have you seen him twitch and jerk like a chicken with its head cut off? Have you watched his eyeballs roll back in his head until all you can see are the whites? Have you ever seen him after he's tried to kill himself?

I have. And believe me, Your Honor, if you'd spend a little more time listening to our law-enforcement people and a little less time listening to the lint-brained bleeding-hearts, there would be fewer pushers vending their venom to adolescents because you'd be throwing the book at them whenever they came before you. Which is what you darned well should have been doing all along.

All right, Mom and Pop. How do you recognize the battle-wounds of this sector of the war against your children? Here's what to look for:

(1) Bloodshot eyes and/or dilated pupils. The problem is getting Susie to look you in the eye once she's on the stuff.

(2) A sudden liking for long sleeves. They hide needlemarks so well.

(3) The "dead fish" syndrome. Apathy sets in like rigor mortis.

(4) Odd hours. Inability to sleep regularly is one of the curses that accompany certain kinds of addiction.

(5) Sudden personality changes. If Junior is on LSD, the changes may not be merely sudden. They may be positively Jekyll-and-Hydeish.

Enough to start with? Oh, there are lots of other possible symptoms, such as a drastic drop in school grades and increasing absenteeism from the family bed and board. But these will be enough to clue you in when the Enemy's barrage starts to roll in on your children.

How do you fight back? What to do about the dope syndrome?

First, recognize it for what it is. Just one more symptom of the nation's unraveling moral fiber. A sign of our times. Then resolve to combat it in your own family, mercilessly, unceasingly, with no holds barred. Remember that souls are actually the things at stake in this war you're declaring, and fight accordingly.

Ride herd on your own kids. Know what they keep in their rooms. Know where they go when they aren't home. Know who their friends are. Know what they're doing when you're not around. Don't be ashamed of "interfering" in your children's private lives. That's one of the things parents are for. The penitentiaries are full of people whose parents didn't "interfere" with them when they were kids.

Next, cut off the Enemy's ammunition. If it's necessary to eliminate all trade with the comic-opera countries that produce the raw opium from which heroin is derived, eliminate it. Completely. If we have to close the Mexican border and seal it hermetically in order to stop the flood of marijuana, close it. And keep it closed. Our kids are more important than all the "Good Neighbor" policies in the universe.

Then talk your legislators into equating the laws covering dope-peddling with those that cover poisoning. And why not? After all, cyanide and strychnine kill only the body. Dope destroys body and soul alike.

Stop worrying about educating kids about its effects. They already know, just as they know all about the evils of alcoholism, chain-smoking, and drag-racing on the county highway at midnight. The schools have seen to that. What the schools have never been able to do and never will be able to do is to make young people want to do the things they know they ought to do and avoid the things they know they ought to avoid.

As I said at the start, humanity has always had its dope addicts. But there's a deadly difference today. The hopped-up hashish-eaters of the Old Man of the Mountain were finally hunted down and put out of business. Thomas De Quincy and Samuel Taylor Coleridge and their fellow Victorian opium-addicts practiced their solitary vice in private agony and in public shame.

Today we justify the addict. We prettify an ancient sin. In a hundred smartly written articles in slick journals we tell ourselves that the marijuana puffer isn't nearly so bad as the drunkard because he doesn't suffer from DTs and cirrhosis. The LSD-tripper, wild-eyed and raving, is simply seeking another dimension of experience, tapping hitherto unplumbed depths of cosmic reality.

What unholy nonsense.

In the last few years we have seen the flower-garlanded lotus-eaters roosting naked and pathetically in trees, flinging themselves frantically from high windows, and shriveling and screaming in self-lighted funeral pyres.

Let's quit kidding ourselves. Marijuana is dope—*Cannabis sativa*. It distorts and twists and perverts. Its users all too often graduate to heroin and morphine. Its pushers deserve the heaviest penalty the law allows. And don't fall for that line about alcohol being worse. Even if it were true, since when is any evil justified by the simultaneous existence of another evil?

LSD is chemical madness. So are its multi-initialed derivatives. Under its influence, one poor, damned creature in my own state recently butchered a fellow-user and carried his bloody, hacked-off arm about for days, a fit symbol of the murderous drug that drove him mad.

So, Mom and Pop, when some fast-talker tells you that marijuana is mild and beneficial and non-habit-forming, call him what he is: a dangerous fool. And when one of your mod friends tries to con you into believing that LSD is a fine, constructive, scientific tool for probing the old subconscious, tell him he's standing in the lurid shadow cast by the piled-up corpses of killed youngsters, and then call him a ghoul. Or worse.

Tough advice? You bet. When I'm in a war with an Enemy who is trying to destroy in the most bestial and loathsome way the persons dearest to me in all the world, you'd better believe I can get tough. Frankly, I'd rather see every dope-peddler dead in his pad than see one more innocent kid rotted and gutted by this toxin we're so tolerant of today.

Feel like a negotiated peace instead of a war of extermination?

Hop to it. I'll watch. I want to see how you go about negotiating with dope. Better not dilly-dally too much, though. Every day, it reaches its leprous fingers a little closer to your children's throats.

SECTOR #3—PARENTS AND THE CAMPUS RIOTS

If I may string a few adjectives on the line, today's ugly, violent, pornographic college conspiracy is the first revolution to be fully financed by its own intended victims.

The conspirators are the dirty, hairy, foul-mouthed white members of the so-called Students for a Democratic Society on the one hand, and the fanatical, hate-filled Negro members of the Black Students Union on the other.

The proscribed and condemned victims are, of course, the parents of America. The ones who pay for the self-same campuses where the conspiracy breeds and burgeons. You and I.

Let's take a quick look at what we're financing. First off, here are some of the things the New Left revolution is *not:*

It's *not* a spontaneous protest by sincere young people against intolerable administrative incompetence and oppression. Our college presidents and deans may not be exactly iron-jawed, lightning-fast men of decision. Just the same, American higher education is undoubtedly the best administered in the world. And anybody who claims to be oppressed on an American college campus today is either completely out of touch with reality or a cynical and deliberate liar. Probably the latter.

It's *not* a genuine demand by black students for more participation in campus policymaking. At San Francisco State, for example, the rioters claimed they were fighting for black-studies courses that the college president was callously refusing to provide. Yet the college board of trustees had okayed the establishment of such classes weeks before the riots started. I know. I happen to be a member of the board that okayed them.

And it's *not* a pardonable display of youthful high spirits, nor a visible manifestation of the generation gap, nor yet an unfortunate by-product of the modern quest for "relevance."

But here are some of the things this revoltion *is:*

It *is* a carefully planned, well-financed plot to take over the entire operation and control of public institutions by a highly organized elite corps. When Mussolini did the same thing in the Twenties, we called it Fas-

cism. When Hitler did it in the Thirties, we called it
Nazism. What shall we call it in the Sixties now that
we have it in our own country, slugging its opponents,
threatening its critics, kidnaping, trespassing, vandalizing?

It *is* contrived anarchy, complete with all the depressing appurtenances of hate, confusion, obscenity, and violence that always accompany the denial of legal authority. The anarchists cannot tell you what they would build
upon the ruins of our fathers' America. They can only
give you their blueprint for destruction, and demonstrate
how admirably they are organized as a wrecking crew.
Nothing about them is positive. Everything is negative.

And it *is* international in scope and design. Berkeley,
San Francisco, Northwestern, Columbia, Paris, Berlin,
the Italian universities—the riots went off around the
world like a 6,000-mile string of firecrackers, one following another with relentless precision and with
identical techniques. Coincidence? Maybe. But I stopped
believing in this kind of miraculous interference with
the laws of probability at about the age of five.

Now that you know what the syndrome is as well as
what it isn't, where do you come into the picture, Mom
and Pop?

Well, you come into it definitely in the beginning and
hopefully at the end, too. As a matter of fact, you have
managed of late to confuse the beginning with the end.
When you bought Junior his new MG, established his
bank account, and sent him off in style to dear old Random U., you decided you could stop worrying for four
years and let the dean look after Junior. In effect, you
quit being a parent. You dropped out.

You are wrong.

Nowadays when your offspring sets out for college,
it's no time to relax. It's a time to get involved. What you
should do right off is to visit the campus to see just where

and how Junior is living. Then, about once a month, drop in on your pride and joy. See what he looks like, what he's smoking, how long his hair is, and whether he's bathing with any degree of regularity. If you are laboring under the delusion that you can stop worrying about a simple matter like personal cleanliness when Junior turns eighteen, disabuse yourself.

If you find your son in pretty constant association with a coterie of bearded brigands reminiscent of Ali Baba and the Forty Thieves, haul him home for a long weekend and talk turkey to him. If the college authorities tell you Junior has been bellowing four-letter words on the quad, wash his mouth out with a reasonable facsimile of the soap you used to use. And if Junior then accuses you of being an acquiescing member of the hypocritical, warloving power structure, move in on him in dead earnest.

Tell him you're paying for his education—the good old S.D.S. isn't. He isn't. Nobody else is. Just you.

Tell him, too, that you're not sacrificing to send him to college so that he can major in obscenity, subversion, and Molotov-cocktail-making.

Remind him that you're sending him to school in order to learn, not to take over the place. If he were educated enough to run a college, there would be precious little point in enrolling him there as a student.

And tell him finally to shape up or ship out. If he refuses, cut off his money. Every nickel of it. Tell him he is an ex-college student as of right now, with a choice of going to work or going into the army if he wants to keep on eating. When and if he decides he wants to go back to college to learn instead of to shoot off his mouth, then you'll be glad to talk it over with him.

Too tough for you? Too cold and heartless? It had better not be.

What's at stake now for all of us is not only the future

of higher education in this country but also the survival of our democratic institutions in the face of mounting student and faculty totalitarianism. I'd infinitely rather yank my son out of school than see him terrorize and subvert that same school on my hard-earned money.

The most important lesson you can teach Junior at any age is that a public institution must be run by the public, through representatives responsible to that public, not run by stray and grimy groups of students and professors responsible to nobody on God's earth except themselves alone.

Granted, it's pretty late to teach Junior this when he's in college. But apparently you didn't teach it to him earlier, and he's never going to learn any younger. And learned it simply must be, for the sake of generations yet unborn.

So get with it. There'll be heartaches ahead, no doubt, if you hit Junior in the pocketbook. But at least you won't be suicidally subsidizing a Reign of Terror in which you yourselves are the first intended victims of Madame Guillotine.

SECTOR #4—PARENTS AND ENTERTAINMENT

The matinee idol is at least as old as Shakespeare. Probably he's as old as drama itself. Every generation has had its quota of theatrical sex symbols who wowed the ladies, especially the callower and downier members of the gentle sex. Burbage was one, back in Elizabethan days. So was Garrick a little later. So in a small way was John Wilkes Booth, before he stopped his ladykilling for bigger game.

Heavy-lidded and dilated-nostriled, the stage messiah trod the boards, filling his palpitating admirers with delicious dreams of dubious dalliance, breathing sighs, telling lies. Usually he was harmless as a cream-puff.

After Valentino and Barrymore, the theatrical stud began to give way to a new phenomenon, the entertainment idol. Rudy Vallee was the first big one. With his wavy hair, nasal croon, and ubiquitous megaphone, Rudy cut a stunning swath through the serried ranks of swooning flappers until the Roaring Twenties looked like the aftermath of the St. Valentine's Day massacre.

Similarly, Crosby dominated the Hungry Thirties, Sinatra the Fighting Forties, and Elvis Presley the Fortunate Fifties. All were magnets for teen-agers, and thus were regarded with considerable suspicion by the jaundiced and dyspeptic Elders of the Tribe. Yet none of them attempted deliberately to corrupt their unfledged worshipers. Such a spectacle was seemingly reserved by fate for our own time.

Oh, they committed certain venial sins. Bing wore atrocious sports shirts, Frank was skinny and uncommonly belligerent, and Elvis swiveled his hips like Little Egypt. But that was about the worst you could say about these original objects of adolescent affection.

They didn't mouth four-letter words over the mike, grimacing the while like a retarded rapist.

They didn't brag smirkingly about how many little girls they had seduced.

They didn't dope themselves up and appear in public looking and acting like graduates of one of the insidious Dr. Fu Manchu's more odorous opium dens.

And most emphatically they didn't go around advising kids to defy their parents, break the law, and hate their country.

My, how times have changed!

Here are some of the more hysterically adulated entertainers of today's "Now" generation:

One prematurely haggard young woman boasts a full head of stringy, greasy hair, a permanently bemused expression, and a repertoire of songs that sound as though they had been written by Kosygin. Her husband dodges the draft, and she herself dodges taxes. She genuflects noisily before the altar of free speech, but when a cartoonist lampoons her mildly in the guise of "Joany Phony," she sues him for his shirt.

A mangy male counterpart regularly gets so looped he practically has to be propped up in front of the mike. He boasts that he's tried everything, and looks it. He urges his wide-eyed audience to go and do likewise. Quite a few foreign countries won't even let him in because they don't want their kids contaminated by an imported creep.

Then there are a couple of brothers who apparently decided a few years back that while comedy had always been their fame, revolution was in fact their game. Everyone who had a kind word to say for patriotism, law and order, or even simple decency became their target for tonight. They leer at morality, sneer at virtue, and howl "Persecution!" at the top of their bad voices whenever one of their victims conjures up enough nerve to fight back, or when they get kicked off the air. They project the fine, constructive public image of two sick termites gnawing intermittently at the skirts of the Statue of Liberty.

So far, I've subconsciously avoided mentioning the myriad rock groups—all sweat, sex, and sound—that multiply like maggots and all too often look like them. Frankly, they're nothing to contemplate if you happen to have a queasy stomach. I used to think these guitar-twanging combos served a halfway useful function, if only because they afforded a profitable refuge for some of our hairier misfits who otherwise would have to be supported from the public purse. More recently, however, and especially since they began taking their clothes off in public, I've had second thoughts about these off-key outfits. Lord knows they were repulsive enough dressed.

In the current war against your children, the Entertainers constitute the enemy's fifth column. They infiltrate the youngsters' ranks with goofy psychedelic lights, sick "in" jokes, and the Big Beat. They soften the kids up for sex, drugs, and treason. They tell your offspring that having a ball is the only thing worth doing, that hard work is laughably square, and that literally anything goes in the brave new world of which they are the grating, twitching, eyeball-rolling harbingers.

All down the long trail of human existence, kids have had two traits in common: love of fun, and a desire to shock. The Entertainers play on these age-old characteristics, and they play on them well. In fact, they're about the only things they do play very well. But it's a far cry from furnishing fun to popularizing pot, and from supplying stimulation to retailing revolution.

One best-selling record in praise of marijuana is thinly disguised as a children's nursery song. Another is a paraphrased paean to homosexuality. Still another is a whining, whimpering attack on the alleged beastliness of Mom and Pop.

A recently deceased comic was so flatulently filthy that even our all-tolerant courts wouldn't have him running around loose. One of his still above-ground colleagues goes all over the country inciting race riots. And a precious pair of so-called innovative comedians specialize in introducing the double entendre and the off-color joke to television, a medium that goes into more homes than the milkman, the plumber, and the family doctor all put to-gether.

Entertainers like these are the Typhoid Marys of mo-rality. They sneak into your home, they infect your fam-ily, and then they're gone to spread the virus to somebody else's kids tomorrow.

What to do about them?

(1) Make a list of the upbeat Entertainers and patron-ize them. There are lots of straight singers, decent danc-ers, clean comics still around. And they're not all dodder-ing old Grandpas, either. Don't make the mistake of lump-ing all the Entertainers in one bad basket. You can do this safely with the pornographers and the dope-pushers. Not with the Entertainers.

(2) Remember that money talks, especially in their highly competitive business. When Junior wants some cash to go to a teen show, find out just what the enter-tainment's going to be. Bone up on who's who with the high school set. If the combo is downbeat, hang onto your wallet. If the guitar-twanger sings vile lyrics, don't give Junior a nickel. If the comedian is telling dirty jokes and promoting civil war, tell Junior to stay home. And make it stick.

(3) When one of these reptilian, hissing, and spitting apostles of hate shows up on your favorite radio or TV show, write two letters: one to the network and one to the sponsor. Tell them you're going to give them one more chance to clean their dirty linen and to improve their image with you and that the next time they permit this kind of poison to pollute the channels, you and your friends are going to boycott them as they've never been boycotted before.

(4) Teach your own children the difference between talent and trash. Make them know that an excellent meas-

ure of a man is what amuses him. Accustom them from infancy to wholesome, intelligent, clean fun. When they grow up, they won't be interested in the other kind.

There's really only one way to fight the Entertainer in his own special sector of the war against your children.

With better entertainment.

SECTOR #5—PARENTS AND RELIGION

We teachers could use a little help from our fellow professionals. Instead, some of the nation's judges, for instance, raise holy Ned with us every time one of our graduating classes wants to hold a baccalaureate ceremony, and they conjure up the combined ghosts of Blackstone, John Marshall, and "Bloody" Jeffreys to frighten us whenever we let some hapless kindergartener say a word of simple thanks to his Creator for his daily cup of milk.

The swingers among our medical friends, on their part, have recently begun to equip junior high school girls with contraceptives in order to remove any possible deterrant to all-out fun and games among the bobby-sox and bubblegum set while simultaneously urging classroom courses in "How to Drink Like a Gentleman" for students who may be more interested in boozing than in bedding.

It's the way-out preachers, however, who are currently handing us educators our biggest crosses to bear. It's tough enough to try to teach moral and ethical values to children who have just read in a national magazine the simpering statement by Rev. A. G. Nostic that God has suddenly died or who have watched on television Bishop Perch's lip-smacking homage to topless burlesque dancers. But when certain of our robed and mitred colleagues start crusading on behalf of organized sexual perversion, we poor pedagogues are indeed, as the French say, given furiously to think.

In fact, I'm thinking pretty furiously right now about a certain Dr. Clarence Colwell, who at last account was president of something called the San Francisco Council on Religion and the Homosexual. The good reverend recently pressed a law suit in the California courts designed to compel the State Fair Commission to grant his gregarious little group the right to distribute its literature on the fair grounds to all comers.

Now, I'll have to admit that I haven't been thinking too much of late about the need to make homosexuals happy. But now that the clerical and canonical Dr. Colwell has taken up the cudgels for the nance and the lesbian, I suppose I'll have to re-examine my attitude toward the third sex.

I've always felt kind of sorry for the sodomite, much as I would feel sorry for a neighbor afflicted with leprosy or even elephantiasis. I'd be willing to go a considerable distance to help him or cure him, just as I'd be willing to nurse a case of catatonia or paranoia. But I have to confess I'd never think it necessary to parade him in public and let him propagandize the uninfected.

To Dr. Colwell I must seem hopelessly square. So it seems that we dull normals must move over and give the homosexual his just desserts. He's not unfortunate or criminal or even sick. He has a perfect right to go around in his miniskirt and high heels, solicit more members for his sad circle, and pass out his literature to the wide-eyed kiddies come to the fair. In fact, he's really just as normal as we are, and maybe in time he will even be considered our superior.

With all due respect to the crusading Dr. Colwell— who, incidentally, has gone the founder of his faith one better by trying to proselytize with writs of mandamus rendered unto him by Caesar—I must respectfully dissent, not only on philosophical but on practical grounds.

An illness is not cured by bragging about it and legalizing it and gussying it all up until the patient has been kidded into believing he's really the doctor.

Also, if homosexuality becomes the righteous rule rather than the sick exception, my teaching colleagues and I will find our professional futures a trifle curtailed, to say the least. As a matter of cold fact, we'll all be out of a job, and the Great Society will have to provide us with expensive vocational rehabilitation, perhaps retraining us as manufacturers of falsies for male transvestites.

Seriously, gentlemen of the cloth, aren't there enough individual souls in need of saving to keep you usefully and vitally employed without messing around with a sociological and biological Pandora's box like this one?

Medicine has its quacks and its fake cancer cures. Law has its shysters and its ambulance chasing. And religion, it seems, has its relativists.

The quacks can kill you. The shysters can rob you. The relativists can shrivel up your faith in everything large, divine, and comfortable until you're left with a little, rotten, shredded ball of shoddy skepticism flavored with an occasional dash of sheer superstition. Relativism is like that.

A child will usually believe what he's told, particularly if you tell him often enough. Education, mine own calling, is built upon the humdrum but necessary ritual of teach and test, reteach and retest, seemingly ad infinitum and now and then ad nauseam. So it must follow as relentlessly as punishment used to follow crime that what the individual is told day after day all through childhood is going to be damnably important, either for good or for ill.

With this primordial truism firmly in mind, those who

came before us on this continent took pains to see (a) that their children went to church regularly, and (b) that while there they were exposed to the time-tested truths of our 5000-year-old Judaeo-Christian heritage, not to the half-baked quasi-existentialist mouthings of some ego-centric jack-bishop.

Until our own time.

Note well the battlecries and the warwhoops of today's relativist preachers:

"God is dead. Nay, brethren, verily he never existed, save in your own childish cravings for supernatural support and solace."

"There is no soul, so forget about the need to save it."

"Get out of the church and onto the picket lines."

"Forget what Christ said about the need to render unto Caesar. Instead, rebel against Caesar, and if at all possible, do Caesar in."

and

"No more celibate, gentle, otherworldly priest, eyes fixed adoringly on Christ and Eternity. Hail instead the advent of the sexy, militant, involved social reformer with reversed collar and inverted Gospels, interested only in the Here and Now."

Some revolting reverends in my own state have within the past few years boycotted some of their own parishioners for the heinous sin of farming their own land as their fathers had farmed it before them. And they have condemned with almost pagan eloquence the earnest efforts of our State Board of Education to set up a few modest moral guidelines for classroom instruction.

Elsewhere, the mod ministers have sneered at the Virgin Birth, poked fun at the divinity of Christ, and mocked at any notion of personal immortality. Some of them invite known atheists to harangue their flocks. Others set up rock combos instead of choirs and frug their way through swinging services right in front of the alter. Hell they have eliminated even as an hypothesis, except, of course, for those who have to listen to their sermons.

In this connection, and apprehensively, I want to make it clear that I love Presbyterians. So I hope they won't cloud up and rain Calvinistic brimstone all over me when I tell them as gently as I can that one of their United Presbyterian church's special commissions is full of apple strudel.

Some months ago the commission members came out with a great gust of hedonism in favor of idleness, play, and just plain lying around as opposed to the corny alternative of industry, diligence, and good hard work. Speaking purely personally, this is fine with me, as indeed it is with most of the Irish, who have traditionally preferred to pluck harpstrings and to go haring off after leprechaun gold rather than to lay bricks and carry hods.

But take a look at some of the commission's further comments: "Part of our mental furniture is that 'every man should work for what he gets.' The man who lives off the labors of others is judged guilty of the sin of sloth: he is somehow less than a man."

And: "Neither toil nor . . . labor is glorified by the Scriptures as the ultimate spiritual necessity."

And finally: "We can take seriously those who suggest that Adam fell when his play became serious—when he became work-oriented."

Come on, fellows! Are you seriously suggesting that a man shouldn't work for what he gets? That he should sponge off some poor devil who isn't lucky enough or irresponsible enough to loaf through life relying on some unfortunate George to do his work for him? Somebody has to raise the radishes and dig the coal, gentlemen, or there will be a drastic and noticeable absence of both.

As for toil being in the scriptural doghouse, I always thought that when Adam got dispossessed from the primeval Garden, one of the promises echoing in his departing ears was that from then on he was going to be eating bread in the sweat of his face. One of the Psalms tells us that God renders to each man according to his work, and although I almost hate to mention it to the worthy reverends on the commission, even a certain commandment says pretty directly: "Six days shalt thou labor, and do all thy work."

Why am I flying into such a snit about the Presbyterian commission's recent Ode to Indolence? Because of the effect of this sort of sanctified buffoonery on schoolchildren. It's hard enough at best to get thirty-odd nimble, restless, fidgety seventh-graders to study regularly, turn in assignments on time, and hit the books every evening without having some full-of-the-devil, cheeky kid in the front row raise his hand and sound off to teacher that Adam got the boot when he became work-oriented.

Troubles we educators have in the normal course of events. Worries we share. Calamities like the Presbyterian commission's praise of folly we don't need.

Do these church-sponsored coveys of clerics and packs of parsons that seem to be spawning like upstream salmon these days have any idea of what they are doing to education when they persist in trumpeting across the land their own weird gospel consisting of the harmlessness of homosexuality, the delights of demonstrating, and the probity of premarital sex?

Do they realize that even if children may be too young to practice any of the new cardinal virtues enumerated in the preceding sentence, they are rarely too young to understand a bunch of muddle-headed ministers who announce that we mortals are put upon this planet to live it up all 365 days every year, and that "work"—if not a positively naughty word—is at least a highly irreligious word under the terms of the New Dispensation?

Let's wearily try to get our semantics straight under this latest onslaught.

Work is what school is all about. Hard work. Regular work. No one can get an education without working at it. Education's daily terminology is as old as the hills: "homework," "schoolwork," "written work."

If you do away with work, you do away with education. And please don't give me a lot of guff about the need for education to be fun. Of course it should. So should work. The most fun in the world.

For churchmen thus to trumpet the delights of doing nothing, the blessings of idleness, and the sanctity of loafing is about as helpful to your kids as it would be for us teachers to come out with a great gust of public praise for playing hookey and dropping out of school.

Equally helpful are the recent burglaries of draft-board offices by foamingly self-righteous members of the clergy, who barge around inside other people's filing cabinets with disgusting buckets of blood and suchlike nastiness. Conduct like this is bound to raise in the child's mind this interesting question: "If it is okay for Reverend Jones to break into buildings, destroy property, and even to walk off with things that don't belong to him, then why shouldn't it be okay for me?"

Then there are the socialized Sunday schools. More and more of them are spending less and less time on the great Bible stories, preferring instead to propagandize the small fry with such highly unspiritual causes as the grape strike, the need for slum clearance, and the iniquity of American foreign policy.

One eminent Anglican theologian, Professor Joseph Fletcher, announced in the kind of stentorian tones formerly reserved for the breaking of the seals in the Book of Revelation: "Sex is clearly in the category of recreation. In sex, we call freedom 'love.' In politics, we call it 'democracy.' "

In short, fellow parents, we now find ourselves in a box where if we preach continence and virginity to our own children we run the risk of being denounced from the pulpit as undemocratic. This equating of free love with free speech would, I'm sure, have intrigued T. Jefferson and A. Jackson no end, and when carried to its logical conclusion, it will no doubt result in the election of *Playboy* magazine's Hugh Hefner to the Presidency one of these days.

The trouble with this kind of church-blessed nonsense is that it erodes one of the great pillars that have always undergirded the superstructure of society: organized religion. Children grow up with no absolute values, no sense of sacred truths, no confidence in the ultimate difference between right and wrong.

There's no deadlier enemy than the Sick Preacher in the war against your children, if only because the churchman down the ages has always been the most steadfast source of strength and inspiration to the young. If a child cannot look to the clergy to set an example of obedience to law, reverence for virtue, and belief in the indestructibility of the human soul, to whom can he look?

So when a man of the cloth goes wrong, no matter what the reason, and when he starts perverting eternal verities instead of preserving them, he's a more dangerous corrupter of youth than the Devil himself. He attains the same doubtful eminence as the policeman who goes on the take, except that the crooked cop usually bollixes up only his own small segment of earthly law and justice, whereas the malfeasant minister may affect the chances of many for the hereafter itself.

A few modest suggestions about what you as an individual can do:

(1) Get active in your local church. Interest yourself more than somewhat in the theories, the thinking, and the theology of your own pastor. If he's a true shepherd of his flock, interested primarily in the salvation of their souls, support him. If he's a Judas goat for the forces of doubt, divisiveness, and decay, fire him.

(2) See that your local church has written policies governing the selection of its next minister. And see that the next man knows precisely the kind of pastor the congregation wants and expects.

(3) Withdraw all contributions from any church that has ceased to concern itself with the Gospel and has become instead a mere critic of government. America has plenty of critics. What we need so desperately today are men and churches who can help us to save our souls.

(4) If you find that your church no longer agrees with you, change churches.

SECTOR #6—PARENTS AND CRIME

These are your children, and they are all colors—white, black, brown, and in-between. A growing number of them are just plain criminals. Whose fault is it?

Yours. Here's why:

As one example of what's wrong, in recent years you've been yanking your kids out of school on the slightest pretext in order to protest some adult grievance. In New York and Chicago, to single out just two from among many, we've seen the ultimate absurdity occur. Black parents teach their offspring to violate the law when they decide that a school is insufficiently integrated, and white parents do the same to illustrate their disagreement with what they consider overzealous attempts by the school board to mix the races.

This attitude on the part of so many parents, if carried to its logical if stupid conclusion, will result in half the pupils being out on strike permanently. It will result in something else, too: Junior will grow up thinking it's okay to behave illegally, because that's the example you're setting for him right now.

If you as a parent tell your child that the law is a lot of eyewash, that something or somebody is more important than the law—and that therefore it's perfectly all right to break the law in order to bring about a better way of life, or equality of housing, or a more relevant college curriculum or indeed anything under the sun including the millennium right here on earth—then your child cannot be greatly blamed if later on in life he applies this rule to other laws as he sees fit.

And I say: "How dare you?" Literally, how do you dare to open a Pandora's box like this one, fraught as it is with such dreadful portent for the future and for the children who must inhabit that future?

It's bad enough when Johnny sees you flout the speed laws whenever the highway patrol is out of sight. It's bad enough when he hears you bragging each April about how much you got away with on your income-tax return. It's bad enough when he watches you roar off in the car after a cocktail party, smelling like a distillery.

But when you encourage Junior himself to break the law for any reason whatever, then you are playing the role of Fagin to your own family.

Of course, it's not just you. You're getting a lot of help these days in raising Junior to be a scofflaw. What about the union teachers, who in many parts of our country are now walking out of schools in complete violation of their signed contracts and often in equal contempt of explicit legislation forbidding such actions on the part of public employees? From New York to California, and in a score of cities in between, teachers who have sworn to help children, not to hurt them, have stalked out on their pupils because they happened to disapprove of certain school-board regulations, leaving their classrooms unattended and the children uninstructed. We need not be surprised if we detect among those same children in future years a somewhat hilarious attitude toward the sanctity of any and all laws, to say nothing about the ultimate altruism and dedication of us educators.

What about those businessmen who conspire among themselves to fix prices or to violate the antitrust laws? These leaders of their communities justify themselves to our youth by stressing the highly technical nature of the ordinances they are engaged in defying, and by pointing to their dollar-spangled respectability in other fields of conduct. But the fact that a man may be kind to animals and a regular churchgoer on Sundays does not excuse him from gypping his neighbors every other day of the week. Indeed, his very high position does much to persuade the children that gypping one's neighbors under certain technical circumstances may be perfectly all right.

What about such fine examples of national leadership as were exemplified in recent years by certain utterances by some of our leading political figures to the effect that America's future leaders will be chosen on the basis of their prison records and experience in civil disobedience rather than on any nonsense about law-abiding rectitude? This is the first time to my knowledge that any American in a high government office has openly advocated violating the law of the land, at least since the days of the late and unlamented Aaron Burr. It opens up fascinating vistas for the youngsters, this cheery, offhand incitement to riot. Apparently our own tots, instead of emulating Washington's truthfulness and Lincoln's honesty, are now to vie with one another for the privilege of clobbering some cop en route to the White House and "national leadership" by way of the nearest reform school.

I guess I'm just not hip to this brave new world we're being urged to adjust to these days. I can see nothing glorious or glamorous about defying the law—any law—much less any built-in guarantee of "national leadership" in 1995. Any cheap hood can break the law, and does, every day.

I can see something else, though: the decline of citizenship, and public ethics, and private morality, stemming from our own gay disregard of any code save our own whims, any law except what we want to follow to gain our momentary ends.

When we teach our children to sneer and to mock at the statutes that alone stand between them and chaos, we are hatching countless chickens that will sooner or later come home to roost. Faced with such upside-down value systems outside the schools, we are simultaneously confronted with a threatened breakdown of discipline inside them. This has been going on for some time, but like most other things, it started first in the home and hit the schools comparatively recently. The prime mover in this change was the "new" psychology, which was widely publicized a few years ago and caused parents to doubt their proper role vis-à-vis their children for the first time in the history of the human race.

Fathers began to hear of the "Oedipus complex," and were urged to search their souls before spanking Junior lest their real motivation turn out to be subconscious rivalry for Mom's affections. Mothers were told about the "inferiority complex," and were frightened out of their wits at the thought of "repressing" Junior. Both Mom and Pop were sternly told to get out of the way and let their child express himself unless they wanted him to blame his parents in later life for the traumatic psychoses that were almost certain to crop up.

The result was the emergence of the least-repressed and worst-behaved generation this world had ever seen. As a child, Junior played with his toys but refused to put them away, threw the spinach on the dining-room floor but got the ice cream anyway, sassed his parents to their faces and got away with it. As a teen-ager, Junior stole the old man's whiskey and shared it with the gang, drag-raced on the county highway at midnight with the family car, and told both the cop and the judge to go to hell when he was finally hauled in. He feared nothing and respected nobody because he had never learned at an early age to do either. The psychologists had been right about one thing: Junior certainly had no repressions. He could have used a few.

The implications for education of the "new" psychology were obvious. The teacher found himself worked over by two formidable conditioners: the psychologists, who naturally couldn't have the schools undoing the "good" that they were so vigorously promoting in the home; and the parents themselves, who naturally couldn't bear to have teacher discipline Junior when they themselves were afraid to.

We're confronted today by the perfectly ridiculous spectacle of the teacher being afraid of some of his pupils, where in the past the situation was the other way around. In several of our big-city schools, policemen have to be stationed in the corridors in order to protect the teacher from his pupils, and the pupils from each other. Education languishes hopelessly in such an environment. I'm reminded of the overly fond parents who sent little Johnny to a new school with a note reading: "Our John is extremely sensitive. At home we never use corporal punishment in any form. If he misbehaves badly in class, just spank the boy sitting next to him. This will frighten Johnny."

A lot of this is just misplaced indulgence. A lot more can be traced to the door of the child "experts." During my student teaching days, I was fed an unmixed diet of complete permissiveness. A teacher who used corporal punishment, I was told, was simply admitting he was a poor teacher, because a good one would have gotten results in some other way. This principle was extended to cover most other forms of externally imposed discipline and jibes perfectly with the rationale of the Progressive Educationists, who scoff at the idea of absolute values or positive standards in anything. "What is of lasting value to one child," they say, "may well be of no value at all to another. Thus the thing to ascertain is the particular need of the individual child and meet that 'felt need' as it becomes apparent to the child himself."

Apply this philosophy to school discipline and it becomes immediately obvious that "standards" of classroom behavior are hopelessly out of date. One child may have the need to engage in more than average "large-muscle activity." In layman's language, this means he wants to run around the room a lot. Another child, probably as the result of unhealthy repression at home, must achieve disinhibition in school through "spontaneous verbal sharings in normally inappropriate group situations." Put crudely, this means that the child shoots his mouth off all the time to his classmates while the teacher is trying to get some work done. Even the pupil who swears at the teacher and who writes dirty words on the blackboard may simply be discharging some pent-up neuroses stemming from an unhealthy family conflict.

The remedy usually prescribed by the educational theorists is some form of psychological approach to the child and his conduct. The teacher may conduct lengthy "sociogram" studies of the individual in relation to his "peer group." She may administer "pupil-personality inventory" tests in order to gain some sort of understanding of the trauma that has led to the undesirable behavior pattern. She may even feel obliged to pry into the most intimate relations of Mom and Pop and attempt to discover which of the two Junior loves more, and why.

Now, if we assume that Junior is running all over the classroom and talking to his friends when he ought to be listening to the teacher, and is engaging in scatological defiance of the constituted authorities because he is mentally sick, then I suppose all this elaborate paraphernalia makes some kind of sense. But suppose Junior refuses to stay in his seat simply because he prefers to run around? Suppose he talks all the time because no one has ever told him to button his lip? Suppose he uses four-letter words because he's full of the devil and wants to shock people? I submit that it's far more logical to make this assumption than it is to assume that Junior is a candidate for the psychiatrist, if only because millions of boys have had the itch to do these things since time began, and relatively few of them have ended up in the booby hatch.

We do get a few truly sick children in our schools and they absolutely do need individual help. The ordinary techniques of discipline are not for these children. But any teacher worth her salt can spot these disturbed pupils within a very short time and try to get special help for them. I question the whole thesis of erecting an elaborate and expensive structure of test-based machinery on the false premise that the needs of the microscopically small minority constitute in fact the needs of the great majority. Most children, as I have known them and worked with them over the last years, are healthy, remarkably tough little organisms. They respond quite well indeed to healthy, moderately tough disciplinary methods, which most school people are still quite willing to supply if we could just get a little support from Mom and Pop.

Recently a junior high school vice-principal caught some thirty of his more extroverted eighth-grade boys staging a knock-down-drag-out brawl in the school cafeteria. The administrator was concerned. Presumably the uproar might cause digestive upsets among the less gladiatorially inclined cafeteria patrons. At the very least it worked considerable wear and tear on the furniture. So he hauled the snarling combatants into his office and proceeded to lay the wood to them. Literally. In fact, he paddled the bejabbers out of them.

The results were horrendous. Tears flowed. Irate parents stormed the school office, demanding that the vice-principal not only be disavowed and censured, but also required to swear a mighty oath on the sacred relics of St. John Dewey that he would never, never lift his hand to one of his pupils again.

The newspapers got into the act. So did television. For more than the traditional nine days, front-page photos featured close-ups of nude gluteus maximuses complete with bruises, and the TV boys went the press one better by lining the thirty martyrs up before the color cameras so that a harrowed public might view the terminal contusions in the original black and blue. One jaundiced surveyor of the three-ring news orgy commented that he hadn't seen so many people with their pants down publicly since the onset of the Bobby Baker case.

Several things about the affair were somehow lost sight of. One was the locale of the student scrimmage. A cafeteria is a mighty poor place to stage a riot, with its inevitable accouterments of sharp knives, heavy crockery, and fires blazing under assorted pots. The uninhibited use of such an arena for gang rumbles might well produce results considerably more lethal than two dozen bruised buttocks.

Another factor is the immemorial role of corporal punishment in teaching kids what to do and what not to do. Prior to our own time, school discipline was built around the liberal use of the rod, and when the small fry discussed a "bircher" they were not necessarily talking about a conservative.

Anyone who has watched a mother bear with her cubs can testify that in the animal kingdom, too, the training of the young is conducted to an obbligato of cuffing and ear-boxing. Our primitive ancestors taught stern survival to their offspring and brooked no nonsense in the process. In an environment where failure to learn what Kipling was to call the "Laws of the Jungle" meant swift death, the Old Man of the tribe was not likely to spare the rod.

Later tribal societies continued enthusiastically to couple learning with larruping. The Bible, in a well-known verse, tells us the best way to spoil a child, and the story of the Spartan boy and the fox affords an object lesson in the way that stark consociation disciplined its young.

Greece and Rome continued to rely on corporal punishment as a matter of course, and during the troubled Middle Ages the whipping boy became an institution and later a metaphorical ornament to half a dozen European tongues.

School in those days was considered a mighty serious business and was conducted that way. Two premises were almost universally accepted: (1) that boys will not behave in school unless compelled to do so and (2) that boys must be made to behave so they can learn things they have to know.

Obviously we can't have teachers committing mayhem on their pupils, but in my more than a quarter of a century in the education business I've never known one who did. They're more apt to harm the child through leniency and mistaken indulgence than they are to hurt him physically. What parents should remember is that in this life there are inner flaws vastly more devastating than a blemished posterior and habits and attitudes potentially more destructive than any reddened rear end.

It's fashionable these days to scoff at punishment, to stress rewards and benefits and "life adjustment." And all these things are fine.

But life is not all rewards. When the vice-principal in the most recent paddling case was called upon the carpet, he said, "I hated to do it. But the boys had to learn that when you do wrong you get hurt. I'd do it again."

Is there anybody who thinks this isn't life? And isn't life what we pay teachers to get our children ready for?

It's within this context, then, that I propose we re-examine the role of the public school in preparing for good citizenship. I submit two premises for your consideration:

(1) That if society is to have a future at all, adults are going to have to respect the rules of the society; and

(2) That children, before they grow up to be adults, must be taught not only to abide by the law, but also to behave generally in a decent, responsible, humane way.

Recently, in communications to every local school board in my state, I urged that time be set aside each day for special instruction in the duties of good citizenship and that greatly increased emphasis be placed by every teacher upon upgrading sharply the everyday standards of pupil conduct and classroom behavior. The whole vast machinery of California's educational system—greatest in the nation—is presently being geared to turn out in the future young people who will honor the law, not defy it, and who will value the safety and the rights of their fellow citizens, not trample on them. I cannot guarantee, of course, that the new stress on individual deportment in the schools will in itself bring about a profound change in our national morality. I can only guarantee that we're going to give it the old college try.

And we can use help from you.

We're going to have to teach our kids to obey laws even when they don't agree with them—*especially* when they don't agree with them—and to try to change those laws only through due process, not through the profoundly alien tactics of intimidation, coercion and violence.

Too many of us are spending too much time harping on how bad things are—how the country is going to pot down the long, long road of Egypt and of Greece and of Rome and of the other civilizations that discarded morals in favor of "anything goes!"—how modesty and morality and virtue are all going down the drain. I propose that instead of continuing to wring our hands helplessly and view with alarm, we get to work, each of us, in our own homes, our own businesses, our own churches, to clean this mess up. This nation still has millions of fine, decent citizens, young and old. They have been for almost two hundred years our most precious national resource. What we've got to do now is to see that the decent get the brass rings. We've got to make respectability popular for a change, and licentiousness bad business. This is a job for all of us.

SECTOR #7—WHY PARENTS ARE RESPONSIBLE FOR OUR CURRENT MESS

Children mirror the conditions under which they are raised. The old bromide about the minister's scapegrace son notwithstanding, a youngster brought up in a sober, studious, courteous, Godfearing family is ninety-nine times out of a hundred going to grow up to be a sober, studious, courteous, Godfearing adult. And the young Abraham Lincoln notwithstanding also, the scion of a drunken, shiftless, ne'er-do-well, uninterested parent is all too apt to take on one or more of these unlovely qualities as he grows older.

This is why I keep saying that most youthful delinquencies go back to Mom and Pop, one way or another. Parental indifference, laziness, and just plain stupidity sow the seeds that blossom into the evil flowers we see blooming in almost every headline these days. Here, for the record, are Mom and Pop's most frequent cop-outs:

(1) *They don't know where their children are.* Every time a tearful mother or a long-faced father comes to me with a dreary account of Susie's unaccountable pregnancy at the age of fourteen or of Junior's brush with the law over a "borrowed" car, I ask the single pesky question: "Did you know where your children were every time they were away from home? And if not, why not?"

(2) *They have a sublimely chuckle-headed faith unequaled since the heyday of Wilkins Micawber that something will somehow turn up to assure a happy ending for their particular offspring.* Other people's children, no. Theirs, yes. Just because they're theirs. Further, that "something," for all the world like Euripides's deus ex machina descending from a stage heaven to the accom-

paniment of creaking machinery offstage, will magically put everything right without the slightest interruption of Pop's televised baseball game or Mom's bridge party.

(3) *As I've said, parents give their children too darned much money to spend and never bother to check up on how it's spent.* Recently I read some interesting complaints from various European police chiefs about nomadic American adolescents who were clapped into *durance vile* a couple of summers ago for sundry misdeeds while roaming the Continent with lots of francs and lire in their pockets and with their nearest parent three thousand miles away across the broad Atlantic.

(4) *They talk a good fight.* Parents find it easy to give orders to Junior, to bicker interminably with him, and to threaten dire consequences. But somehow the orders don't get carried out, the bickering remains devoid of anything but wind, and the consequences are still hanging fire in some purely hypothetical future.

Reason: It's just too unpleasant and tiring to really go to the mat with Junior.

Result: Junior regards his parents as a couple of blowhards. And why not?

(5) *Too many of them set a perfectly lousy example.* Some parents chide their sons for drinking while they themselves are brandishing their third predinner martini, and they counsel sagely with their daughters on the evil effects of tobacco while half-hidden in a choking cloud of their own cigarette smoke. A child can't be blamed too much, after all, if he views with a slightly jaundiced eye his father's uplifting lectures on the depravity of sexual promiscuity delivered in a context dominated by the old man's notorious pursuit of every good-looking stenographer in the downtown office. What all this boils down to is simple selfishness. Too many

parents today are saying, "Don't do as I do; do as I tell you."

You want to bask in the warm aura of a happy home, but you don't want to give up anything in order to make the basking possible. You want the privileges of domesticity without sacrificing any of the carefree joys of bachelorhood. You want to enjoy your children, but you don't want to become overly involved with them.

You dropped out of the sex puzzle by refusing to give your children the ancient rules of morality, modesty, and simple decency and then enforcing those rules justly, swiftly, and drastically.

You dropped out of the dope hangup by fat-headedly assuming that your kids would never stoop to drugs and turning them loose with plenty of pocket money in a jungle of teenage addicts and pushers.

And you dropped out of the college orgy of violence, obscenity, and subversion by washing your hands of Junior after you got him safely registered and in residence at good old Random U.

What's to be done about it? Plenty.

If Junior hasn't yet passed the point of no return, rein him in. If he has, concentrate on his younger brothers and sisters. Institute strict household rules on conduct and behavior and stick to them. Starting at about the age of three, make sure that every child you're responsible for from here on knows the difference between such old-fashioned words as "right" and "wrong," "virtue" and "sin," "honor" and "dishonor," "good" and "evil." Make sure, too, that their virtue is promptly rewarded and that their sins are swiftly punished.

Above all, make them earn the money you give them, and even then don't give them too much. And try to get together with the parents of your child's friends and talk them into doing the same thing.

In closing, I trust that any possible youthful reader will take due heed of all these parental peccadilloes I've been dwelling on and avoid them when he, too, becomes a parent. If all his peers could somehow be brought to a rough likemindedness, then in about one generation we could eliminate all our reform schools, most of our prisons, and a good many of our asylums.

Anyone want to bet on the enigmatic future?

I'll be glad to hold the money.

CROSSROAD #6

The Struggle over Reading

SHORTLY AFTER 1965's bloody rioting in Los Angeles, I asked a leading Negro educator what the schools could do to help prevent similar outbreaks in different places. His answer was illuminating enough to pass on to you in six parts:

First, do whatever is necessary to get your finest, most inspirational teachers into the slum schools, where they are most needed. If this means educational "flight pay," so be it.

Second, hunt up the best-qualified educators you can find who are themselves members of minority races and put them into some of your school district's top administrative and supervisory positions.

Third, tell them to get into the slum areas and spend some time there instead of just driving through once in a while in the district limousine. Have them hold meetings with parents and visit classes and set up priority listings of local problems and work out ways to solve them.

Fourth, see that each classroom teacher has enough time, incentive, and protection to get out of his classroom every so often and into the homes of his pupils. This may be a traumatic experience for some of us, but we teachers have never been known as namby-pamby milksops. In the old days, we followed the first Conestoga wagons westward, long rifle and McGuffey reader in the same saddlebag, fighting big, raw-boned boys bare-knuckled for the right to teach them Latin conjugations, trading grammar for grain, Chaucer for chickens, arithmetic for apple cider. What we did once, by thunder, we can do again, and we had better, because nobody else will.

Fifth, forget bird-cage building and bookcase construction in the high school shop classes and teach these bewildered youngsters vocational English, vocational mathematics, vocational spelling—yes, and even vocational filling-out-of-job-application forms. Above all, teach them the old, old truth that when you finally get a job you show up on time with a decent haircut, a shave, clothes that don't make you look like a delegate to a Hell's Angels' convention, and a willingness to keep your mouth shut and your nose to the grindstone for eight hours every day.

Sixth, try to make these kids feel a sense of belongingness, of community identity. The Watts riots were conducted largely by teen-agers and they had no more feeling of identification with their nation, their state, their city, or even their own neighborhood than my cat. They were rootless, motiveless, and hence shameless. Surely the schools can give them some roots, motives, and pride.

As he left my office, my Negro friend looked back over his shoulder.

"And don't forget," he said gently, "that about twenty-five percent of those rioters could neither read nor write."

In the greatest city of the West, this is an infernal disgrace. Oh, I know the reasons given—the great flooding in of illiterates from the Deep South, the lack of funds, the shortage of qualified teachers, and all the other excuses. But somehow these vast cities like Los Angeles, Chicago, and New York are going to have to get these people to read. This is the first and great prerequisite to everything else. Even if we have to postpone "social studies" and "language arts" and "sharing with the peer group" and teach reading to these mute and frustrated kids every living minute they're in school until they get it, then that's what should be done.

Let's teach them to *read*—not to try to recognize thousands of words by their "configurations" and "contours." This means phonics and the alphabet and syllables, not the "look-say" method that has done so much for the past twenty-five years to produce a generation of quasi-illiterates.

California was the first state to mandate statewide comparative testing of reading. It's still the only state that has any idea how good or how bad its reading achievement really is. This drastic step was taken about eight years ago, and was resisted by the California educational hierarchy the same way a hippie resists gainful employment. Over two years ago, our biggest California city found itself low man on a twenty-city totem pole of test results. Its schoolchildren just didn't know how to read very well. The subsequent outcry was more than considerable.

These test results didn't come as a surprise to those of us who for almost ten years had been begging the City of Los Angeles to junk its obviously inadequate reading techniques and start teaching phonics to its first-graders as soon as they arrive in school.

Neither were we surprised by the initial reaction to

the horrendous test scores. Everybody denounced the tests. This is precisely comparable to the patient with a high fever who denounces the doctor's thermometer.

Fortunately, Reaction Number 2 was more interesting. Los Angeles promptly invested in several thousand "phonics kits" and distributed them to its elementary teachers. Aside from the fallacy involved in assuming that phonics is something that can be packaged and handed out like tranquilizers, this action by the school board triggers several highly intriguing questions.

If instruction in phonics is really the answer to the reading problems, why didn't the teaching profession recognize the fact decades age and do something about it? Conversely, if phonics isn't the answer, why did the nation's third-biggest city spend so much money and energy supplying its teachers with phonics kits?

And while we're giving poor Los Angeles a bad time: When are the other forty-nine states going to wake up and start testing the reading ability of their own kids? Los Angeles might look pretty good by comparison.

For years beyond counting, the leaders of my profession have been dosing the country with anesthetic bromides like these:

"Teaching good citizenship is more important than teaching mere subject matter."

"Competence in reading as in other subjects will spring naturally from the felt needs of the child, and when the proper maturation level of the individual has been reached."

"A teacher's effectiveness can never be measured by objective testing in the so-called fundamentals."

Every one of those platitudes is demonstrably false:

(1) Subject matter, especially reading, is far and away the most important thing the schools exist to teach. Good

citizenship comes from familiarity with our nation's history, knowledge of the structure of its government, at least a nodding acquaintance with great literature, and lively interest in current events. None of these wellsprings of good citizenship, you will note, can be tapped by the nonreader.

(2) Competence in reading does *not* spring spontaneously from the felt needs of the child. It springs from an efficient, inspirational, no-nonsense teacher, and from good, interesting, challenging books, both dedicated to the proposition that learning the letters of the alphabet, the sounds of those letters, and how to combine them into syllables is the best possible way to teach anyone to read.

(3) And bosh to the comfortable theory that good teaching is so intangible and fragile a commodity that it can't be measured objectively. Right now, in dozens of our biggest cities, an effective elementary school teacher is one who sees that the children in her class learn to read easily and fluently before she ships them on to the next grade. In other words, if she's effective, her kids can read. Period.

What we need right now is a crash program in reading for our slum schools. If necessary, cut out everything else until the children know how to read. And for as long as necessary.

Reading is the great prerequisite for everything else, not only in school but also in life itself. The teacher who gets her pupils to read has done the biggest job a teacher can ever do.

And you'd better believe that this kind of effectiveness can be measured. We're certainly measuring it in California.

For instance, when the 1968 Los Angeles test results

came in, for the first time in umpteen years the reading scores were up. Out in the sprawling San Fernando Valley, reading achievement went up a whopping 16 percentage points in one year. In West Los Angeles, it was up 14 percent for first-graders alone. On the city's north side, reading ability rose 9 percent for first-graders and 19 percent for second-graders. Among racial-minority children, the percentage of rise was from 1 to 4 percent.

So in the greatest city of the West, the slump in reading at last had been arrested. How was it done? Here is a rough chronology:

(1) Years ago, Los Angeles opted for a reading program that started in Grade 1 with the "word recognition" approach, which brought in phonics later on instead of the other way around.

(2) Under this system, the tests showed a steady decline in reading ability that eventually scared even the Los Angeles reading experts.

(3) Finally, the "phonics kits" I mentioned earlier were passed out by the thousands to elementary teachers and an intensive program of concentrated reading was initiated.

(4) After a year of this, the reading scores went up.

There are several lessons to be learned from the Los Angeles experience. One is that phonics actually does what its advocates have claimed: It teaches children to read. Another is that even the enemies of phonics will reluctantly use it to pull their chestnuts out of the fire if the fire finally gets hot enough. Personally, I hope that still a third lesson will be the logic of a permanent phonics-based reading program instead of a sporadic fire-alarm approach to the problem of poor reading.

Yes, the lessons are there for my colleagues to read,

emblazened by the Los Angeles experience like hand-
writing upon a highly visible wall. The question of
whether any attention will be paid to them is another
matter altogether.

What may prevent it?

The same thing that has always roadblocked it, at least
for the past thirty years: the unwillingness of the so-
called reading experts and curriculum consultants to
admit they've been wrong all their lives.

Each grade school teacher will swear on an Everest-
size stack of Bibles that she uses phonics in her reading
classes, and she will be right. The trouble is that she
uses it at the wrong time. She should start using it on the
first day of the first grade. Instead, she usually follows
the admonitions of her teachers-college professors and
drags phonics in by the scruff of the neck months after
the "look-say" damage has been done.

What to do about it? Change the way teachers are
taught to teach. But that is another book.

Meanwhile, two facts are incontrovertible:

(1) Before the crash phonics program, Los Angeles
reading scores were low and getting lower every year.

(2) Since the passing out of the phonics kits, the scores
have gone up, in some cases dramatically.

Yet what I heard from every "look-say" exponent in
southern California was: "Why, phonics really had nothing to do with the improvement."

Ho-hum. 'Twas ever thus.

Another thing that makes me yawn more than a little
these days is the wriggling and squirming currently
going on in regard to the Challe Report. The unmatched
ability of educators to spout ink all over their past mistakes like a cagey cuttlefish dodging a shark is brilli-

antly pointed up by the recent Carnegie research study on how to teach children to read. Having receipted for more than my share of this squid-ink treatment in recent years, I guess I shouldn't have been surprised at the technique resorted to by the semanticists who wrote up the report, but I was.

The study starts out with an air of refreshing and wide-eyed surprise by revealing that the "look-say" method of teaching reading has failed. I was mildly gratified but hardly amazed at the finding that the "meaning emphasis" that compels the poor little first-grader to draw pictures of hundreds of new words and then try to remember what each one looks like has been a national flop the like of which has not been seen upon our continent since Black Friday, 1929.

Inasmuch as everybody from Admiral Rickover to Rudolf Flesch, including me, has been saying this for the last fifteen years, I may be excused for concluding this conclusion to be conclusive but not cataclysmic. But hold on. What turns out to be the brand-new, revolutionary, bold way to instruct Junior in the nuances of the first-grade primer? Why, teaching him the letters of the alphabet, the Challe Report announced excitedly. Working with vowels and consonants. Stressing the sounds of letters and syllables, believe it or not.

Team director Jeanne Challe is a Harvard lady education professor. And when, shining in all her Cantabridgian aura of Revealed Certainty, she says that the best reading results are achieved by focusing the child's attention on a printed word and stressing that his word is made up of little units called letters that represent sounds that stand for the spelling of the word in question, you'd better believe it.

Sound vaguely, even hauntingly familiar? It should.

Long before McGuffey, this was known as the "phonics" approach to reading, and it has been the way Western civilization taught its kids to read ever since the Phoenicians invented the alphabet and the Egyptians stopped writing in hieroglyphics.

Until our own time. We, of course, knew better.

But here's what sent my blood pressure up like the Saturn rocket. The eminent educators who made the new study couldn't being themselves to admit that what our profession has been doing so busily and defending so frantically ever since the 1930s was dead wrong. They concluded solemnly that concentrating attention upon letters and their sounds is something absolutely novel and unprecedented, and so they coined a nice fresh title for it, redolent of the Computer Age and the Psychedelic Society: "code emphasis."

It isn't phonics, you see, that stresses vowels and consonants. Perish the thought. It's "code emphasis." It isn't phonics that focuses on individual letters. No. It's *code emphasis.*

And it really can't be phonics that has finally won the generation-long battle against "look-say" picture-writing. It's—what else?

Knowing my colleagues' sheeplike willingness to go along with exotic gimmicks and semantic eyewash, I foresee a bright educational future for code emphasis. But not for phonics, of course. That would be asking too much.

Okay, fellow teachers. The old blood pressure has long since gone back to normal. Teach the small fry the letters and the sounds and how to put them together, will you? Call it code emphasis or intrastructured identification— or even flower power, if you wish. Forget phonics. Never mention that horrid little word again.

Just teach it! And starting on the first day of the first grade. After all, it's never too early to begin emphasizing that old code.

While we're dwelling on jargon like this, I have to say that I've been waiting a long time and with growing hopelessness for somebody with expertise to tee off on Progressive Education's latest excuse for poor reading: dyslexia.

For any of you who are not of the Inner Sanctum of education, dyslexia is the tendency of certain children to see letters in reverse. Obviously, it would nicely explain inability to read, and equally obviously this makes it alluringly attractive to "look-say" reading teachers, who are compelled now and then to explain why their pupils can't read.

To ward off a Niagara of letters from furious parents of allegedly dyslexic children, let me hasten to state that I do indeed believe in dyslexia. During my thirty years in education, I have known precisely one case. But of late, as reading difficulties have burgeoned despite our gloriously "modern" teaching methods, the learned estimate of persons affected by dyslexia has grown enormously, from practically none a few years back to as high as 30 percent of the population today!

Dyslexia neatly fits education's classic definition of the perfect alibi: It's scientific-sounding, it's mysterious, and it's something the teacher can't be expected to do much about.

I've been somewhat caustic about this latest entry in education's growing stable of ringers in the race to justify poor reading, but every time I've sounded off about it I've been snowed under by a barrage of protests that accuse me of everything from child abuse to ignorance of scholarly research.

Now at last help has arrived. A short time ago the Los Angeles *Times* reported this statement by one of the nation's leading authorities: "I have yet to meet what is described as the classic dyslexic. My experiments with

thousands of children have never brought me to the conclusion that dyslexia explained anything or clarified anything or offered any corrective program."

My authority is Dr. Melvin Howards, director of Northwestern University's Center for Educational Development.
And he's furious as a result of the "unscientific, biased,
and inaccurate" diagnoses of so-called dyslexic children.

Welcome to our small but select group of angry educators, Dr. Howards. When we succeed in getting a majority
of America's teachers equally furious about the tragic
waste of teacher time, public tax money, and pupils' lives
that is bound up with our present method of teaching
reading, then maybe those of us who have been getting
Excedrin headaches banging our skulls against the stone
wall of professional stubbornness can take a much-needed
vacation.

Let me prescribe a few drops of medicine:

It isn't dyslexia that afflicts your little nonreader, unless he's literally one in a million.

It isn't that he lives in a slum.

It isn't because he has a low IQ. Anyone above the imbecile level can be taught to read.

It isn't the books you're using, nor the flash cards, nor
the fact your school doesn't employ a psychometrist.

Your pupils aren't reading properly because you're not
teaching them properly how to read. You're repeating
parrotlike the tired old rationalizations you learned in
your teachers-college training classes about "the need for
a multiple approach to reading," the necessity for "meeting individual pupil needs," and the rest of the shibboleths
and slogans that multiply like rabbits.

Teach your pupils the letters of the alphabet.

Then teach them the sound of those letters.

Then teach them to combine those sounds into syllables.

Then teach them to sound out whole words from the printed page.

They'll read, all right. That's the way every generation of Americans since Jamestown Colony learned how to read, right up to our own time. Those other generations didn't do too badly, either. In the little red schoolhouse, at least, the nonreader was unknown.

And just leave dyslexia to the experts. You may teach on and on, clear to the golden days of retirement, and never see a true case.

So much for reading methods. The great American public that supports and populates the schools, however, should be equally concerned with *what* the children read, not alone with *how*. In this connection, I'm happy to report that not all the nutty psychiatrists who are slithering and swooping about are in the United States. Australia has at least one running around loose. His name is Dr. Francis McNab, and he thinks Little Red Riding Hood was a sex delinquent.

"A sexually tempted young girl," he solemnly warned the Melbourne kindergarten teachers recently. "The big, bad wolf doesn't need much interpretation, either."

Oh, brother!

Little Red Riding Hood, along with Cinderella, has been around for a long, long time. Nobody until our own foolish time ever thought either of the wolf as a sex symbol or of Red as a possible principal in the Profumo case, and I can darned well assure you that no kid does today.

The ancient tale stems from a far-off time when children were actually carried off by real, live wolves, and when woodchoppers often had to use their axes for other purposes than chopping down trees. Only a pretty sick society would read into a child's simple adventure story a mess of Freudian folderol.

A little scary, Red may be.

A little stupid, too, not to know a wolf from a grand-mother.

Sexy, Red's not.

This is the sort of guff that would be a real thigh-slap-per if it weren't for the fact that a lot of my fellow teachers actually believe it. At least they do in Australia, apparently.

For instance:

"Jack and the Beanstalk" is on the kindergarten black list Down Under because Jack disobeys his mother, steals private property, murders the giant, and finally commits vandalism by cutting down the beanstalk itself.

The giant, in his turn, with his doggerel about blood-smelling and bone-grinding, is preparing the young mind for the concept of cannibalism, and everyone knows that Her Majesty's dominions just can't have five-year-olds run-ning around devouring people. Simply isn't done, you know.

But it's not just Jack. Goldilocks needs some therapy, too. After all, didn't she first trespass and then steal the bears' porridge?

And nursery rhymes such as "Who Killed Cock Robin?" are, considering the subject, not even for the birds.

Couple the rhyme with the usual kiddie-book illustra-tion showing poor C.R. all done in, with his claws up in the air, flat on his back, and a king-size arrow sticking out of his chest, and we have a Hollywood horror guaranteed to send little Willie into a fine fit of the screaming meemies, don't we?

No. We don't.

What we really have is a bunch of so-called child ex-perts gumshoeing around seeking childhood causes for the massive rise in adult violence throughout the West-ern world.

I question whether any youngster ever had the seeds of

violence planted in his little mind as a result of Mom reading him fairy tales or nursery rhymes. The Age of Victoria had the same childhood stories we do, and before it the so-called Age of Reason. Yet past centuries were not beset by our current plague of criminality, probably because the would-be criminal in those days knew there was an excellent chance that he would be strung up if he acted up. Today's thug, for the first time in history, gets lots of understanding and whole dollops of ego-satisfaction instead of swift, stern punishment.

Result: Crime marches on.

But not because of nursery rhymes and fairy tales.

The only trouble with the nursery-rhyme classics and the great children's stories is that we rarely mention them in school at all, even in the primary grades.

How many of you remember "Jack the Giant-Killer"?

I do. Somehow, when I was a boy, Jack always seemed to be just my age. He had a Sword of Sharpness and a Cloak of Invisibility, and he went around chopping the heads off wicked giants, many of whom seemed to possess a multiplicity of heads. One of the worst of these ogres I remember to have been the Welsh Giant, who was constantly in a temper, possibly as a result of having to speak his native language all the time.

Anyway, Jack went in and out of castles rescuing fair maidens, and the corridors ran knee-deep in giant blood. It was all very violent and very gory and altogether wonderful. My mother used to have to lead me to the table in order to get me to eat, and even than I brought "Jack" with me to prop up alongside my plate.

How long has it been since you've seen a kid do this? How long, in fact, has it been since you've seen a copy of "Jack the Giant-Killer"? Unless you've got an old one around the house handed down from childhood, it's been quite a while, hasn't it?

The child psychologists and the Progressive Education-ists combined forces to outlaw Jack from the children's books a long time ago. The mere mention of his name to-day suffices to send them off into a whole barnyard series of clucking remonstrances.

Jack's hairbreadth escapes, it seems, created anxiety neuroses. His magical weapons represented a flight from that deadly literal reality that simply must surround us constantly these days. His violent reactions to unheard-of villainies served as a trigger to latent aggression on the part of the child.

Nonsense. My own generation grew up with Jack, and I believe statistics will bear me out when I claim that the incidence of both giant-decapitation and castle-burgling not only did not increase during our era, but indeed actually lessened somewhat in comparison with previous generations.

In contrast, I'd like merely to indicate in passing and without comment the delinquency record and the rate of violent crime prevailing today among our teen-agers, none of whom have ever heard of Jack.

One of the great questions in American education to-day is simply this: Do the children get this precious part of their cultural birthright in the schools?

Have your sons and daughters been introduced to the great Friends of the Children—those towering authors out of our past who loved the young enough to write im-mortal lines and stories for them?

Have the little ones, for instance, walked with Stev-enson in *A Child's Garden of Verses:* "I have a little shadow that goes in and out with me"; "In winter I get up at night and dress by yellow candlelight"; "When I was sick and lay abed, I had two pillows at my head"? Do they watch, with the Brothers Grimm, while Rapun-zel from the enchanted tower lets down her golden hair? Are they on familiar terms with "Cinderella" and "Puss in Boots" and "Jack and the Beanstalk"?

When the youngsters have grown older, what about their acquaintance with the Mad Hatter and Hiawatha, the Pied Piper and Robin Hood, and Sinbad the Sailor and King Arthur? Have they met Lilliputians with Gulliver and thrilled to the footprint in the sand with Robinson Crusoe? Have they charged "half a league, half a league, half a league onward" with the Light Brigade at Balaclava? Do they know the wonderful verses that start with the lines "Under the spreading chestnut tree," and "It was the schooner *Hesperus*," and "Oh, young Lochinvar is come out of the west"? Will they always look back with feelings of fellowship on names like David Balfour and Jim Hawkins, Captain Nemo and Little Alice?

If your local schools have opened the doors into the magical, sun-drenched world of the Children's Classics for your sons and daughters, you should be both glad and grateful. For during the past two decades and more, the philosophy of Progressive Education has belittled and downgraded the importance of all of these treasures. The "life adjustment" cult, which dictates the contents of our elementary "readers" in the schools, has succeeded in substituting for the deeds of the heroes before Troy something called "A Brand New Job for a Tractor"—for the wanderings of Ulysses an account of "How Billy Helped His Team"—and for the epic feats of Beowulf a story titled "The Attic's Treasure."

There is a pernicious plot apparently afoot to disembowel the grand old fairy tales and to emasculate the classics by expurgating them and bowdlerizing them and "improving" them. If some of them—like Jack—turn out to be so intractable as to be past reclaiming, they are quietly Orwelled out of the kids' books altogether. The results of this organized effort to create a brave new world of togetherness by filling the children's minds with mush and pap are ofttimes calculated to make the angels weep!

Treasure Island has recently been rewritten. One version substitutes more "realistic" easy words for Stevenson's tough ones. Another eliminates the "sordid" passages. Blind Pew doesn't get trampled to death by a horse anymore. In fact, he's not even blind. And the grim massacre aboard the *Hispaniola* is toned down out of all recognition.

A child's version of *Ivanhoe* in manuscript form recently passed across my desk enroute to the publisher. Remember Isaac of York? Well, he isn't Jewish anymore. This retouching of Sir Walter Scott does relieve his masterpiece of any taint of anti-Semitism. It also, of course, denationalizes Isaac's gallant and beautiful daughter, Rebecca, who has more brains than all the rest of Scott's cast of characters put together.

It's somehow appropriate for our generation to amputate all that is wonderful and thrilling and mysterious from the kids' books, preferring instead to subject our youngsters to the sublimely uplifting influence of the evening television programs.

The ancient myths and legends—so necessary to any sort of understanding of literature in later life—have passed out of the curriculum. Not one child in a thousand today can tell you about Perseus and the Gorgon's Head, Theseus and the Minotaur, or Jason and the Golden Fleece. Metaphor and symbolism are passing, too—out of the schoolbooks, out of the consciousness and experience of the generation now growing up all around us.

What a shame it is that for the little ones there will be no magic, singing memories of the Black Knight thundering with his axe upon the stubborn gates of Torquilstone, nor yet the haunting cry of "Pieces of eight!" from the feathered throat of Captain Flint as he perched malevolently upon the massive shoulder of the seafaring man with one leg.

Three things have all schools, and no more than three: pupils, teachers, and books. So long as humans remain human, there is little one can do to alter the first two members of the trinity. But there is a very great deal that can and should be done about the third. The books must be improved.

Some of them are fine, to be sure, and getting better. Many of our geography and science texts are a whole world superior to the rather primitive tomes I used to yawn over during my grammar-school days. World-history books, too, have gotten better at the same time that many American-history books, unfortunately, have gotten worse, electing to become mere transmission belts for propaganda of various ilks and isms.

But it's the elementary readers I'm worried about. More than a decade ago, I was writing *Suffer, Little Children,* which harped largely on the theme of the retarded reading books we were using and their stupefying effect upon children in general and upon smart children in particular.

They've grown grudgingly a little better in the last ten years. No more Dick and Jane, at least. And a few— a very few—publishers are doing a good job of stressing the phonics approach and featuring the Children's Classics. But not enough of them, alas, for me to get very excited.

Here are the ulcers still afflicting the nation's readers:

(1) *"Me-Tarzan-you-Jane" vocabulary.* There's a perfectly pernicious practice prevailing among textbook

publishers that may be summarized as the Condescension Syndrome—the outrageous assumption that children will refuse to read any stories that have unfamiliar words in them.

Youngsters learn new words by getting so interested in the story that they're willing to look up the meaning of the new words.

Moral: Make the stories interesting for a change.

(2) *The contemporaneousness fetish.* The theory here is that today's kids are titillated only by the here and now. So the books have to deal with such themes as racial unrest, slum clearance, peace marches, and open housing.

For little children? Come off it, publishers!

Give them the wrath of Achilles. Horatius at the bridge. Scott in the Antarctic. Joan of Arc. Alfred and the cakes. Boonesborough.

They'll read your stories, and they'll learn valor and decency and self-sacrifice while they're reading, which is more than they can learn from most of the drivel you're placing before them now.

(3) *Insipidity.* The dreariness of it all! The sheer, mind-numbing, deadly dullness! Jerry making up his vapid argument with little Ronald. Betty learning to share her cookies with Billy. Bobby's trip to the farm. Linda's cocker spaniel having puppies.

No wonder kids don't have fun reading anymore.

Whatever happened to excitement in reading? To *The Three Musketeers? Treasure Island? Alice in Wonderland? Lancelot of the Lake?*

Don't take my word for it. Ask your own kids. Better yet, ask the neighbor's kids. It's more fun that way.

"How did Hector die?"

"Who was Long John Silver?"

"What did Ulysses do to outsmart Plyphemus?"

"Who said, 'All for one and one for all'?"

Go on. Ask them. And when you get that blank stare back, don't blame the children. Blame their books.

By the time the kids graduate from high school, the damage is done. For a long look at the nature and the causes of that damage, permit me to refer you for a few moments to Dr. William W. Witt, the affable, down-to-earth chairman of the Lafayette College English department. His views on how not to teach teen-agers to write the mother tongue should be engraved in twenty-foot neon letters atop Mount Rushmore.

For years I've been saying that high school graduates know as little about how to express themselves coherently in English as I know about Etruscan tomb carvings. Professor Witt says it better:

"They can't write."

Take a long, incredulous look at some of his other heresies:

"The problems of student writing are not solved by mixing them all together in one great catchall called 'Language Arts' or 'Communication'—labels that may encompass every conceivable act of human utterance from conducting a Hi-Y meeting to answering the telephone."

Shocked? Here's his "composite caricature" of the new breed of freshman in his writing courses:

"This student's dominant system is intellectual slovenliness. . . . He is apparently convinced that the world has given him a poetic license, which he flashes as freely as a traveling salesman with a credit card. He merely opens a little door in the front of his teeming brain and out pours the flotsam and jetsam onto the paper with indiscriminate abandon."

Hallelujah! And amen! The iconoclast from the Key-

stone state has some pointed advice for his fellow instructors, too:

"The teaching of writing will not improve until we
get more teachers who [are] strict disciplinarians to
whom a shoddy, lazy performance is an insult to human
intelligence."

And just to put the whipped cream on the banana
split:

" 'Creative writing' usually stands for brave ventures
in narration rather than humble exposition. It means
poetry and short-short stories for the school newspaper
and the yearbook. And if the school neglects him for his
brilliance by exempting him from discipline, his writing may be incurable."

By voicing these astounding sentiments, Witt has automatically cut himself off from the mainstream of permissive Progressive Education, and he will probably
end up in the academic Coventry already inhabited by
Rudolf Flesch. Admiral Rickover, the Council for Basic
Education, and the rest of us few unregenerates.

For what he says is blasphemy, of course.

Everyone knows that "discipline" is a nonword with
the life-adjustment cult. Just as everyone knows, too, that
the only important thing about expressing oneself is
the airy freedom and downright abandon with which one
goes about it.

Foggy diction? Unimportant.

Dizzy spelling? Who cares?

An allergy to cold, hard facts and plain, simple words?
So what?

Dr. Witt has put a prodding forefinger upon the cardinal sin of modern education: its rejection of memorization and drill and practice and hard work in favor of the
pursuit of such blithe and glittering butterflies as self-

expression, creativity, and personal communion with the Cosmic Significance Of It All.

It's more than just not knowing how to write a decent paragraph.

It's not being able to place Waterloo in its proper century—or country, for that matter.

It's not really understanding the difference between a simile and a metaphor or between Boyle's Law and Gresham's Law.

It's not quite mastering the "i-before-e" rule in spelling or the rules of square root or the table of elements.

To sum up, I think W.W.W.'s wry message to American educators is this: "Before your starry-eyed charges can build stately pleasure domes in Xanadu, they've got to roll up their sleeves and bake the bricks. It's your job to get both the oven and the kids fired up to do a long, hot job."

College English instruction is affected increasingly by the sloppy disregard for reading and writing disciplines that starts in the elementary grades and which the university professors perpetuate and intensify on their own prestigious and stratospheric level.

The survey by the National Council of Teachers of English unveiled the horrendous facts that half of all English teachers in this country never majored in the subject in college, and that the average elementary teacher spent exactly 8 percent of his college time on English.

This may explain why I get letters from teachers now and then complaining about building custodians who inadvertently leave things "laying" around their classrooms. Lying, apparently, is something done only by liars.

Comes now Dr. Michael Shugrue of the Modern Language Association to place the blame for this Tobacco

Road syndrome on the typical college English Department.

"Our profession has grossly neglected American public education. If English loses its central place in American education to such fields as reading or guidance, the fault will be largely that of college departments of English."

Dr. Shugrue doesn't come right out and say so, but I will. The college English Department conspicuously and resoundingly fails to teach potential English teachers two things:

(1) *Plain old-fashioned grammar.* This includes such previously taken-for-granted skills as spelling, syntax, punctuation, and the humdrum ability to write a simple, no-nonsense paragraph without gross errors either in form or in meaning, or in both.

(2) *The classics.* It's not at all uncommon for the future English teacher to sail blithely through college without ever having opened *The Divine Comedy,* read the *Aeneid,* or even heard of the *Nibelungenlied.* Quite often he is turned loose on a captive audience of hapless high-schoolers without knowing the difference between trimeter and tetrameter, or between Excalibur and Durandal, for that matter.

The task of an elementary teacher of English is to teach every child to spell correctly, learn sentence structure, conjugate verbs, and become familiar with the parts of speech. If somewhere along the line she can introduce the children to Alice in Wonderland and Jim Hawkins, D'Artagnan and Huck Finn, so much the better.

The high school English instructor's job is to hold out staunchly for student essays that don't read as though they had been written by retarded LSD-trippers, and in addition to get into the skulls of his pupils the difference between similes and metaphors, transitive and intransitive verbs, and active and passive voice. He should also demand as a prerequisite for a passing grade at least an equally passing acquaintance with the wrath of Achilles, the hunger of Oliver Twist, and the pride of Captain Ahab.

English does not exist to teach children sociological clichés and abecedarian stereotypes. Neither is its purpose to abet the facile and comforting assurances we're hearing now on all sides from "authorities" who really ought to know better that, after all, it doesn't make any particular difference how you say or write something just so long as you manage to make yourself understood.

It makes all the difference in the world.

English is not just what a consensus of the lazy and the nihilistic want it to be. It has its own standards and its own rules, some as old as Chaucer, some as new as tomorrow's editorial. It evolves, true. But it is not subject to whimsical mutations at the beck of back-alley slang. If a child speaks bad English, teach him good English. Don't con him into thinking that the two are the same.

Finally, and still in connection with what's happening to the "WHAT" part of our literature, a brief digression Hollywoodward:

The late dramatic and erratic Charles Dickens is universally acknowledged to have been one of the four greatest novelists of all time. Critics often squabble over Tolstoy, Cervantes, Fielding, Thackeray, and Emily Brontë for inclusion in the other three top spots in the hierarchy of supreme fiction writers, but there's no argument about old Charles.

That's why I was mightily impressed and more than a mite taken aback a few months ago when I read a statement attributed to Screen Gems president Jackie Cooper. Cooper, who has never previously been ranked alongside Dr. Samuel Johnson as a literary critic, had the following winged words to say about his film company's upcoming spectacular, *A Christmas Carol.*

"Christopher Isherwood is writing it," he said. "Dickens was a terrible writer. In the original, Scrooge is mean and stingy, but you never know why. We're giving him a mother and father, an unhappy childhood, a whole background which will motivate him."

Now, there's a mouthful. Consider the vistas it opens up:

A background of racial discrimination for Gunga Din.

Old age as a retired shipping magnate for Jim Hawkins.

Madame Dufarge frightened by a hedge-clipper at the age of three.

Think of Isherwood's opportunity! His supreme, unmitigated, pluperfect gall. Rewriting Charles Dickens indeed! *A Christmas Carol* is probably the greatest thing of its kind ever written. It's about as nearly perfect as a literary tour de force can possibly be.

The hack who seriously believes he can improve on Dickens belongs in the same padded cell with the nutty poet who offers to rework Shakespeare's sonnets and with the screwball artist who proposes adding a mustache to the Mona Lisa. Hollywood has long had strange, even eerie effects on certain unstable characters, but this is ridiculous.

Still and all, I must confess to being fascinated by this bald-faced admission of genius on the part of Cooper and his minions. Presumably they will now proceed to pschoanalyze Scrooge, supply him with sexual anxieties complicated by a latent Oedipus complex, and pack him off at the end of the story to a class in sensitivity training.

It should be a grand movie, all right. Sort of a Victorian version of *Peyton Place*.

I guess I shouldn't have been surprised, however. In my office are copies of Henry James's *Turn of the Screw* and Stephen Crane's *The Red Badge of Courage*. Except that they aren't really. The publishers, you see, brag in the foreword that they have successfully mutilated these classics for school use by managing to use only two thousand different words in each book.

When I pause to consider how many thousands of ringing, glowing words were poured like molten gold by these literary titans into the painting of their prose pictures, I begin to comprehend the extent of the "Me-Tarzan-you-Jane" syndrome epitomized by these emasculated little horrors that are going into our schools disguised as the real thing.

The theory behind all this deliberate, driveling reduction of our great classics is, of course, the monstrous assumption that such wholesale cutting and slashing will somehow make the books simple enough to be "acceptable" to the student mind. No one seems to be even remotely interested in the alternative theory, which is that the student should be aided in building up his own vocabulary so that he can "accept" just about anything in the way of great writing without having it pablumized and pre-chewed for him by some officious ass. Meanwhile, that whirring noise you hear in the distance is probably poor Charles Dickens, revolving in his grave like an electric fan.

We don't need team teaching to teach kids to read. Nor teaching machines. Nor code emphasis. Nor limited-vocabulary classics.

We do need decent-size classes, a phonics approach that

is grounded in a thorough knowledge of the techniques, and books that are exciting and mysterious and challenging and fun.

Are these too much to ask for? They had better not be. Upon the belt of reading hang all the keys to the future for the millions of children who wait to inherit this thronging, clangorous, clamorous planet. It's up to us to continue this fight for better reading just as long as children are prevented from doing so by stupidity or indifference.

Knowing the problems and the roadblocks as we do, it promises to be a long fight but not a hopeless one. We educators have dedicated our lives to the service of the young. Surely we can render them no greater or nobler service than to open for them and with them the doors that lead to the enchanting, the radiant, the infinite world of books.

CROSSROAD #7

Higher Education and the New Fascism

Conspiracy, n. A combination of persons for an evil or unlawful purpose.
—*The New Century Dictionary*

YES, WE CONSERVATIVES believe the so-called student activism is a conspiracy. Everything we've read that emanates from the Chicago headquarters of the S.D.S. confirms us in our belief that the ugly violence at San Francisco State was directed and organized by a group that also directs and organizes such skull-cracking and arson at Berkeley, Northwestern, Columbia, and a score of convulsed campuses in between. I have before me an S.D.S. handbook detailing methods of subversion for the faithful, and a letter signed by one Michael Klonsky, National Secretary for the Students for a Democratic Society, in which he describes his national organization as an "enemy of the state."

Hitler took over the schools first. His first casualties were the true teachers. His allies were the false teachers,

ﾉ

puffed up with the poison of intellectual arrogance and seduced by the will o' the wisp of power over the institutions that employed them. The goal of today's "enemies of the state" is to subvert the control of our institutions of higher learning by the people who support and populate those institutions and to turn them over to groups and individuals who represent nothing more nor less than anarchy.

The weapons used are violence and threats of violence, blackmail, arson, and kidnaping. In my own state, I can document the violence at San Francisco State College, the blackmail at San Jose State College, the arson at San Fernando State College, and the mob terror at Berkeley.

Here is the way it all begins:

(1) The anarchists of the Students for a Democratic Society, the Black Students Union, and the so-called Third World Foundation infiltrate the campus newspaper staff and take control of news coverage and editorial policy.

(2) A series of "causes" are unearthed, ranging from mixed parties in men's dormitory rooms to alleged campus police brutality. If some racial angle can be dredged up, you can bet it will be.

(3) Underground pamphlets and hastily printed sheets will be distributed and pinned to college bulletin boards. They will be obscene. Any attempt to ban them will be branded a violation of free speech and academic freedom and will be puffed into a cause célèbre.

(4) Fraternities, sororities, and the R.O.T.C. will be next on the target list. They will be attacked and their disbanding demanded.

(5) Then it will be the turn of the athletic teams. Mistreatment of Negro athletes will be claimed, and the replacement of white coaches by black coaches will be insisted upon.

(6) The right of the student anarchists and their faculty allies will then be asserted to control the entire college curriculum and to rewrite the courses of study completely.

(7) Neutralization of the college president and the board of trustees will then be sought. Object: to render all outside control meaningless.

(8) Finally, a general strike will be called. Confrontation with police will be welcomed. Students and faculty members who resist the strike call will be intimidated and roughed up.

(9) College buildings will be invaded, occupied, and set fire to. When martial law is declared and the troops move in, the goal of the anarchists will have been achieved.

(10) When the troops are withdrawn, the riots and the burnings will then start all over again. Ultimate object: to close down the institution permanently.

If all this gives you the eerie feeling that you may possibly be living in a nightmare, don't panic. You really are. At least if you're around many college campuses these days.

Within the last two years in California, the following incredibilities have blossomed in full horror on tax-supported college and university campuses:

(1) An armed and disciplined band of storm troopers invaded a college newspaper office and sent the student editor to the hospital with a brain concussion because his editorials were not rabid enough to suit the activists.

(2) Another student newspaper office was firebombed with Molotov cocktails.

(3) Two college administration buildings were set on fire and valuable records destroyed.

(4) Representatives of a private business establishment, invited by college authorities to present job information in a college building, were beseiged by a baying band of bearded bums and forced to climb out a back window in order to escape the mob.

(5) A college instructor threatened his president with violence and announced his intention to "burn the place down" if his demands were not met.

(6) In Berkeley, the fountainhead and spawning-ground of student fascism, youthful mobs fought pitched battles with the National Guard for the right to trespass upon property that did not belong to them.

All this in one state! Multiply by approximately fifty and you'll get some idea of the positively hair-raising state of higher education in this land today.

What we are witnessing in some of our colleges today is not only a horrendous waste of money, time, and energy, but also an ominous reversal of the whole image of American higher education, from research to revolution, from inquiry to insurrection, from serious study to sheer slapstick. In California, I can say from personal experience that it has become physically unsafe for peaceful citizens to set foot on certain campuses on certain days. Not long ago, one of our West Coast colleges canceled its opening football game.

Reason: A Negro professor and a few Negro students suddenly decided that not enough Negroes were being pledged by the local fraternities, so they threatened to "burn down" the football stadium unless the game was called off. The college prexy, fearful of mass mayhem, blew the whistle on the ballgame before it could get under way.

I am not going to scatter my fire on side issues. The main question is:

When should an educational institution permit threats of violence from individuals to force it to revise its carefully planned programs?

My answer: never.

Such activities exist presumably for the benefit of the whole student body and are painstakingly thought out and set up a long time in advance. Granted this, it follows that a small minority of the institution's inmates cannot possibly be allowed to disrupt the entire campus machinery, regardless of whether their grievances are as sound as a McKinley dollar.

The alternative: chaos.

If racial discrimination was being promoted or perpetuated by the college in question, then the protesters should have brought their beef before the school administrators and the board of trustees months earlier, and in a peaceful manner. As a member of the latter group, I can testify that this wasn't done. Had it been, there would have been no need for threats, since all the trustees were and are as devoted to nondiscrimination as was Martin Luther King.

But how can anyone be expected to know that grievances exist if the aggrieved parties clam up, refuse to seek orderly redress, and spend their time instead writing Black Hand notes and mixing Molotov cocktails?

When someone walks into my office and asks for help, I'm going to drop what I am doing and try to give it to him. But when he walks in and asks for trouble, then by the shillelagh of old St. Patrick, that's what I'm going to give him.

I present to you three propositions:

(1) Violence works both ways.
(2) Threats of any kind are beneath contempt.
(3) A college president who knuckles under is simply

laying up a vast store of rapidly escalating woe both for himself and for his entire profession.

Thanks to the truism that nothing succeeds like success, I suppose we'll now be regaled with a long, dreary series of basketball games halted by Rap Brown brandishing a cigarette lighter or track meets panicked by Stokely Carmichael tossing rocks into the pole-vault pits.

The people of my state have recently reacted sharply to this kind of dangerous nonsense by voting to cut off all further money for college and university construction. But this is like cutting off a hospital patient's food supply when what he really needs is a different doctor. To stretch the simile a little further, the problem is how to change doctors when all of them have seemingly graduated from the same medical school.

Incidentally, with Columbia and Northwestern and a score of other convulsed institutions in mind, let me say that it's not just California that's on a solo flight from reality. It's happening in other states, too, and in states where it hasn't happened yet, it's getting ready to.

As for the Black Students Union, the Panthers, the Muslims, and their ilk, everyone who has really paid any attention to these groups puts them in exactly the same category as the Mafia in modern times and the infamous Molly Maguires of my own Irish ancestors prior to the turn of the last century. They thrive on terror, they batten upon fear, and they live by threats and intimidation. I regard them with the same mingling of reprobation and contempt that formerly I reserved for the Ku Klux Klan.

A wry commentary on the endless list of "demands" and "confrontations" these days is to be found in the straight-faced proclamation issued recently by the Italian Student Fratellanza at the University of San Francisco, which has managed to go its humorless exemplars one better:

I. The immediate hiring of two Italian professors, one from Northern Italy and one from Southern Italy.

II. Raise in pay of all instructors of Italian descent.

III. A three-unit seminar course to be offered in "Divorce—Italian Style," including a two-hour lab period.

IV. The establishment of the Sicilian Defense Workshop, which shall encourage legal aid to members of the Mafia and Cosa Nostra who have allowed their syndicate protection insurance to lapse.

V. Immediate cancellation of all intramural basketball and football games, and the creation of a Bocci Ball League.

VI. Background tarentella and opera music at lunchtime.

VII. Vending machines to offer pizza (both sausage and pepperoni), ravioli, garlic bread and 8-oz. cans of Dago Red.

VIII. School holidays on Columbus Day, the birthdays of Benito Mussolini and all other Italian war heroes (a total of two days off).

IX. Paid-up term life insurance policies, issued by Mafia Mutual, with assignment of dividends to the Al Capone Memorial Foundation.

X. All female students and secretaries must submit to pinching in the hallways.

To show their unflinching determination to achieve these goals in the face of the bigoted—if unnamed—anti-Italian forces in our midst, the Fratellanza warned solemnly that "if these demands are not acceded to by the time the next boat leaves for the mother country," it would call for a protest march around the campus chanting such "Italian power" slogans as:

"Galileo was right!"

"Olive skin is beautiful!"

and even

"Garlic power!"

Obviously a major crisis is upon us. Demand No. 7 alone would double the per-capita student consumption of bicarbonate in this country.

I've been expecting this ever since Rap, Stokely, and Eldridge started posting their hourly ultimatums anywhere they would stick. It was only a question of time until everyone else got into the act. Now the Italians have served notice, and the pasta is in the mozzarella. Or vice versa.

You can't fault the Italian students, however. After all, if it makes sense to set up special courses in "black history" and "brown literature," why not "olive culture"? Or even "blond civilization," for that matter? Shades of old Adolf!

Seriously, although the Student Fratellanza has its tongue firmly lodged in its cheek, it has done us all a favor, if only by showing so hilariously how stupid this whole "color power" syndrome really is. The same thing may be said of the "national origin" complex.

The only reason most of us were born in America was because our forebears wanted to get away from their respective homelands. They were sick of the rigid caste systems and repressive governments that had inspired them to look longingly westward in the first place.

Black Americans are no exception to this rule. While they were transplanted overseas against their will, as were the first Australian settlers, few of them want to return to Africa today. My own ancestors were literally driven out of Ireland by the Great Famine, but their involuntary emigration doesn't mean that I want to set up "Irish power" college courses now.

Any group that barges around shouting power slogans and flexing its muscles is doing the whole nation a grave disservice. None of us needs more power. We do need more tolerance, more understanding, and more human kindness. And we can't get these things—ever—by swearing at other people and making them afraid of us.

What, then, makes student activism worth commenting upon philosophically? To me, it is one question: How can we really tell just which laws should be obeyed today?

As the French say, this gave me furiously to think, and it put the whole sorry farrago of campus lootings, burnings, and assaults in a much more serious light. Maybe it's because a conservative just naturally respects government by laws and distrusts government by groups of individuals.

Every time our college students open a campus newspaper they are regaled not only with four-letter words but also with dime-novel anecdotes of starry-eyed, unwashed Galahads who are currently demonstrating their invincible idealism by smashing windows, assaulting deans, and setting fire to ivied halls of learning, all in the holy name of deeply held personal convictions.

The laws are no good. They're irrelevant. Or the Regents' regulations are oppressive. So we'll make our own personal laws and rules. We'll do it ourselves. So goes the refrain, from San Francisco to Columbia.

Almost weekly, different student delegations visit me in my Sacramento office. Oddly enough, they seem little concerned with curriculum changes, racial discrimination, absentee professors, impersonal administrators, and the like. Oh, these may be the headline issues of the moment, but they're actually just flotsam and jetsam on the underlying sea of student discontent. What the activists really want is power. Power to control policy. Power to spend tax money. Power to hire and fire professors.

So I ask them these pertinent questions:

(1) "In any tax-supported institution belonging to the people, who should set policy for that institution?"

The immediate, unthinking answer I always get is: "Those who attend the institution."

But this thesis will withstand only about thirty seconds of logical analysis. If a public institution should indeed be turned over to its inmates, then the orphans should operate the orphanage, the insane should set policy for the asylum, the convicts should run the penitentiary, and the patients should govern the hospital.

A tax-supported institution must be controlled by those who pay the taxes. Who else could possibly control it? And this means *all* the people of the state, not just a microscopically small minority of students and professors. If certain groups of students want to set up a college of their own, then by all means they should do so. It's a free country. But they should do it with their own money, not with their neighbors' money.

(2) "If the people's institutions should indeed be controlled by the people who support and populate them, then under what circumstances should these institutions have their policies determined by anyone except the representatives of the people themselves?"

And the answer to Question 2 has to be: "None." Under no conceivable concatenation of circumstances can a democratic society permit the policies of its institutions to be determined by anyone except its own legally selected servants, responsible to all the people. Most assuredly, democratic institutions cannot be run by stray groups of students and professors who are responsible to nobody on God's earth except themselves.

Certainly students and professors should have an important voice in policymaking. After all, they are the ones most directly affected by the policies. But to say that they should be consulted is a far cry from saying that we should turn over the whole shebang to them, lock, stock, and barrel, as the more rabid among them are currently demanding.

These are my two questions. Quite often they are met with blank looks and puzzled head-shakings, mute indictments of the failure of these youngsters' professors to teach them the most important things any citizen needs to know. Then, as punishment, I usually launch into a brief if unsolicited lecture on life in a democratic republic, which goes this way:

The only glue that holds a society like ours together is mutual respect for the democratically enacted laws that alone stand between us and anarchy. When any one of us unilaterally defies the will of the majority as embodied in the laws and regulations that the representatives of all of us have enacted, then what that individual is really doing is demonstrating his disbelief in and his contempt for the democratic process. And this is Fascism.

It is widely agreed that the individual's rights must be protected, and I agree. This is the whole reason for the Constitution and the courts. But when it is argued that because a man sincerely believes himself to be right and everyone else to be wrong, including the courts, this gives him the right to defy the law, then I must disagree profoundly. Yet this is precisely the claim of the campus activist, black or white. Because he doesn't agree with the will of the people as expressed through their representatives, he has the right to bring the orderly machinery of the institution to a grinding halt, or even to burn the place down.

Poppycock. This is the argument of some moronic arsonist or a twitchy-eyed bomb-thrower. It is not the argument of a rational adult, or even of a reasonably thoughtful child. It is, however, the argument of a Hitler, as some of us ruefully recall.

Take the campus draft-card burner, for instance. He may not like the Vietnam War. With my only son on active duty in Vietnam, neither do I, I assure you. However, I don't happen to like paying my taxes, either. Does the fact that a given law or enacted regulation excites my dislike, my mistrust, even my uncontrollable loathing, entitle me to disobey it? Does my conscientious objections to several of the features of the graduated income tax give me the right to refuse to obey it?

It does not.

It gives me the right to change it, if I can persuade the majority of my fellow citizens that I am right and the law is wrong. It gives me the immemorial right to petition, to remonstrate, to demonstrate peaceably and legally. It emphatically does not give me the right to set my own convictions, no matter how passionately or belligerently held, above the law of the land or the rules of the institution that I am attending.

Remember this: When any man places himself above the law, to that extent exactly he weakens the protection of the law for all his fellow citizens. To that extent also he throws open the gates to wholesale defiance of laws in general, and to the eventual rampancy of crime triumphant.

And this, students, is where we all came in. About 1,000,000 B.C.

End of lecture.

Lawlessness, collegiate or otherwise, is as old as the human race. Yet today's collegiate activists and their more mature apologists act as if lawlessness were something breathlessly mod. They are equally confused about the true purposes of higher education. Columnist James Reston chortled a few months ago: "Columbia University will never be the same. It went on for a long time operating like a medieval university, concerned primarily with the history of man through the ages, but indifferent to man in the slum outside its gates."

Now, let's stop and define our terms, as John Stuart Mill used to say. What is a university, anyway?

My dictionary defines it as "an institution of higher learning of the highest grade, having various schools or facilities concerned with instruction in all or many of the highest branches of learning."

Odd, isn't it? Not one word about the university as a disseminator of black- or white-power propaganda. Nothing to the effect that a university exists to revolutionize singlehandedly the nation's social, political, or economic order. Not even a hint that a university is supposed to clean up the slums, burn down the Pentagon, or even repeal the Selective Service Act.

No, my dictionary apparently doesn't believe that a university is set up to make young people either contented or rebellious, liberal or conservative, affluent or poverty-stricken.

It's set up to make men learned.

Insofar as the black student is concerned, the university affords him access to the tools of learning so that in later life he will be equipped to solve his own problems. It offers him a way out of the ghetto by opening the gates that have been closed to him for so long. So great a promise does it hold for the black student that it is heart-rending to see him smashing and burning down the very institution that alone offers him salvation.

But to Mr. Reston, the university is a cross between urban development and a Che Guevara rally, preoccupied always with the "men in the slum outside the gates."

It isn't, you know. In this country, we have Offices of Economic Opportunity and Job Corps and Urban Redevelopment boards coming out of our ears. Their mission in life is the "man outside the gates."

The university, on the other hand, concerns itself quite rightly with the man *inside* the gates, with the would-be scholar—black or white, rich or poor—who has come to it for learning. All it should ask of him is that he maintain scholarship standards, permit the institution to meet the intellectual needs of others, and emerge from its halls after four years a more learned man than when he entered them.

This implies, of course, that (a) the university must not be used for any purpose except to provide the individual with the intellectual tools he needs in order to pursue the truth, and that (b) in order to do this, the university cannot forever be charging madly off in all directions like Stephen Leacock's famous horseman to solve vast socioeconomic problems that it was never designed to deal with in the first place.

After a man becomes truly educated, he then possesses the mental lumber he needs in order to build either a conservative temple or a liberal pad. He is equipped then to become a reformer or a revolutionist, or even a Republican.

But while he is still in school—in other words, while he is still accumulating the relevant data for his next fifty or so years—he should be exposed with beautiful impartiality to all possible points of view on every controversial subject from Keynesian socialism to the origin of the ancient Etruscans.

A university is simply too important to each individual to be turned into a slum-clearance project, as Mr. Reston would apparently like it to be. This nation already knows how to eliminate its slums and can so do whenever it really feels like spending the money. What we don't know very much about is the truth in regard to life and the universe, and how to equip ourselves in order to pursue that elusive Grail. Only higher education can supply the greatly prized and highly specialized equipment needed in the search.

The proper menu of the university, then, is not Mr. Reston's proposed hash and slumgullion. It's nothing less than nectar and ambrosia, the food which alone can make men like gods. This being so, why all the rioting and the revolting, the burning and the barnyard rhetoric? Where is the academic leadership that we have nurtured so long and so expensively, and of which we have a right now to expect much better things than we have been getting of late?

The really nightmarish part of this entire phenomenon is not the irrational and obscene actions of the student activists, nasty though these churls are. It's rather the lip-smackingly eager acquiescence in anarchy on the part of some of the professors, who purposely promote the disruption of their own institutions by aiding and abetting the rioters and pornographers. In the name of academic freedom, they have surrendered their own futures to advocates of academic license. American college professors, you are guilty of the mess we are currently in. And remember: Like nature, the public will not long tolerate a vacuum. If you can't police your own profession, someone from outside will certainly come in and do it for you.

When and if such action comes, don't claim a violation of academic freedom. What we will be witnessing instead is an abdication of academic responsibility—by you and by no one else.

Of course, there are plenty of good professors still browsing about the meadows of academe. One of them is Dr. John A. Geddes, of the University of California, and he recently lifted his voice and told it exactly "like" it is in the pages of the San Diego *Union*.

"Most campuses are devoid of any active anti-Communist group. The opposition and criticism that students should be hearing to counter what the leftists tell them does not exist. The minority of faculty holding conservative beliefs are generally reluctant to speak out."

Let me interpolate my complete agreement. The good profs are scared green. Not of Commies. Not of Black Panthers. Not even of the dope-ridden, hairy student activists. No, they're scared that some of their own fellow professors won't love them anymore.

John Howard, president of Rockford College, has the answer: "The academic leadership, like the national leadership, is immobilized by fear of militant criticism."

Isn't that quaint? They might become unpopular. Whatever happened to the concept of the professor as a dedicated seeker after truth, his eyes set on a goal far higher than mere popular approval? Or the immemorial duty of the educator to present all sides of controversial questions to his captive audience?

But let's listen to Dr. Geddes again: "Conservative faculty members are discriminated against. Some Republicans are viewed as right-wing extremists and fascists."

And one more observation: "A critical amount of power has been delegated to faculty senates. Citizens no longer have a decisive voice through their own elected or appointed board in the conduct of campus affairs. They cannot influence or balance the political-social values that are passed on to students. This is a fatal error. It can destroy the university system. . . ."

In the jargon of my youth, you said a mouthful, Professor. As a long-time member of two of America's biggest college and university governing boards, I can attest personally to the truth of everything Dr. Geddes says about his own profession.

College governing boards no longer govern. They have turned the institution over to the inmates. The boards, too, are afraid of being censured by the academic senates. Why? Don't ask me. For years I've been censured on an average of once a month by academic senates, teacher unions, principals' associations, librarians' conventions, and various political-action committees, with no noticeable ill effects to date.

So, ye boards of college trustees, buck up. The solution to this mess lies with you. Listen to the good profs, men like Dr. Geddes. Toughen up. Clean house. Reclaim the powers you've surrendered to the cap-and-gowned Pied Pipers. If the leftist professors threaten to censure you, let them. If they want to leave, hand them their hats and buy their tickets. Otherwise, you're going to fool around until someone gets killed. And, grievously, it will almost inevitably be the wrong someone.

War has been declared against us on our own campuses. Let's get rid of the warmongers before some decent kid's life becomes a sorry monument to our own adult cowardice and vacillation.

If the current mess in higher education were not so truly messy, I would be grimly savoring the exquisite dilemma in which the left-wing professors now find themselves. The classic Jacobin dictum that every revolution winds up devouring its own children like old

Saturn is being borne out, this time in the hallowed halls of academe.

Last year's lurch-ins, smash-ups, and lock-outs on a dozen chaotic campuses from Cornell to San Francisco had several elements in common. One was the abject spinelessness of most of the college presidents, who vied with one another to see who could take the least action. Another was the Neanderthal lawlessness of the student storm troopers who brought physical fascism into our colleges for the first time.

But the real common denominator was the covert encouragement given the neo-Nazis by certain professors. It amounted to a surreptitious, back-patting, "Go-ahead-and-bust-things-up-we'll-stand-behind-you" prodding, which some critics have charitably described as irresponsible but which I prefer to call evil. Any teacher who abets violence and lawbreaking on the part of students is a Pied Piper of destruction—and a coward to boot.

Why a coward? Because his own future isn't in danger. He can always fall back upon academic freedom, his local faculty senate, or the American Association of University Professors, if anyone dares to question his role as a corrupter of the young. His students, however, have no protection against the lifelong police records they acquire as a result of listening to their professor's advice to loot, smash, blaspheme, and trespass.

Quite recently, the chairman of the board of trustees of one of our largest state-college systems ventured to tell a Commencement Day crowd that Communist speakers on campus should be rebutted, in his opinion, by speakers of equal importance and persuasiveness from the other end of the political and economic spectrum.

The result was predictable: a rash of resolutions from horrified faculty associations demanding that the chairman resign, on the grounds that he was infringing upon academic freedom. I'm sure that if the *chairman* had suggested that one of the *professors* resign, there would have been anguished breastbeatings and Macedonian outcries from every professional group in the country, from the American Association of University Professors on down. But the professors had no scruples whatever about trying to get the president's job, did they? And without even attempting to argue the merits of the case he was endeavoring to make.

Academic freedom cuts both ways. I've always believed that a teacher, operating within the scope of his special competence, lecturing on his assigned subject, clearly identifying his personal beliefs as such to his students, giving the pros and cons of controversial issues fairly, should be protected to the utmost by the institution that employs him. His superiors should have an obligation to defend him against cranks and pressure groups and crusaders in behalf of personal causes.

On the other hand, an instructor who is more interested in promoting a certain ideology than he is in seeking truth, who parades a train of whimsical crotchets and beliefs in the guise of facts, who neglects or ridicules all facets of argumentative issues except the one to which he is personally committed, is *not* entitled to the protection of academic freedom.

Indeed, he is not an educator at all but a promoter. And who ever heard of a promoter being entitled to academic freedom? Anyone who deliberately places himself beyond the pale of his own profession's ethics can hardly expect that same profession to spring to his defense when he runs into trouble. If the profession does so spring, it is laying up a store of potential mischief for itself.

The purpose of an educational institution is to instill in young people a reverence for accurate and logical thinking, to share with them the intellectual artifacts of the past that combine to form the firm foundation of our cultural present, and above all to inspire within them an insatiable curiosity about life and learning.

The graduate who leaves the hallowed halls of academe convinced that his teachers have found the answers for him and have shared those answers with him has failed to get an education, regardless of what those answers may be or how feverishly they have been promulgated.

If we educators insist upon indoctrinating kids with certain points of view, we have opened wide the door to every way-out outfit that has a doctrine to put over and the votes to take over. The schools do not exist to pander to a certain point of view—even ours.

Recently, I'm happy to say, the professorial chickens have begun coming home to roost. The social-science department at one institution has been plaintively piping that demands for new and comprehensive courses in black art, culture, and history will expose them to logically irrefutable demands for equal time for Icelandic, Tibetan, and even Irish courses. And where is the time for all this to be found? Or the money? Where indeed?

An economics prof found himself the target of resignation demands because one of the militant groups didn't appreciate his lectures on existing federal-aid programs. His harried superiors duly receipted for the usual threats, bullying bluster, and dictatorial demands for his immediate ouster, on penalty of unspeakable consequences. On the West Coast, one dean was actually so intimidated physically that he handed in his enforced resignation.

What price academic freedom now, O professors?

The cream of the jest is that the beleaguered instructor is almost certainly a flaming liberal. After all, a conservative economics professor is as hard to come by these days as a clean word from Norman Mailer. So here we have an academic Dr. Frankenstein who has undoubtedly spent his life nurturing and coddling the fevered ego of a little monster named Student Activism, only to find himself chivvied from pillar to post today by a gruesome grown-up golem who makes the late Boris Karloff look like Harold Stassen by comparison.

The consternation among the professors is growing daily and is pathetic to behold. Or at least it would be if some of us didn't remember how these mixed-up mentors encouraged their present tormentors to rebel for the sake of rebelling, to demonstrate for the sake of demonstrating, to flout authority for the sake of anarchy.

A teacher's job is to get enough logic, learning, and factual data into the immature heads of his students so that in later life if they still want to protest, they will at least know what they are protesting about. And all the academic senates in Christendom notwithstanding, the teacher's job is definitely not to use his students as surrogate sluggers, sit-downers, and saboteurs for his own tweedy, pipe-puffing, comfortable, Olympian self.

Your bully-boys are like all the rest, professor. They strike first at the target closest at hand. And you're it. Better cool 'em, or find yourself at trail's end teaching only what these draggle-tailed Dantons and ribald Robespierres will let you teach.

Recently, Dr. Arthur Jensen managed to titillate the jaded Berkeley campus of the University of California by saying that Negroes have inferior intelligence. While I am sure Professor Jensen's statistics are accurate, I do not have equal confidence in the conclusions he drew from them. The good doctor was promptly placed on the special red-hot gridiron reserved by the liberal Establishment for anyone who dares to question its *a priori* assumptions, and he proceeded to step up the red heat to glowing white by stating that the alleged black intelligence lag was not only innate but also genetic. This I doubt,

but what I don't doubt at all is a scientist's right to pub-
licize and discuss his own research.

Some people do, however, notably the so-called Students
for a Democratic Society. These spiritual descendants of
the Hitler "Jugend" are currently calling upon the university to fire Professor Jensen forthwith, if not even
sooner, on the grounds that he is a racist pig, a running
dog of the white-power structure, a soulless lackey of
the bourgeois honkies, and just about everything else in
the book except a Trotskyite revisionist. They don't agree
with his research findings, so of course they want him
fired.

So much for academic freedom, S.D.S. style.

I've already referred to my Irish ancestors. For some
years now, quite a few anthropologists and sociologists
have been pointing with alarm at the high incidence of
alcoholism among the sons of old St. Patrick, and some
of them have claimed that undue fondness for the cup
that cheers is, among the great Gaels of Ireland, both innate and genetic.

As it happens, I don't believe this, either, for obvious
reasons. Now, whether it's worse to be accused by the
scientists of being genetically stupid or genetically soused
is a question I'll let my readers decide, but I'd like to
point out that we of the Ould Sod are not shillelagh-
ing around trying to terminate the gainful employment
of those savants who are studying our drinking habits
and duly commenting on them, favorably or unfavorably.

It's downright odd how the student-activist movement
has changed in four years. In 1965 it called itself the
"Free-Speech Movement." Remember? Now it's free
speech for everybody except Dr. Jensen. And the Dow
Chemical Co., of course. And the Marine Corps recruiters.
And, in the end, anybody who doesn't agree lock, stock,
and barrel with the S.D.S. I wonder how the activists

reconcile their impassioned defense just last year of Eldridge Cleaver's sacred right to spew his abominable obscenities all over the Berkeley campus without even the
benefit of a college degree with their present equally impassioned attack against the free-speech rights of Dr. Jensen, who is a distinguished authority, after all, with more
degrees than a thermometer.

Isn't it strange how academic freedom works these
days? If somebody tries to keep Professor Jensen from dis-
cussing a scientific hypothesis, he's a noble friend of freedom.

What we're witnessing nationwide is an exercise in
discriminatory dialectic. Bishop Warburton once put it
this way: "Orthodoxy is my doxy; heterodoxy is another
man's doxy." Similarly, my favorite speaker must be heard
because he is right; yours must be silenced because he is
wrong.

That this kind of bat-brained illogic leads straight to
thought-suppression and eventually to a Fascist dictatorship should be crystal clear even to the most severely
retarded member of the S.D.S. And this truism leads in
turn to the inescapable conclusion that such a totalitarian
state of affairs is precisely what the S.D.S. leaders are working for.

What's wrong with letting Dr. Jensen state his case
without simultaneously trying to intimidate him and get
his job, and then inviting those who disagree with him
to shoot his case full of holes, if they can? As I seem to
recall, this used to be what higher education was all about.

The question I'm asked most frequently these days, however, is not about the professors; it's about the college
presidents. I'm beginning to believe that we college trustees should seriously consider adding an extra dimension to
our hitherto rather prosaic hiring procedures. In addition

to screening dignified would-be college presidents or chancellors for earned degrees, administrative experience, scholarly expertise, and moral probity, I suggest that the aspiring candidates be required to submit to a searching physical exam.

Object: to find out whether they have backbones.

From the timorous, fluttery, maiden-aunt way our most prestigious leaders of higher education have been squealing, averting their eyes, and hiding under their desks every time some squalid squad of unkempt undergraduates trees them in their own offices, I've been wondering whether they have anything between their neckbones and their hipbones more solid than a little gristle.

Teddy Roosevelt once snorted in regard to a Supreme Court justice who had disappointed him, "I could have carved a judge with more backbone out of a banana."

Just a few months ago, the president of a great American university wrote an unbelievable letter to one of his state legislators. The gist of his argument was that the assemblyman was out of bounds for venturing to suggest that students and professors be held to account for outraging everyday standards of simple decency and civilized decorum on a public campus.

"The legitimate theater and cinema stage scenes portraying erotic matters which skirt the antipornography statutes," the prexy pointed out, "but when students put on similar productions, the public is offended."

Note the implication. If the local Main Street burlesque house features a smelly little production titled *Girls in the Raw,* which happens to be popular with the blearier-eyed members of the bald-headed row, it's okay for the college dramatic club to do the same. And if the Bijou drive-in is showing Susan Smut in *Lust Alley,* this automatically gives the green light to the junior class to put on a stag movie in order to finance the annual prom. After all, nothing can possibly be wrong if everybody does it, and everybody's doing it now. So goes the president's plaintive refrain.

He wasn't joking, either. Several institutions of allegedly higher learning have recently permitted *The Beard* to be performed within their hallowed walls. *The Beard,* incidentally, is so depressingly and monotonously filthy a play that it makes outhouse scrawlings read like the *Meditations* of Marcus Aurelius.

But let's pursue the learned president's line of reasoning a little further:

"Citizens outside a university can take the most extreme positions on public issues and indulge in any kind of behavior they wish, whether or not it is insulting or close to treason, provided only that it is lawful, but students are expected to be more-than-lawful."

You're darned right they are. They're expected to be students, with all the word implies. They're expected to become better, finer, nobler persons than the rank-and-file, not to wallow in a four-year state-supported slough of sex, drugs, and treason. They're expected to do more than just obey the law, which, after all, is obeyed more or less automatically by most of the rest of us, without our necessarily having the benefit of an expensive college education. A college man is supposed to be a gentleman, and there's a lot more wrapped up in that word than mere concern with the letter of the law.

I guess my dispute with this particular academician originates with the essential narrowness of his outlook insofar as the purpose of his own institution is concerned. A university has a higher aim than he seems to think it has. It's intended to be a beacon, not a mirror. It's purpose is to perpetuate the wonderful and the uplifting and the inspiring portions of our cultural heritage, and, if 'possible, to add to them and to enrich them in our own time.

But the goal of a university is not to slavishly and sniggeringly reflect the baseness and violence that is the other side of the coin that is our everyday environment, just because these things are there. Neither is its objective to emulate a Minsky runway, a gladiatorial arena, or even a cracker-barrel spit-'n'-argue club.

The purpose of any institution of higher learning is to give young people the intellectual tools that the human race over the centuries has found to be indispensable in the pursuit of truth. And this it cannot do in an atmosphere that is a cross between a love-in and a Mafia meeting.

In the final analysis, Mr. College Administrator, the climate on your own campus is uniquely and precisely what you make it. Or at least what you permit it to become. And in the last few years, you've permitted it to become a caricature of higher education. So it is with most of our college prexies these days. That's why I did a double take a short time ago when someone sent me a copy of a letter put out to the public at large by the chancellor of the University of Denver. It started out: "This letter is to inform you that this university has dismissed more than forty students on this day. Their dismissal is the result of willful disobedience of the rules and regulations for orderly and proper conduct."

It went on to state that the usual assortment of punks had threatened to sit-in and disrupt in the dishearteningly familiar pattern of today's distracted campuses. As a result, the Denver chancellor expelled every one of them, saying: "This university will not be run by threats and intimidation. It will not respond to ultimatums from students, and it will not be intimidated by groups who are dedicated to the disruption of institutions of higher learning or seek disorganization to the point where such institutions can be controlled by violence and run under constant threat of disruption."

By the Eternal, it's about time some college administrator said this, and followed it up!

I've had it with college presidents who refer everything to their academic senates, who apologize to students because they haven't been permitted to put on dirty plays in the Greek theater and orgies in the dorms.

The Denver chancellor's name is Dr. Maurice Mitchell. He ought to be given a $10,000 raise, a new ten-year contract, and encouraged to hold a series of nationwide seminars entitled "How to Be a Real Chancellor," which would be made compulsory for all other college administrators. Some of these courses could be given by Dr. S. I. Hayakawa, president of San Francisco State College, apparently the same kind of a man.

I know it's going to be hard for some of these prexies to acquire backbones when they were born without them. But it should at least be possible to firm up the gristle a little.

On the students' part, activism stems from three causes: affluence in the form of parental largesse; exhibitionism on the part of the activist; and permissiveness by the college authorities. Take away any one of these three legs, and the activist stool falls to the ground. Many of the hairy rioters, exuding a visible aura of unwashed disinhibition and looking remarkably like so many unmade beds, get monthly allowances on the condition that they stay as far away from home as possible.

Most of them are hypocrites. They hanker wistfully and vocally after public martyrdom, but they take care to go first class. Who ever heard of a genuine, 14-karat martyr demanding amnesty, for example? Or flying sobbing to the motherly apron of the ACLU every time a sit-in fails or a slugging victim fights back unexpectedly? Shades of St. Joan!

This hypocrisy was first brought home to me when the Russian rape of Czechoslovakia evoked nothing but thunderous silence from the collegiate champions of peace, love, and egalitarianism. When the Soviet tanks rolled into Prague and splashed the curbs of that suffering city with the blood of its innocent citizens, I waited with bated breath for the Russian embassy to be stoned, the picket lines to march, the placards to sprout. Surely those who had been so frantic in their protests against America's involvement in Vietnam would howl their rage to the four winds and write their indignation on the very heavens in letters of fire at this cynical and brutal act of Russian aggression.

I waited. And I waited. I'm still waiting. But, at least in California, nothing at all happened. No demonstrations. No picket lines. Nary a placard. The silence was positively tumultuous. And it was total.

What made the difference? In one instance it was poor old Uncle Sam who was involved, and it's the "in" thing for the protesters to foul-mouth their own country. But when holy Communist Mother Russia decides to invade and enslave and torture and kill her defenseless neighbors, then the campus bleeding-hearts piously avert their gaze, cross over gingerly to the other side of the street, and walk rapidly in the other direction, whistling hurriedly as they go.

This is why I refuse to take this particular sort of white activism seriously. It is made possible only by the jelly-like supineness of college presidents and boards of trustees. If the latter really wanted to blow the whistle on this sort of nonsense, all they need do is instruct their administrators to prepare a list of students who advocate or practice campus violence and then expel them. Every one of them. Permanently. There is no place in higher education for the incendiary or the plug-ugly. And if necessary, get court orders keeping them from returning to the scene of their crimes.

The same treatment should be meted out to the professors who abet the junior-grade Fascists. Fire them. If some classes have to be closed until some responsible instructors can be recruited to take their place, close them. And if a strike is called as a protest, announce that the institution is in business for those who want to use its facilities, and that anyone who doesn't want to attend it will be permanently accommodated.

The sincere student who is honestly confused is another matter.

Amid all the violent and obscene guff we've been getting from the S.D.S., the B.S.U., and the umpteen other multi-initialed front organizations of the New Left, have you ever wondered what the vast and silent majority of our young people are thinking these days?

A couple of months ago I decided to get off my swivel chair and out from behind my desk and find out. Since then I've been meeting with representative high school and college student groups from California to New York. In the process, I've tried to keep my mouth shut and my ears open, a hard job for any educator.

Result: I can say with all due modesty that I'm one of the few Americans over fifty who know what the decent kids want. I know because they've told me.

The demands of the indecent, of course, are so well publicized that they have come of late to evoke only cavernous yawns in the way of responses:

"Set up racially segregated classes."

"Abolish college entrance requirements for a favored few."

"Let the students run the university with the public's tax money."

"Bring back Eldridge Cleaver."

But these weirdo causes aren't what most of your young people are seeking at all. Here, for the record, are the "demands" of the decent, with my own comments added as a kind of obbligato:

(1) "Get that Vietnam mess over with. We Americans had rocks in our heads when we sent 600,000 of our boys 10,000 miles away to slog around in a swamp."

(Not much disagreement on this anymore, is there?)

(2) "Give eighteen-year-olds the right to vote."

(A lot of older folks agree with this one, too, including a fellow named Richard M. Nixon.)

(3) "Establish more school courses on the history and culture of racial minorities."

(And why not? This is one of the things schools are for.)

(4) "Recruit more school administrators who will find time to listen to student problems and suggestions."

(The kids really feel strongly about this. One bright-eyed, highly attractive young lady who is vice president of the nation's biggest high school student-body organization delivered herself of this heartfelt observation: "We wanted to talk seriously with our principal. We had some ideas we thought would improve our school. It took two weeks to get an appointment, and then he was able to give us only fifteen minutes. To add insult to injury, all the time he listened to us, he kept looking at his watch.")

(5) "Give our elected student officers more real responsibility. Too often they're just used as front men and as window dressing by the school administration."

(From thirty years' experience in public schools, I've observed that when student-body organizations are encouraged to administer extracurricular activities financed by the students' own money, they generally do a darned good job. We hear a lot about the relatively few instances in which anarchistic activists have succeeded in infiltrating student governments and even in taking them over at places like San Francisco State, but for every case like this there are a hundred others where the exact opposite is true.)

Another matter, too, is the Black Power activist, differing from both the sincere worrier and the cynical anarchist.

He has apparently decided to visit upon the rest of us the sins of our slaveholding great-grandparents and to make our universities battlegrounds in his current war against men long dead. As a monument to this tour de force in futility, the Black Power student is trying to destroy the only institution that can really help him and which only recently has come to be open to him in large numbers.

The Panthers and the Muslims, then, are self-declared enemies of the state. They add nothing to the American dream; they only subtract from it and try to muck it up. Therefore every effort must be made to subtract them in turn from our campuses, if only to safeguard the lives and safety of the serious students and professors of all races. It would be as stupid to allow such advocates of racist mass murder to infiltrate our student bodies today as it would have been to permit the bundsters of the Third Reich to do so in 1939.

Aside from this, what can be done to arrest the sickening decline and fall of America's once great system of higher education? Quite a few of us in the profession have been waiting for what seems an eternity for someone to come up with a solution—almost any solution—to the current campus convulsions. I guess that all along I had subconsciously expected the answer to come from somebody high in the inner councils of academe: a fed-up university president, an indignant college chancellor, or even a daring dean.

But despite the fine work of men like Mitchell and Hayakawa, of all unlikely people, a politician finally tackled the problem head-on and offered a thoughtful, forceful, no-nonsense remedy. California's governor, Ronald Reagan, recently came out with this five-point plan for ending the campus riots:

(1) Isolation of so-called hard-core rebels by remedying legitimate grievances, thus denying the rebels temporary allies.

(2) Expulsion of "those assuming the student role but whose real goals are patently not academic."

(3) Dismissal of faculty members "who betray their academic calling through disruptive or violent activities on the campus."

(4) Action by the "vast majority of students and faculty members who are loyal to academic goals" to assure that the rights of law-abiding members of the college community are safeguarded.

(5) Continued public and governmental concern to insure that colleges are not used "as a staging area for insurrection."

After six years' membership on the governing boards of the biggest university and state college systems in the land, I can testify that Reagan's formula would work, if we could just persuade some embattled and beleaguered institution of higher learning to adopt it.

Some colleges do have antiquated curricula and poor lines of communication with their students. Before anything else will work, these open invitations to unrest have to be corrected by the institutions themselves. Then, when every ailment has been prescribed for and when every student knows the channels by which his suggestions, criticisms, and grievances can be conveyed to the powers that be, move in on the sneering rioters and the sniggering pornographers. Expel them.

And when the faculty inciters to riot and disorder threaten to strike or to shake the oppressive dust of your college quad from their sandals and to seek greener and obscener pastures elsewhere, let them. In fact, encourage them. And if they won't leave voluntarily, fire them.

So you may be short-handed for a while. So what? Better to close down a few classes than to keep them open the way they are now. Better to deny admission to a few students now than to have to close down the whole colledge later on and deny everyone an education permanently.

The commonly heard objections to this draconic regimen for higher education are that it would cause wholesale faculty resignations and that it would stifle a free and unfettered intellectual climate on campus. Such objections ignore the obvious facts that any institution would be far better off for the departure of cap-and-gowned advocates of violence and law-breaking, and that there can be precious little intellectual freedom in an atmosphere of brooding terror.

California's governor, of course, is now the object of the same tired old epithets "anti-intellectual" and "enemy of education" which the Far Left fringe of the academic community currently reserves for anyone who tries to do anything to clean up the appalling mess in higher education today. Oddly enough, the professors never seem to come up with any clean-up solutions themselves. Except more tax money for salaries, of course.

The time has come to act. In any democratic society, the minority that forcibly attempts to subvert the will of the majority does so at its own peril. Conservatives understand the proper role of a minority group, for we are one ourselves. And never do we threaten or blaspheme or smash. This is why the groups now trying to restore dignity and peace to our afflicted campuses are mostly conservative in nature. The liberals, as usual, spilled the milk in the first place. Also as usual, we conservatives are having to mop it up.

It's time we *all* woke up. There's a conspiracy to close our colleges down, and it's up to the people themselves to keep open the people's institutions. In the process of doing this, here are a few things to remember:

(1) There is no inalienable right to attend college. College attendance is a privilege, not a right.

(2) Remember that only the people can run their own colleges. In a democratic society, we cannot turn the control of tax-supported institutions over to anyone except the chosen representatives of the people themselves.

(3) Remember that when any individual or any group attempts to subvert the people's institutions and take them over for their own use to use against the people, this is fascism.

The question being asked us today is the old, homely, American query: Who's going to run the store?

We do not pay our taxes to subsidize thugs or saboteurs or pornographers who infest our institutions of higher learning in the guise of students. Let us remove the false students to make room for the true students, who wait by the thousands outside our college walls trying to get in.

Support these true students when they try to make themselves heard.

Support the true professors when they try to free themselves from the bonds of academic tyranny in the guise of academic freedom.

Support your legislators when they pass stern laws to restore order to our campuses.

Above all, support the opportunity of your own children and grandchildren to get an education, for this in fact is the issue now at stake. If we sit idly by and turn our institutions of higher education over to our enemies by sheer default, we will deserve what we get.

But will our children?

In Africa, when a noble beast of the forest or veldt falls lame or ill, he sooner or later finds himself ringed about with bristling, slavering hyenas, which first hamstring him and then drag him down and devour him. America's vast system of higher education today is just such a noble but stricken beast, and the hyenas are already giggling and slashing.

Before our unbelieving eyes there is being painstakingly reenacted the fall of the Weimar Republic (1919–1933), this time with America instead of post–World War I Germany in the starring role. Remember how the Communist wolf-packs roamed and ravaged unhindered throughout the early Thirties until the inexorable systole and diastole of history inevitably evoked the brutal counteraction of the unspeakable Nazis? Remember how the street gangs of the Left clashed bloodily and continually with the armed thugs of the Right until a dazed and desperate citizenry finally gave full power to the one man who seemed capable of restoring order?

It's an old, old pattern. Caesar knew it well. So did Cromwell and Napoleon and a long list of other "restorers of order" whose "order" usually turned out to be even more fatal to the liberties of the people than had been the senseless brawlings of the rioters, whose violence made their rise to power possible. Always the thunders of one group of extremists brought down upon everyone concerned the lightnings of its opposite number.

So it is today in American education. The obscene hysteria of the left-wing longhairs has predictably called forth its own equally adrenal reaction from the other end of the spectrum. In San Francisco last year, for example, a meeting of the local board of education was broken up by flying squads of disciplined bully-boys.

"So what's new?" you shrug ruefully.

Just this: The goons this time were rightist, not leftist. And I don't know about you, but this rings all the historical alarm bells in the fire station as far as I'm concerned. The Weimar Syndrome is with us now, complete with nearly all its old, unlovely appurtenances: roving packs of punks, arsonists destroying public buildings in the dead of night, peaceful assemblages dispersed by terrorists, law-enforcement officers waylaid and beaten, democratically enacted laws defied by organized bands of criminals.

One thing only remains to make the parallel complete: the ultimate clash between the red guards of the Left and the storm troopers of the Right, with our cities serving as blazing, bloody battlegrounds where two equally irrational ideologies will fight it out until the betrayed and bitter populace finally opts for the "Man on Horseback" who will save them from anarchy and fierce civil strife.

And this final, ugly thing will come to pass unless we Americans wake up and act now to quarantine the carriers of the disease. For sheer survival's sake, let's stop pussyfooting around on this issue. If the germ-carriers are college students, expel them. If they're rioting and revolting against the laws of the republic, jail them.

It's no accident that the Weimar Syndrome has hit our college campuses first. The Nazi terror hit the German universities early in the game, too, and shortly thereafter the world was treated to the emetic spectacle of one formerly respectable "herr professor" after another testifying publicly to the virtues of National Socialism and publishing learned papers on the validity of Aryan supremacy. Extremism has always thrived when it has gone to college because it appeals both to the immature and to the disillusioned. And only in higher education can the plague-spreaders find so many adolescents who are half-educated and so many adults who are half-baked.

Sinclair Lewis said ironically, "It can't happen here." Some of us who are old enough to remember Weimar know that it can happen anywhere. The tragedy of our times is that our youth is too busy demonstrating to read the history it needs so badly to understand. Thus the ancient adage threatens to prove its horrid accuracy yet once again, and to our heavy cost: "Those who will not learn from history are condemned to repeat it."

INDEX